OUR

HARSH

LOGIC

OUR
HARSH
LOGIC

Israeli Soldiers' Testimonies
from the Occupied Territories
2000–2010

Compiled by
BREAKING THE SILENCE

Metropolitan Books
Henry Holt and Company
New York

Metropolitan Books
Henry Holt and Company, LLC
Publishers since 1866
175 Fifth Avenue
New York, New York 10010
www.henryholt.com

Metropolitan Books® and m® are registered trademarks of
Henry Holt and Company, LLC.

Library of Congress Cataloging-in-Publication Data

Our harsh logic : Israeli soldiers' testimonies from the occupied territories,
2000–2010 / compiled by Breaking the Silence.—1st ed.
      p. cm.
   ISBN 978-0-8050-9537-1
  1. Palestinian Arabs—Civil rights.   2. Palestinian Arabs—Crimes against.
3. Palestinian Arabs—Government policy—Israel.   4. Palestinian Arabs—Social
conditions—21st century.   5. Soldiers—Israel—Anecdotes.   I. Shovrim shetikah
(Organization : Israel).
   DS119.76.O82 2012
   956.05′4—dc23   2012010531

First Edition 2012
Designed by Meryl Sussman Levavi
Printed in the United States of America

10 9 8 7 6 5 4 3 2 1

Contents

PART THREE
The Fabric of Life: Administering Palestinian Civilian Life

PART FOUR
Law Enforcement: A Dual Regime

A Note on
Breaking the Silence

In June 2004, some sixty veteran soldiers of the Israel Defense Forces presented an exhibition of written testimonies and photographs from their military service in Hebron in the Occupied West Bank. The exhibition led to the founding of Breaking the Silence, an organization that is dedicated to exposing the day-to-day reality of military service in the Occupied Territories through testimonies by the soldiers entrusted with carrying it out. The organization interviews men and women who have served in Israel's security forces since the outbreak of the Second Intifada in September 2000 and distributes their testimonies online, in print, and through the media. Breaking the Silence also holds events and lectures and conducts tours in the West Bank, with the aim of shedding light on Israel's operational methods in the Territories and encouraging debate about the true nature of the Occupation.

This volume contains 145 testimonies and is representative of the material collected by the organization (through more than 700 interviews) since its inception. The witnesses represent all strata of Israeli society and nearly all IDF units engaged in the Occupied Territories. They include commanders and officers as well as the rank and file, and both men and women.

All the testimonies published by Breaking the Silence—including those in this book—have been collected by military veterans and verified prior to publication. Unless noted otherwise, they were reported by eyewitnesses and are published verbatim, with only minor alterations to the language to remove identifying details and clarify military terms. The organization keeps the identities of witnesses confidential; without anonymity, it would be impossible to make the information published here public.

Although the soldiers' descriptions are limited to their personal experiences, the cumulative body of their testimony allows a broad view—not only of the IDF's primary methods of operation but also of the principles shaping Israeli policies in the Occupied Territories.

Breaking the Silence considers exposing the truth of those policies a moral obligation and a necessary condition for a more just society. For Israelis to ignore clear and unambiguous firsthand accounts of the Occupation means surrendering a fundamental right of citizens—the right to know the truth about their actions and the actions of those who operate in their name. Breaking the Silence demands accountability regarding Israel's military actions in the Occupied Territories, which are perpetrated by its citizens and in their names.

A Note on *Our Harsh Logic*

In this book, readers will find themselves immersed in the ordinary speech of Israeli soldiers, which is dense with jargon, idiom, and a frame of reference specific to their particular experience. The testimonies in the original Hebrew are transcribed verbatim, preserving the words of the testifying soldier as he or she spoke them. The English translation has stayed as faithful as possible to the original, only adding clarification where it is critically necessary for understanding.

Our Harsh Logic was edited in Hebrew by Mikhael Manekin, Avichai Sharon, Yanay Israeli, Oded Naaman, and Levi Spectre.

OUR

HARSH

LOGIC

Introduction

The publication of *Occupation of the Territories: Israeli Soldiers' Testimonies, 2000–2010*—the report on which this book is based—marked a decade since the outbreak of the Second Palestinian Intifada. Drawing on the firsthand accounts of hundreds of men and women soldiers interviewed by Breaking the Silence, the report exposed the operational methods of the Israeli military in the West Bank and the Gaza Strip and the impact of those methods on the people who must live with them— the Palestinians, the settlers, and the soldiers themselves. Moreover, the IDF troops, who are charged with carrying out the country's mission in the Territories, revealed in unprecedented detail the principles and consequences of Israel's policies, and their descriptions gave clarity to the underlying logic of Israeli operations overall.

The testimonies left no room for doubt: while the security apparatus has indeed had to respond to concrete threats during the past decade, including terrorist attacks on citizens, Israel's actions are not solely defensive. Rather, they have systematically led to the de facto annexation of large sections of the West Bank through the dispossession of Palestinian residents and by tightening control over the civilian population and instilling fear. The widespread notion in Israeli society that control of the Territories is exclusively aimed at protecting citizens is incompatible with the information conveyed by hundreds of IDF soldiers.

In the media, in internal discussions, and in military briefings, the security forces and government bodies consistently refer to four components of Israeli policy: "prevention of terrorism," or "prevention of hostile terrorist activity" (*sikkul*); "separation," that is, Israel remaining separate from the Palestinian population (*hafradah*); preserving the Palestinian "fabric of life" (*mirkam hayyim*); and "enforcing the law" in the Territories (*akifat hok*). But these terms convey a partial, even distorted, portrayal of the policies that they represent. Although they were originally descriptive, these four terms quickly became code words for activities unrelated to their original meaning. This book lays bare the aspects of those policies that the state's institutions do not make public. The soldiers who have testified are an especially reliable source of information: they are not merely witnesses; they have been entrusted with the task of carrying out those policies, and are—explicitly or implicitly—asked to conceal them as well.

The testimonies in this book are organized in four parts, each corresponding to one of the policy terms: "prevention," "separation," "fabric of life," and "law enforcement."

In the first part, "Prevention," the testimonies show that almost every use of military force in the Territories is considered preventive. Behind this sweeping interpretation of the term lies the assumption that every Palestinian, man and woman, is suspect, constituting a threat to Israeli citizens and soldiers; consequently, deterring the Palestinian population as a whole, through intimidation, will reduce the possibility of opposition and thereby prevent terrorist activity. In this light, abusing Palestinians at checkpoints, confiscating property, imposing collective punishment, changing and obstructing access to free movement (by setting up transient checkpoints, for example), even making arbitrary changes to the rules (according to the whim of a commander at a checkpoint, for instance)—these can all be justified as preventive activities. And if the term "preventive" applies to almost every military operation, the difference between offensive and defensive actions gradually disappears. Thus most military acts directed at Palestinians can be viewed as justifiably defensive.

Part Two covers the second policy term, "Separation." On its face, the principle of "separation" seems to involve the defense of Israelis in Israel proper by driving a wedge between them and the Palestinian population in the Territories. However, the testimonies in this part show that the policy does not only mean separating the two populations, but also separating Palestinian communities from each other. The policy allows Israel to control the Palestinian population: Palestinian movement is channeled to Israel's monitoring mechanisms, which establish new borders on the ground. The many permits and permissions Palestinians need to move around the West Bank also serve to limit their freedom of movement and internally divide their communities. The often arbitrary regulations and endless bureaucratic mazes are no less effective than physical barriers. The policy of separation is exposed as a means to divide and conquer.

The soldiers' testimonies also reveal a third effect, which is the separation of Palestinians from their land. The Israeli settlements and surrounding areas are themselves a barrier. Palestinians are forbidden to enter these territories, which often include their own agricultural land. The location of these multiple barriers does not appear to be determined solely by defensive considerations based on where Palestinians live, but rather on offensive calculations governed by Israel's desire to incorporate certain areas into its jurisdiction. In the West Bank, checkpoints, roads closed to Palestinian traffic, and prohibition against Palestinian movement from one place to another are measures that effectively push Palestinians off their land and allow the expansion of Israeli sovereignty. The soldiers' testimonies in this part make clear that "separation" is not aimed at withdrawal from the Occupied Territories, but is rather a means of control, dispossession, and annexation.

The reality of Palestinian life under Israeli occupation is the subject of Part Three, "The Fabric of Life." Israeli spokespeople emphasize that Palestinians in the Territories receive all basic necessities and are not subjected to a humanitarian crisis, and that Israel even ensures the maintenance of a proper "fabric of life." Such claims, along with assertions of economic prosperity in the West Bank, suggest that life under foreign occupation can be tolerable, and even good. On the basis of these claims, those who support Israeli policy argue that the occupation is a justifiable means of defense, and if harm is regrettably suffered by the population, the damage is "proportionate" to the security of Israeli civilians. But, as the testimonies in Part Three confirm, the fact that Palestinians require Israel's good grace to lead their lives shows the extent to which they are dependent on Israel. If Israel is able to prevent a humanitarian crisis in the Gaza Strip, when considered necessary, then Israel also has the power to create one. Israel's claim to allow the maintenance of the "fabric of life" in the West Bank reveals the absolute control that it has over the Palestinian people. On a daily basis, the Israeli authorities decide which goods may be transferred from city to city, which businesses may open, who can pass through checkpoints and through security barrier crossings, who may send their children to school, who will be able to reach the universities, and who will receive the medical treatment they need. Israel also continues to hold the private property of tens of thousands of Palestinians. Sometimes property is held for supposed security considerations, other times for the purpose of expropriating land. In a significant number of cases, the decision to confiscate property appears completely arbitrary. Houses, agricultural land, motor vehicles, electronic goods, farm animals—any and all of these can be taken at the discretion of a regional commander or a soldier in the field. Sometimes IDF soldiers even "confiscate" people for use during a training exercise: to practice arrest procedures, troops might burst into a house in the dead of night, arrest one of the residents, and release him later. Thus, as this part shows, the Palestinian fabric of life itself is arbitrary and changing.

In Part Four, which covers the "dual regime," the soldiers' testimonies show how, in the name of enforcing the law, Israel maintains two legal systems: in one, Palestinians are governed by military rule that is enforced by soldiers and subject to frequent change; in the other, Israeli settlers are subject to predominantly civil law that is passed by a democratically elected legislature and enforced by police. The Israeli legal authority in the Territories does not represent Palestinians and their interests. Rather, they are subordinate to a system through compliance with threats that reinforce Israel's overall military superiority.

The testimonies in this part also reveal the active role played by settlers in imposing Israel's military rule. Settlers serve in public positions and are partners in military deliberations and decisions that control the lives of the Palestinians who live in their area of settlement. Settlers often work in the Ministry of Defense as security coordinator for their settlement, in which case they influence all kinds of details affecting the area, such as transportation, road access, and security patrols, and even participate in soldiers' briefings. The security forces do not see the settlers as civilians subject to law enforcement but as a powerful body that shares common goals. Even when the wishes of the settlers and the military are at odds, they still ultimately consider each other as partners in a shared struggle and settle their conflict through compromise. As a consequence, the security forces usually acquiesce in the settlers' goals, if only partially. Thus settler violence against Palestinians is not treated as an infraction of the law. It is instead one more way in which Israel exercises its control in the Territories.

It is sometimes claimed that the failure to enforce the law among the settlers is due to the weakness of the Israeli police force. The testimonies in this section strongly suggest otherwise: that the law is not enforced because security forces do not treat settlers as regular citizens but as partners. In the process, the security forces also serve the settlers' political aspirations: annexation of large portions of the Occupied Territories for their use.

"Prevention," "separation," "fabric of life," and "law enforcement" are some of the terms the Israeli authorities use to signify elements of their policy in the Territories. But rather than explaining the policy, these terms conceal it under the cover of defensive terminology whose connection to reality is weak at best. The accounts of the IDF soldiers cited here show that the effect of Israel's activities in the Territories is not to preserve the political status quo but to change it. While Israel expropriates more and more territory, its military superiority allows it to control all strata of Palestinian life. Contrary to the impression the government prefers to give, in which Israel is slowly withdrawing from the Territories securely and with caution, the soldiers portray a tireless effort to tighten the country's hold on both the land and on the Palestinian population.

Despite its scope, this book is limited to the information brought to light in the soldiers' testimonies. It does not describe all the means by which the State of Israel controls the Territories and should not be read as an attempt to address every aspect of the Occupation. The full picture is missing the activities carried out by the General Security Services (Shabak) and other intelligence agencies, as well as the military courts, which constitute an important component of military rule, and additional facets of the military administration. Rather, the purpose of this book is to replace the code words that sterilize public discussion with a more accurate description of Israel's policies in the West Bank and the Gaza Strip. The facts are clear and accessible; the testimonies oblige us to look directly at Israel's actions and ask whether they reflect the values of a humane, democratic society.

Prevention: Intimidating the Palestinian Population

An Overview

Since the outbreak of the Second Intifada in September 2000, more than one thousand Israelis and six thousand Palestinians have been killed. The considerable escalation in violence between Palestinians and Israelis both in the Occupied Territories and within Israel prompted the security system to develop new, more aggressive methods of action, which were intended to quash Palestinian opposition and prevent attempted attacks on Israeli civilians and soldiers on both sides of the Green Line.

The testimonies in Part One address the IDF's offensive and proactive military action in the Occupied Territories during the past decade. Although the security forces claim they are "preventing terror," the soldiers' testimonies reveal how broadly the term "prevention" is applied: it has become a code word that signifies all offensive action in the Territories. As the testimonies here attest, a significant portion of offensive actions are intended not to prevent a specific act of terrorism, but rather to punish, deter, or tighten control over the Palestinian population. But the term "prevention of terror" gives the stamp of approval to any action in the Territories, obscuring the distinction between using force against terrorists and using force against civilians. In this way, the IDF is able to justify methods that serve to intimidate and oppress the population overall. These testimonies also show the serious implications of blurring this distinction for the lives, dignity, and property of Palestinians.

The actions described include arrest, assassination, and occupation of homes, among others. Also revealed here are the principles and considerations that guide decision makers to take those actions—both in the field and at high levels of command. Early in the Second Intifada, the IDF established the principle behind its methods, calling it a "searing of consciousness." The assumption is that resistance will fade once Palestinians as a whole see that opposition is useless. In practice, as the testimonies show, "searing of consciousness" translates into intimidation and indiscriminate punishment. In other words, violence against a civilian population and collective punishment are justified by the "searing of consciousness" policy, and they have become cornerstones of IDF strategy.

One particular action identified with the IDF's efforts at prevention is targeted assassinations. The IDF has claimed repeatedly that assassinations are used as a last resort, as a defensive measure against people who plan and carry out terrorist attacks. However, the soldiers' testimonies reveal that the military's undertakings in the last decade are not consistent with statements made in the media and in the courts. More than once, a unit was sent to carry out an assassination when other options, such as arrest, were at its disposal. Also, it becomes clear in this part that at least some of the assassinations are aimed at revenge or punishment, not necessarily to prevent a terrorist attack. One testimony describes the assassination of unarmed Palestinian police officers who were under no suspicion of terror. According to the soldier testifying, the killing was done as revenge for the murder of soldiers the day before by Palestinian militants from the same area. Other testimonies describe a policy of making Palestinians "pay the price" of opposition: missions whose goals are, to quote one of the commanders, to "bring in the bodies."

Arrests are another instrument of the effort to "prevent terror." During the last decade, tens of thousands of Palestinians were arrested in almost nightly operations conducted deep in Palestinian territory. According to testimonies, arrests are frequently accompanied by the abuse of bound detainees, who are beaten or humiliated by soldiers and commanders. Arrests are used to accomplish a variety of aims, and in many cases, the reason is unclear to those being arrested. For example, during IDF invasions of some Palestinian cities and villages, all the men were detained in a specific place, although the army knew of no connection to any misdeeds and had no intelligence about their intentions; they were held, bound and blindfolded, sometimes for hours. Thus, under the guise of "prevention of terror," mass arrests are used to instill fear in the population and tighten Israeli military control.

Arrests are often accompanied by destruction or confiscation of Palestinian property and infrastructure. The testimonies demonstrate that destruction is often the result of a mistake or occurs in the course of operational need, but it may also be inflicted intentionally by soldiers and commanders in the field, or by orders coming from higher up. In every case, destruction is an additional avenue for control of the population.

Invading and taking control of Palestinians' private domains has also become common in the last ten years. Nearly every night, IDF forces invade families' homes, often taking up posts there for days or even weeks. This action, known as creating a "straw widow," is aimed at better controlling the territory by capturing positions and creating hidden lookouts. As revealed in the testimonies, though, the aim of taking control of a house is often not to prevent conflict but to cause it. Testimonies in this chapter describe "decoy" missions, whose goal is to force armed Palestinians out of hiding and into the streets in order to strike at them.

In addition to assassination, arrest, and destruction, the testimonies describe a method of intimidation and punishment called "demonstrating a presence," one of the IDF's primary means of instilling fear. A conspicuous expression of "demonstrating a presence" is the army's night patrol in Palestinian cities and villages. Soldiers are sent to patrol the alleys and streets of a town, and they "demonstrate their presence" in a variety of ways: shooting into the air, throwing sound bombs, shooting flares or tear gas, conducting random house invasions and takeovers, and interrogating passersby. Field-level commanders call these "violent patrols," "harassment activity," or "disruption of normalcy." According to the soldiers' testimonies, "demonstrating a presence" is done on a frequent and ongoing basis, and it is not dependent on intelligence about a specific terrorist activity. Missions to "demonstrate a presence" prove that the IDF sees all Palestinians—whether or not they are engaged in opposition—as targets for intimidation and harassment.

"Mock operations" are another example of a "disruption of normalcy." In the course of drilling and training, military forces invade homes and arrest Palestinians: they take over villages as a drill in preparation for war or to train for combat in an urban setting. Although the Palestinians affected might experience these incursions as real, the testimonies show that they are not carried out in order to make an arrest or prevent an attack but are explicitly defined as drilling and training activities. Finally, the term "prevention" is also used to suppress nonviolent opposition to the Occupation. During the past few years, a number of grassroots Palestinian protest movements have developed in the Territories, often with the cooperation of Israeli and international activists. These movements rely on demonstrations, publications, and legal action to make their protest—all forms of nonviolence. Yet IDF "prevention" extends to using violence against protesters, arresting political activists, and imposing curfews on villages in which political activity takes place.

The different objectives and methods revealed here form part of the logic of IDF activity in the Territories over the last decade. Underlying the reasoning governing this activity is the assumption that distinguishing between enemy civilians and enemy combatants is not necessary. "Demonstrating a presence" and the "searing of consciousness" express this logic best: systematic harm to Palestinians as a whole makes the population more obedient and easier to control.

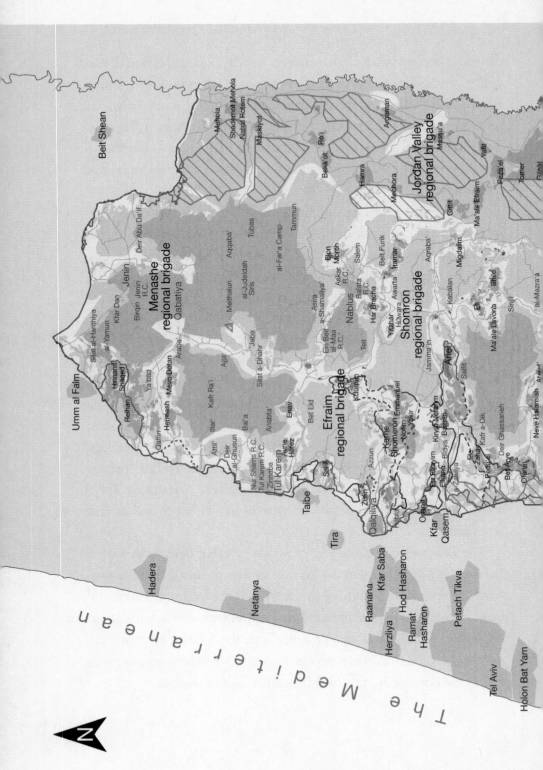

The Occupied West Bank

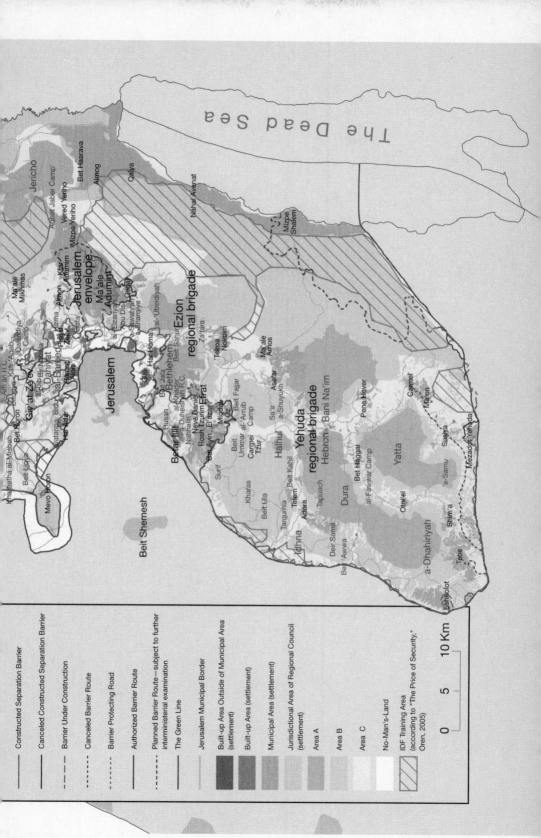

Map by Shai Efrati

1. Stun grenades at three in the morning

UNIT: PARATROOPERS
LOCATION: NABLUS DISTRICT
YEAR: 2003

We did all kinds of very sketchy work in Area A.* That could mean, for example, going into Tubas on a Friday, when the market is packed, to set up a surprise checkpoint in the middle of the village. One time, we arrived to set up a checkpoint like that on Friday morning, and we started to spread out: inspecting vehicles and every car that passed. Three hundred meters from us some kids start a small demonstration. They throw rocks at us, but they come maybe ten meters and don't hit us. They start cursing us and everything. At the same time, a crowd of people gathers. Of course, this was followed by aiming our weapons at the kids—you can call it self-defense.

What was the purpose of the checkpoint?

Just to show our presence, to get into a firefight—we didn't know whether that would happen or not. In the end we got out without a scratch, without anything happening, but the company commander lost it. He asked one of the grenade launchers to fire a riot control grenade toward the demonstrators, the children. The grenade launcher refused, and afterward he was treated terribly by the company commander. He wasn't punished, because the company commander knew he'd given an illegal order, but he was treated really disgustingly by the staff. That's what happened. Another time we went into Tubas at

---

*Territory in which, according to the terms of the 1995 Washington Agreement, security-related and civilian issues are under control of the Palestinian Authority; in Area B, the Palestinian Authority controls only civilian affairs; Area C, which includes the Israeli settlements, the Jordan Valley, buffer zones, and bypass and access roads—a majority of the land—remains exclusively under Israeli control.

three in the morning in a Safari and threw stun grenades in the street. For no reason, just to wake people up.

What was the point?

To say, "We're here. The IDF is here." In general, they told us that if some terrorist heard the IDF in the village, then maybe he'd come outside to fight. No one ever came out. It seems that the goal was just to show the local population that the IDF is here, and it's a common policy: "The IDF is here, in the Territories, and we'll make your life bitter until you decide to stop the terror." The IDF has no problem doing it. But we didn't understand why we were throwing grenades. We threw a grenade. We heard a "boom," and we saw people waking up. When we got back they'd say, "Great operation," but we didn't understand why. This happened every day—a different force from the company did it each time, it was just part of the routine, part of our lives.

2. To stop the village from sleeping

UNIT: ARTILLERY
LOCATION: GUSH ETZION
YEAR: 2004

Normally, the point of "Happy Purim"* is to stop people from sleeping. It means going into a village in the middle of the night, going around throwing stun grenades and making noise. Not all night long, but at some specific time. It doesn't matter how long you do it, they don't set an end time. They say, "Okay, they threw stones at you today in Husan, so do a Happy Purim there." There weren't that many of those.

Is that what's called "demonstrating a presence"?

I'm sure you've heard the term Happy Purim before. If not, you'll hear it. Yes, demonstrating a presence. Sometimes we got instructions from

---

*On the Purim holiday, Israeli children celebrate by making tremendous noise and creating chaos in the streets.

the battalion to do something like that. . . . It's part of the activities that happen before—

What's the rationale behind that kind of operation?

If the village initiates an operation, then you're going to initiate a lack of sleep. I never checked how much this kind of operation actually stops people from sleeping, because you aren't in the village for four hours throwing stun grenades every ten minutes—if we did that three times the IDF would run out of stun grenades. These are operations that happen at a specific time, and if you throw a single stun grenade at point X in Nahalin, it probably won't make much noise a hundred or two hundred meters away. In general, maybe this creates the impression that the IDF is in the village at night, without having to do too much, but I don't think it's more than that.

3. They came to a house and just demolished it

UNIT: KFIR BRIGADE
LOCATION: NABLUS DISTRICT
YEAR: 2009

During your service in the Territories, what shook you up the most?

The searches we did in Hares, that was the straw that broke the camel's back. They said there are sixty houses that have to be searched. I said that there had to have been some warning from intelligence. I tried to justify it to myself.

Was this during the day or at night?

At night.

You went out as a patrol?

No, the whole division. It was a battalion operation, they spread out over the whole village, took control of the school, smashed the locks, the classrooms. One room was used as the investigation room for the

Shin Bet,* one room for detainees, one room for the soldiers to rest. I remember it particularly annoyed me that they chose a school. We went house by house, knocking at two in the morning on the family's door. They're scared to death, girls peeing in their pants with fear. We bang on the doors, there's a feeling of "We'll show them," it's fanatical. We go into the house and turn everything upside down.

What's the procedure?

Gather the family in one room, put a guard there, tell the guard to keep his gun on them, and then search the whole house. We received another order that everyone born after 1980 until . . . everyone between sixteen and twenty-nine, doesn't matter who, bring him in cuffed and blindfolded. They yelled at old people, one of them had an epileptic seizure. They carried on yelling at him. He doesn't speak Hebrew and they continue yelling at him. The medic treated him. We did the rounds. Every house we went into, they took everyone between sixteen and twenty-nine and brought them to the school. They sat tied up in the schoolyard.

Did they tell you the purpose of all this?

To locate weapons. But we didn't find any weapons in the end. They confiscated kitchen knives. What shocked me the most was that there was also stealing. One person took twenty shekels. People went into the houses and looked for things to steal. This was a very poor village. At one point, guys were saying, "What a bummer, there's nothing to steal." "I took some markers just so I could say that I stole something."

That was said in a conversation among the soldiers?

Among the soldiers, after the action. There was a lot of joy at people's misery, guys were happy talking about it. There was a moment where

---

*"Shin Bet" and "Shabak" are used interchangeably. Both names are acronyms for Sherut Bitachon Clali, or General Security Services, which is responsible for internal intelligence.

someone they knew was mentally ill yelled at the soldiers, but one soldier decided that he was going to beat him up anyway, so they smashed him. They hit him in the head with the butt of a gun, he was bleeding, and they brought him to the school along with everyone else. There were a pile of arrest orders signed by the battalion commander, ready, with one area left blank. They'd fill in that the person was detained on suspicion of disturbing the peace. They just filled in the name and the reason for arrest. I remember there were people with plastic handcuffs that had been put on really tight, and I'd cut them off and put on looser ones. I got to speak with people there. There was one who worked thirteen hours a day, and another one a settler had brought into Israel to work for him, after two months he didn't pay him and handed him over to the police.*

All the people came from that one village?
Yes.

Anything else you remember from that evening?
That bothered me? A small thing, but it bothered me. There was one house that they just demolished. There's a dog that can find weapons but they didn't bring him, they just destroyed the house. The mother watched from the side and cried, the kids sat with her and stroked her. I see how my mom puts so much effort into every corner of our house, and suddenly they come and destroy it.

What do you mean, that they just destroyed a house?
They smash the floors, turn over sofas, throw plants and pictures, turn over beds, smash the closets, the tiles. There were other, smaller things, but this really bothered me. The look on the people whose house you've gone into. It really hurt me to see this. And after all that, they left them for hours tied up and blindfolded in the school. The order came to free them at four in the afternoon. So that was more than twelve hours.

---

*It is illegal for Palestinians from the Territories to work within Israel without a permit.

During an army operation near Jenin, this teenaged boy wandered into the area. When the soldiers discovered that he was related to a man they were looking for, they took him back to their post (seen here) to deliver him to the Shin Bet for interrogation.

There were investigators from the security services who sat there and interrogated them one by one.

Had there been an earlier terrorist attack in the area?

No. We didn't even find any weapons. The brigade commander claimed that the Shin Bet did find some intelligence, and that there are a lot of guys there who throw stones, and that now we'd be able to catch them . . . Things from the operation in Hares are always surfacing in my mind.

Like what?

The way they looked at us, what was going through their minds, their children's minds. How you can take a woman's son in the middle of the night and put him in handcuffs and a blindfold.

4. The deputy brigade commander beat up a restrained detainee

Unit: General Staff Reconnaissance Unit
Location: Nablus area
Year: 2000

It was in Kfar Tal, we went to look for a few suspects, a Nassar Asaida and his brother Osama Asaida. And we were at a house where Osama was supposed to be, we surrounded the house and closed in. The procedure is that you yell and make noise . . . and if that doesn't do it— you throw a stone at the door so they'll wake up, and if that doesn't work, then you shoot in the air or at the walls . . . In the end you throw bombs on the roof, but the procedure is clear that you start the . . . the action with . . .

Not with shooting?

Not with shooting but . . . really at the end . . . there was fire from a machine gun, maybe a Negev, I don't remember what there was, at the wall. A burst of fire, you know five, six times: rat-tat-tat-tat, like that . . . like they fired a lot and again, it was against procedure and against . . .

So what then happened to the suspect?

The suspect came out . . . and we interrogated him, and it really was him, and they restrained him with his hands behind his back and blindfolded him, I don't remember what we put on him, um . . . and I took him to the northeastern corner of the courtyard and some kind of, they sent some kind of armored jeep from the deputy brigade commander, the brigade commander at that time was ——, but he wasn't there. I don't know who the deputy brigade commander was. He arrived with a driver and a radio man or some other guy, and when I took [the detainee] I certainly wasn't rough but I also wasn't gentle, I was very assertive. I took him and made things clear, so it was totally clear who's the boss in this situation, but when I got to the deputy brigade commander, then he decided that instead of just being aggressive, he'd also remind him who's the boss, who's the Jew and who's the Arab, who's the prisoner, and he gave him some two, three, four blows, elbow to the ribs, a kick to the ass, all kinds of . . .

The deputy brigade commander himself?

The deputy brigade commander himself. It wasn't just "See who's the boss," which, say, would mean hitting him once to show him. I don't understand it, it could just be the guy, just a way of releasing tension. The deputy brigade commander letting off tension with the . . . this son of a bitch who probably sent suicide bombers . . . In that situation it was me standing between these two people, the terrorist or the suspected terrorist, and the deputy brigade commander, so that he wouldn't . . . to prevent abuse of the detainee. I also found myself threatening the . . . two or three times I threatened the driver and the radioman, when they put him into the back of the jeep or whatever it was, that if I heard that something happened to him, I would personally take care of them. I don't know where he is, and how this ended. But I remember that afterward I thought that as a soldier who's there to protect the State of Israel, in the end I found myself wondering, what's the difference between the deputy brigade commander abusing a . . . a Palestinian detainee who, it doesn't matter what he did, who is now restrained and blindfolded? Of course I reported it as well, it didn't lead to anything.

5. They kicked a cuffed man in his stomach and head

UNIT: ARMORED CORPS
LOCATION: GENERAL
YEAR: 2000

There's some law that it's forbidden to hit a Palestinian when he's handcuffed, when his hands are tied. When the Shabak guys take people from their homes in the middle of the night, they'd blindfold them and kick them in the stomach while they're handcuffed. Three in the morning, they open the door, burst into the house. The mother's hysterical, the whole family's hysterical . . . the Shabak sends someone in to check, it's not always a terrorist, but they grab him, they bring him out—you can't imagine what's going through the guy's head—he's blindfolded, there's two soldiers holding him from behind, and other soldiers follow. These are standing army, fifteen people in the company who're a problem, a minority. And they just, here's this man handcuffed, and they kick him in the stomach and the head . . . those guys really liked doing it.

Was it reported to the staff?

This was an officer! A serious officer, part of the staff! During your regular service, you don't understand what's going . . . If this guy wasn't allowed to do it, he wouldn't do it! It's just because that's how it is. It's the Wild West and everyone . . . does whatever they want.

And most of the soldiers, they just take it as given?

. . . The truth is, when I think about it, I should have done something. I really should have stopped it . . . but you don't think like that . . . You say that's the reality, it doesn't have to be that way, they're shits for doing it . . . but you don't really know what to do. You don't feel like there's anyone to turn to.

You go back home. Did you tell your mother and father?

Are you kidding? You suppress it.

Your parents knew nothing at all?

What are you . . . ? You're part of it. Really, there isn't much you can do. Especially when they're officers and you're in the Tank Corps who they wouldn't even piss on, so what? You're going to fight? You're going to stop it? You can't start messing with company loyalty or the group like that, you can't start fighting with people in the middle of it all. It wouldn't happen now. I wouldn't let it happen, but that's not saying much because I'm in the reserves.

6. He's hitting an Arab, and I'm doing nothing

UNIT: NAHAL

LOCATION: HEBRON

YEAR: 2009

The forward command team . . . kept telling us they hit Arabs for laughs all the time. On patrols and . . . they always hit them, but there was one time that was my main event . . . One day we got an alert. We jumped up, began to gear up, me and the medic were getting the gear for the jeep, and the company commander opened his office door, came out, and said: "Scram everybody, only me and —— are going." He told me to leave my gear and come as I am. He wasn't wearing his bullet-proof vest or anything, just his uniform and weapon. We drove to the Pharmacy checkpoint. There were two or three kids there who wouldn't go through the metal detector. We stopped the jeep, he got off, took a boy to the alley.

One of the kids who wouldn't go through the machine?

Yeah. And then he did what he did.

What?

He . . . I can see it, like a film. First he faced the kid, the kid was close to the wall, he faced him, looked at him for a second, and then choked him with the . . . held him like this with his elbow.

Against the wall?

Choked him up against the wall. The kid went wild, and the company commander was screaming at him, in Hebrew, not in Arabic. Then he let him go. The kid raised his hands to wipe his eyes, and the commander gave him a blow. The kid dropped his hands and stopped wiping his eyes, he left his hands at his side, and then the slapping started. More and more slaps. Blows. And yelling the whole time. The kid began to scream, it was scary, and people started coming around the checkpoint to look in the alley. Then I remember the commander coming out and telling them "It's okay, everything's okay." He yelled at the kid: "Stay here, don't go anywhere." He came out, said everything was okay, called over the squad commander from the checkpoint, stood facing the kid and told the squad commander, "That's how you deal with them." Then he gave the kid another two slaps and let him go. It's a crazy story, I remember sitting in the vehicle, looking on, and telling myself: I've been waiting for a situation like this for three years. From the minute I enlisted, I wanted to stop things like this, and here I am doing nothing, choosing to do nothing, is that okay? I remember answering myself: Yes, it's okay. He's hitting an Arab, and I'm doing nothing. I was really aware of doing nothing because I was scared of the company commander, and what could I do? Jump off the jeep and tell him to stop, because it's stupid, what he's doing?

How old was the boy?
A teenager. Not eighteen. More like thirteen, fourteen, fifteen years old.

How long did it go on?
The beating? I don't remember.

Ten minutes? An hour?
It wasn't . . . Something like ten minutes of hitting. Then he called over the squad commander.

The squad commander at the checkpoint?
Ten, fifteen minutes, then he got into his vehicle and drove off.

The kid stayed in the alley?
Yeah. In the alley. You know the one I'm talking about? The alley in front of Pharmacy checkpoint.

When you're coming from Gross?
Yes.

On the left?

On the right. There's the checkpoint, the entrance to old Abu Sneina.

Tell me, did you talk about this with anyone, another officer, someone else, friends?

I remember returning to the post, getting off the vehicle, I was like . . . I got off and went into the room where the rest of the platoon was, and said: "Listen, you can't imagine the insane thing that just happened, he came along and beat him up." That's it.

Did they say anything?

The thing is, I was on really good terms with the deputy commander. I talked to him about it after he got out of the army and after I'd been reassigned to the brigade training base. I told him and he said, as a civilian: "How come you never said anything? You know we'd have done something about it, we'd never have let it pass." That's how it is.

7. We would send their neighbors to disarm explosives

UNIT: ENGINEERING CORPS
LOCATION: RAMALLAH
YEAR: 2002

So there was an uproar when the Qassams* arrived in the West Bank. They called us to some location, they found Qassams in the minaret of a mosque. What do you do? You look for someone to go up to the mosque and take down the Qassams because it's dangerous for us. So they knocked on doors in the area. There's always someone with us who speaks Arabic. There's an army unit of Arabic speakers who are like mediators, they go with the force and make all the announcements. So they knocked on doors and found someone. He was retarded. They said, "Go up to the mosque. There are pipes in the minaret. Bring them

---

*The term is used for artillery rockets launched into Israel by Palestinians during the Second Intifada.

down." They didn't even tell him it was explosives. It turned out it was motors for Qassams. It wasn't so dangerous but it certainly wasn't work for someone like that. The reason it happened was because the "neighbor procedure" was a basic combat procedure. I think that even today it's basic procedure . . .

You used it a lot?
A lot. All the time.

You really used him as a human shield?
Yes, a human shield, in the sense that if there were something danger-ous . . .

But you have a robot.
But the robot takes a ton of time to operate and bring everywhere. You need a special vehicle. Our vehicles aren't armored, and to put it on an armored vehicle is a whole other problem. And then, just getting it to move, and there are a ton of malfunctions. Bringing a robot to a minaret, even the best engineers can't create a robot that can do that. "Neighbor procedure" was certainly central when dealing with suspicious objects.

That's very strange. The basis of your job is to know how to approach a bomb and neutralize it.
Our job is to remove the threat. Okay, I could also shoot. Tell everyone to take cover and . . . When they were considering what to do, in opti-mal conditions, that could have worked, but to start shooting at a minaret at one in the morning in the middle of Ramallah or to get one of the neighbors take it down . . . We aren't a command authority . . . we go to the commander and tell him our options in our order of pref-erence: "Either you bring a tank and fire at the minaret, or you bring a neighbor, or I'll go in and get it down." It's hard for me to remember what we said in that situation.

What was your preference?
For a neighbor to do it.

Were you afraid?

What? Presumably. With improvised explosives a small mistake is extremely dangerous. If you have a telephone with you it's extremely dangerous, static electricity is extremely dangerous. Explosives are very, very dangerous, nearby friction is very dangerous. When you know how dangerous they are you don't want to go near them. So many times they used . . . I remember a time when there was a really big argument in the unit. It was around Hebron. They had shot at someone who was wearing a flak jacket.* Now I'm trying to remember if they took the jacket off of him. I think they did, but now you have to destroy it because you don't know what's inside, you don't want to endanger yourself by opening it. It's better to blow it up.

Are you talking about a terrorist?

Yes. So one of the soldiers in the unit gave one of the neighbors a block of explosives that was ready to explode . . . he took the brick with the electric wire or maybe it was wireless, there were all different kinds. "Take it, put it down, and go." I'm like . . . as the army we don't take a risk. There was a big argument if it was right or not. I don't think there were many cases like that. But [the soldier] said: "I'm not going near explosives for no reason."

If there is someone else to do it.

Yes. If there is someone else. They did the same thing routinely with the South Lebanon Army. I don't know if you know about it. They created a unit of South Lebanon Army soldiers who basically . . . were trained on a very low level. They gave them short training . . . to deal with the explosives in Lebanon. It's a similar routine here if there is someone else prepared to do it.

Prepared?

Yes.

---

*A jacket packed with explosives.

So what was the argument?

If it's right to let someone else do it from a professional standpoint. It's considered a professional job.

So it was a professional argument?

Yes.

The argument wasn't on an ethical level?

No.

Is that what you learned in training?

Yes, absolutely.

If there's no possibility of doing the neighbor procedure, do you do things yourself?

How is there a situation where that's not an option?

If there are no people?

Just understand that the argument was solely professional, if it's professional to let someone go instead of you in a place where there are suspected explosives. Could he activate something or set off something. Nothing to do with ethics.

8. I couldn't believe how an order to kill could be carried out in a minute

UNIT: SPECIAL FORCES
LOCATION: GAZA STRIP
YEAR: 2000

The story which brought me here happened in Gaza. After these two incidents, I think there was a period at the beginning of the Intifada where they assassinated people with helicopters, a huge media frenzy because sometimes it would miss and kill other people. They decided to send people in, ground forces, and we started to get ready.

This was at the beginning of the Intifada?

Yes, it was at the beginning of the Intifada. Until then there were a few assassinations with helicopter missiles . . . from a media perspective . . . I remember it was a huge mess because there were mistakes and they hurt other people and they informed us we were going to do a ground elimination operation.

Is that the terminology they used? "Ground elimination operation"?

I don't remember. But I remember that we knew it was going to be the first operation of the Intifada. That was very important for the commanders and we started to train for the operation, the plan was to catch a terrorist on his way to Rafah, block him in the middle of the road, and eliminate him.

Not to arrest him?

No, direct elimination. Targeted. That operation was canceled and a few days later they informed us that there is an operation, but we're going on an arrest operation. I remember the disappointment that we were going to arrest him instead of doing something groundbreaking, unusual in combat, changing the terms—instead we're going to arrest him. The operation was planned . . . Can I have a pen and paper?

Yes.

[Drawing] This is the road, here is where the APCs always are. We were supposed to relieve the guys in the APCs, and when the car arrives, and then intelligence from the drone, we move here with the armored truck, cross the road, there are also dirt paths here from the bases, and inside the armored truck there's a hole on top and a step for the soldiers to pop their heads out of the truck like in the *A-Team* and basically block the road here. He'll stop here and we'll shoot at him from here.

To arrest him or shoot at him?

I'm now talking about the first plan—to arrest him. When everyone gets out [of the truck] like that with their weapons to stop him, to say,

"Get out of the car," and that's it. Very simple. When there are jeeps here, they're supposed to be security jeeps, pretty big ones. And that's it, we went out on the operation, when I . . .

Which force are you in?

I'm in this force, two soldiers and the operations commander—here.

Do you have a sharpshooter's rifle?

No, an M16. There's another vehicle here but I don't remember where it was located.

What kind?

A jeep or an APC. Anyway, we're waiting inside the APC, there are Shin Bet agents with us, and we can hear the updates from intelligence, and it was amazing: "He's sitting in his house, drinking coffee, he's going downstairs, saying hi to the neighbor"—all kinds of stuff like that. "He's going back up, coming down again, saying this and that, opening the trunk now"—really detailed stuff—"he's opening the trunk, picking up a friend"—he didn't drive, someone else drove, and they said his weapon was in the trunk. We knew he didn't have the weapon with him in the car, which made the arrest much easier. At least it reduced my stress, because I knew that if he ran to the trunk to take out the weapon, they'd shoot at him. It was reasonable to assume he wouldn't do it.

Which force did the Shin Bet agent sit with, with the jeeps?

With me. In the APC. He didn't see. Maybe there was also another Shin Bet agent there, I don't remember. We were in contact with command and they informed us that he'd arrive in five more minutes, four more minutes, one more minute. And then there was a change in the orders, apparently from the brigade commander: elimination operation. A minute before. They hadn't prepared for that. They'd prepared for something unexpected, like if maybe he didn't have a weapon—a minute to go and it's an elimination operation.

Why do you say "apparently from the brigade commander"?

I think it was the brigade commander. Looking back, I think the whole operation seems like a political trick by our commander, who was trying to get bonus points for doing the first elimination operation, and the brigade commander trying, too . . . everyone wanted it, everyone was hot for it, for this kind of business. The car enters, and not according to plan: really their car stops here, and in front of it another car, here. That's the car we need, and here's another car coming into the section. From what I remember, we had to shoot, he was three meters from us. We had to shoot, and after they stopped the cars I fired from three meters through the scope, and the gun fire made an insane noise, just crazy. And then this car, the moment we started shooting, started speeding in this direction.

The car in front?

No, the terrorist's car started speeding—apparently when they shot the driver his leg was stuck on the gas, and he started flying. The gunfire increased, and the commander next to me is yelling "Stop, stop, hold your fire," and I see that they don't stop shooting. They don't stop shooting. In those cars, they get out and start running, they're running from the jeep and the armored truck, shoot a few rounds, and then go back. Insane bullets for a few minutes. "Stop, stop, hold your fire," and then they stop. In that car, the car in front, they fired dozens if not hundreds of bullets.

Are you saying this because you checked afterward?

Because we carried the bodies. The armored truck brought the bodies. There were three people in the car, and nothing happened to the person in the back. He got out of the car, looked around like this, put his hands in the air, and the two bodies in front of him were hacked to pieces. He sat in the back.

In the car with the suspect?

Yes. I checked afterward, I counted how many bullets I had left—I shot ten bullets. It was terrifying: more noise and more noise and more noise. It happened in a second and a half. And then they took out the bodies, we carried the bodies, I have no idea why. We went to a debriefing. I'll never forget when they brought them out at the base, I don't remember which one, they brought out the bodies, and we're standing two meters away in a semicircle, the bodies are covered in flies, and we're having a debriefing. The debriefing was, "Great job, a success. Someone shot the wrong car, and we'll do the rest on the base." We went back to base, I'm in total shock from the bullets I saw, from the crazy noise there. We saw it on the video, it was all documented on video for the debriefing. In the debriefing I saw all the things that I told you, the people running, it's clear, the minute of gunfire, I don't know if it's twenty seconds or a minute, but it was hundreds of bullets and it was clear that everyone died, but the gunfire went on and the soldiers are running from the armored truck, fire a few bullets and run back. They show it in the debriefing and I see a bunch of bloodthirsty guys firing insane amounts of bullets, and at the wrong car, too. The video was just awful, and then the unit commander gets up, who we'll be hearing a lot about.

What does that mean?

He'll be a regional commanding officer or the chief of staff one day, and he says, "The operation was not carried out perfectly, but the mission was accomplished, and we had a call from the chief of staff, the defense minister, and the prime minister"—we're all happy, getting compliments, it's good for the unit's prestige and the operations it gets, and you know, just "great job." The debriefing was just cover-up after cover-up.

Meaning?

Meaning they don't stop and say, "Three innocent people died." Maybe with the driver there was no choice, but who were the other two?

Who were they, in fact?

At that time I had a friend at a course with the Shin Bet, I remember he told me about the jokes that went around about the terrorist being a nobody. He probably took part in a shooting, and the other two just had nothing to do with the whole thing. What shocked me was that the day after the operation, the newspapers said that "a secret unit killed four terrorists," and there was a whole story on each one, where he came from, who he'd been involved with, the operations he'd taken part in. And I know that on the Shin Bet base, jokes are going around about the nobody we killed and how the other two aren't even connected, and at the debriefing itself—I'm going back a bit—they didn't even mention it.

Who did the debriefing?

The unit commander. They didn't mention it. It's the first thing I expected to hear, that something bad happened, that we did the operation to eliminate one person and ended up eliminating four. I expected everything would stop and he'd say, "I want to know who shot at the first car. I want to know why A-B-C ran from the vehicle to join in the bullet party." And that didn't happen. At that point I understood that it just doesn't bother them. These people do what they do and it doesn't bother them. The next day, when the operation was published in the newspapers—I was in shock.

Did the guys talk about it?

Yes. There were two others I could talk to and tell them that I don't understand how it happened . . . The second guy was really shocked but it didn't stop him from carrying on. It didn't stop me, either. It was only after I was released from the army that I understood. No, even in the army I understood that something very bad had happened and I didn't know how it would affect me. When I was released from the army, I couldn't believe that I'd gotten to the point of shooting at people. It's not practical and it's field security, but I couldn't imagine myself getting an order to kill someone without knowing who it was. I don't know how I got to that point. And today I can say, even if it was Osama bin Laden I wouldn't shoot him. The Shin Bet agents were as happy as kids coming back from camp.

What does that mean?

So happy, high-fiving and hugging. Pleased with themselves. Smiling, they didn't even join in the debriefing, it didn't interest them. I couldn't believe how an order to kill someone could be carried out in a minute. What exactly was the politics of the operation? How come my commanders, not one of them, admitted that the operation failed? It failed so badly and the shooting was so all over the place that the ones in the truck got shrapnel from the bullets. They just shot at them, at the truck itself. It's a miracle we didn't kill each other. They didn't mention it.

9. Death sentence for a man who wasn't armed

Unit: Paratroopers
Location: Nablus
Year: 2002

We took over a central house, set up positions, and one of the sharp-shooters identified a man on a roof, two roofs away, I think he was between fifty and seventy meters away, not armed. I looked at the man through the night vision—he wasn't armed. It was two in the morning. A man without arms, walking on the roof, just walking around. We reported it to the company commander. The company commander said: "Take him down." [The sharpshooter] fired, took him down. The company commander, ——, basically ordered, decided via radio, the death sentence for that man. A man who wasn't armed.

You saw that he wasn't armed?

I saw with my own eyes that the guy wasn't armed. The report also said: "a man without arms on the roof." The company commander declared him a lookout, meaning he understood that the guy was no threat to us, and he gave the order to kill him and we shot him. I myself didn't shoot, my friend shot and killed him. And basically you think, you see in the United States there's the death penalty, for every death sentence there are like a thousand appeals and convictions, and

A Palestinian boy feeding pigeons on the roof of his house in the casbah in Hebron, 2003. The photo was taken through a rifle sight by a soldier trying to break up the boredom of eight hours of guard duty. Nahal Brigade, Battalion 50.

they take it very seriously, and there are judges and learned people, and there are protests and whatever. And here a twenty-six-year-old guy, my company commander, sentenced an unarmed man to death. Who is he? What do you mean, a lookout? And even if he was a lookout? So what, you have to kill him? And how did he know he was a lookout? He didn't know. He got a report from the radio about an unarmed man on the roof, and he gave an order to kill him, which I think is an illegal order, and we carried out the order, we killed him. The man died. And listen, to me it's murder. And that's not the only case. We'd laugh about it, we had code names: "the lookout," "the drummer," "the woman," "the old man," "the boy," and what was the other one? I'll remember later.

And these are all people you killed?

These are all people we killed. Oh, "the baker."

10. The battalion commander gave an order to shoot at people trying to recover the bodies

UNIT: PARATROOPERS
LOCATION: NABLUS
YEAR: 2002

There's something else: shooting at people trying to recover bodies. I definitely remember that in Nablus. It was on the main road, they killed two, two armed men. They identified two armed men in Nablus, toward the end of the operation, they killed them, and then shot at the people who came to recover them.

That was the instruction?

I was with the battalion commander there. The battalion commander is now a colonel.

What's his name?

——. He definitely gave the order to shoot at people who came to rescue the bodies.

Were they armed, the people rescuing the bodies?

I think they were, but I'm not sure.

Did they endanger anyone?

They didn't endanger anyone, but in general the order there is to shoot at anyone armed. Like, anyone armed was . . .

To be killed?

Yes. So it seemed reasonable to me.

You don't know if they were armed?

I don't remember whether they were armed or not, but I definitely remember that people came to recover the bodies and they fired on them. At the time it didn't seem so terrible to me, today it seems a little, it's . . . I understood that it's also something, a logical procedure. You leave bodies in the field—they told me they did it a lot in Lebanon—you leave a body in the field, and you wait until they come to recover it so you can shoot at them. It's like you're setting up an ambush around the body. But those are things I heard about Lebanon. So it happened here, too. I remember something shocking there, like it's gotten to the point of contempt for human life. We got an order on the radio telling us how to get to the head of the breach. So we get it, and it's: you cross this tunnel, the tunnel opens to a road, you turn left, and at the end you turn right. And then it's, like, really, someone wrote, marked the direction you have to go with arrows because those are places where they met up and split and whatever, and every company had its own arrow, and then someone comes and makes an arrow: →.

What about the guys who were shot recovering the bodies? Did someone then go to kill them?

Yes, we verified the killings. If it's a body that's been lying in the field for a long time, then probably not, but even after they've fired, they shoot to kill, and it's really a problem.

We're in Nablus?

We're in Nablus again. After you kill someone—he's already lying on the ground—you shoot through the scope to take him down for certain.

And the guys who went to recover the bodies who you shot at, did you verify their deaths?

I think so, it was procedure.

You weren't in that situation?

I didn't see it. I was in the same room as the guy doing the shooting, but I didn't . . .

You didn't bother going to the window . . .

You try to stay low, if you don't have to.

11. He took down an eleven-year-old boy

UNIT: PARATROOPERS
LOCATION: JENIN
YEAR: 2003

It affects some one way and some another. Some people are like . . . "Okay, I killed a kid, okay." They laugh . . . "Yeah, now I can draw a balloon on my weapon. A balloon instead of an X. Or a smiley face."* Some people take it hard. I remember I was in Jenin during squad commander training, and let's say we were in the middle of doing a straw widow and they tell us whoever climbs on the APCs or armored vehicles—shoot to kill. And the whole point was that people would climb up, because there are APCs under the house all the time. Of course they tell us that the aim is to bring out the wanted men. But what armed man is going to shoot at an APC just like that? They also say that if anyone jumps on the APC and takes the machine guns . . . shoot to kill. And then a friend of mine came with his M24, a sniper's weapon, and just then a kid climbed up. He shot him, all happy—"I took someone down." And then they told him he took down an eleven-year-old kid or something like that. He took it very hard.

He was happy he killed someone? Why?

Because you've proved yourself. You're a man.

Do they know he's not armed?

Of course he's not armed and he climbs on the APC . . . No one asks you why you've got two Xs, and whether they were armed, and if it was by the rules. It could have been two guys throwing Molotov cocktails.

*Soldiers often put a mark on their weapons for every person they kill.

12. Her limbs were smeared on the wall

UNIT: GIVATI BRIGADE
LOCATION: GAZA STRIP
YEAR: 2008

There was an operation in the company next to mine where they told me that a woman was blown up by a fox,* her limbs were smeared on the wall, but it wasn't on purpose. They knocked and knocked on the door and there was no answer, so they decided to open it wet.† He put down a fox and just at that moment the woman decided to open the door. And then her kids came over and saw her. I heard about it during dinner after the operation, someone said it was funny, and everyone cracked up, that the kids saw their mother smeared on the wall. That's an example. I was also screamed at by my platoon in our *Achzarit*§ when I thought about giving the detainees we had with us some water from the platoon's canteen—the field canteen, twenty-four liters. They said "What, are you fucked in the head?" I don't know what their reason was, but they said: "Germs, come on." In Nahal Oz there was an incident with kids who'd apparently been sent by their parents to try to get into Israel because their families were hungry, to try to find food or I don't know what. Anything like that, it's a hunt, fresh turkey. We did a patrol at Nahal Oz. There were fourteen- or fifteen-year-old boys, I think. I remember a boy sitting blindfolded and then someone who everyone knew was a jerk came and hit him, here.

On the legs.

And he spilled some oil on him, the stuff we use to clean weapons, I don't remember where.

---

*Explosives used to break through doors and walls.
†With live ammunition.
§An *Achzarit*, or "evil lady," is a heavily armored personnel carrier that is mostly used by the Golani Brigade.

Did anything happen?

He did it in the middle of the company, but there was no officer to see it. I said something to him in the moment, but I didn't yell at him and I didn't tell my officer that he did this and that. Theft was very common as well. Souvenirs, flags, cigarettes.

The commanders and officers didn't notice it, even though it was common?

I think they did, and if not, my company commander knew because I told him.

And what did he say?

Good that I brought it to his attention.

And was it stopped?

I don't think so. It wasn't stopped.

Earlier you brought up the issue of slaughtering animals.

It was during one of the operations in the *Achzarit*, even the first, I think. The company sergeant major was commander of one of the APCs, and there were horses and sheep there, maybe even donkeys, and he sprayed bullets with the MAG out the window and maybe even ran them over, I don't remember. He shot the animals.

Did anyone ask any questions?

No, it wasn't in my APC, but I know about it.

How do you know about it? Can you repeat the story?

The whole company was in the APCs there, or in the houses where the operation was—first of all, I think I saw dead sheep, things get mixed up in my head. Someone told me that someone shot them. During the operation we talked about what happened, and he told me about shooting the sheep. It wasn't something I needed to verify, it didn't sound illogical that it happened.

Was it a one-time occurrence?

I think so.

13. A well-known procedure

UNIT: PARATROOPERS
LOCATION: NABLUS
YEAR: 2004

There were a few operations where we went into Balata during the day-time in the alleys in the market, to take out armed guys. That's the target. Once we did a mock arrest in a shop in the market. We just went into a shop. Whichever one looked the most convenient. At the same time, snipers went into the houses nearby and we stay there for forty minutes in the shop like idiots, hoping no one would shoot us there in the middle of Balata. It's very . . . it's a refugee camp . . . the deputy commander of a paratrooper company was killed there a month ago . . . so we're in the same alley, hoping our snipers take them down before—

Hold on, is there a reason why you're doing this?

I don't know. There's no intelligence or anything, Just something the company commander decided.

What, while you're on the move?

No, no, no. There's a battle procedure of three days. You look at the aerial photos, you say, "If I choose this shop, then this is the house where I'll set him up," and, sort of strategically, this shop is the most convenient. It's got the best entrance, the best emergency exit.

And is there curfew or not?

What, there's no curfew. This is a year later.

Are there people in the alley?

People everywhere. That's the point. Everywhere. The alleys in the market in the middle of the day, full of people. Like any market . . .

And you go in.

We go in with stun grenades, shooting in the air. The shop is something about this size, with the whole wall open to the street. Here's a door, and here's a door, and all this is open to the street. And the moment we go in, people start fleeing.

What's the point?

To bring out the gunmen, and the guys will take them down first. We're the ducks.

Okay, so what do you do in the meantime?

Nothing, take positions inside the shop, try to find cover. In case they come to the alley opposite us and . . .

Scary?

Yes.

How long?

Forty minutes. The point is to make it look like an arrest right up till the end. So they won't get our method. And so you also arrest someone. Arrest someone inside the shop, go through the whole procedure of . . . take him into detention blindfolded, to the regional brigade headquarters, they'll interrogate him and release him at the end of the process. So they think it was a real arrest and we just got the wrong man. There was one time where we went in once and the shop was empty, and another time there were three people there, one seventy-year-old, one fifty-year-old, and a sixty-year-old woman.

You had no one to detain, just . . .

Yes, but it didn't stop the platoon commander from blindfolding and handcuffing the seventy-year-old and taking him with us.

And detaining him and . . .

Yes, but then we didn't take him, we saw it wasn't necessary. But what we did was send him to open up the house for us.

I don't understand.

They say we don't do the "neighbor procedure" anymore. So they don't call it that now. They call it "bring a friend" or something like that. There's a name . . .

What does it mean?

It means that if I've come to arrest someone and I know the guy is dangerous, he's armed and all that, then there's nothing to stop me from going to his neighbor . . . and I go in and I don't exactly know the location—I have five houses, let's say in the casbah or in Balata. Intelligence tells me that the guy's supposed to be on this block. So I knock on the door: "Which family is this?" Okay, that's not the one. "Okay, you come with me." Make him knock on the door and get everyone out.

So now he walks around the block—knocking on every door?

No, he goes to one house, and then we take someone else. From the second house.

And when he does that where are you?

A bit behind him. He goes first.

You aim your weapon at him?

No. He goes first and you aim, but not specifically at him. He knows he's got nowhere to run. He knocks on the door: "Ya Salaama . . ." He gets them to come.

What . . . that's still happening?

Yeah, it's a well-known arrest procedure in case of—

When was the last time you did this?

April . . . I don't remember exactly.

Did it seem strange to you when you did it?

It's clear to me that it's not okay, but not strange. It's something that happens all the time. A well-known procedure.

14. You want to kill him but he's crying

UNIT: NAHAL BRIGADE
LOCATION: HEBRON
YEAR: 2009

Once we did an arrest. They were throwing stones at Gross Square, so we were alerted and this boy suddenly appeared, so the lookout got on the radio and told us to stop, he was right near us.

How old was the boy?

Fifteen years old, called Daoud. So we arrested him. Stopped our vehicle, ran after him, and he was in total shock. We took him to Gross, to the Jewish side, and he began to cry, scream, he was screaming on the ground, all sweaty and crying. And there was nothing we could do with him, suddenly you've got a weeping kid on your hands who only a second ago at Gross had been throwing tiles, and you're dying to beat him to a pulp, and you've been called out in this crazy heat. You want to kill him but he's crying. We didn't know what to do so we took turns guarding him because every one of us lost it when we were with him and did something, then left. At some point I was with him, I tried to calm the kid down because he was tied and blindfolded and crying and it was streaming down his face. I began shaking him, then the deputy company commander got hold of him and shook him, "Shut up, shut up already, enough!" Then we took him to the police station and he was still crying and the police wouldn't take him in for interrogation. They just wouldn't take him in and it was so annoying, insane. And the middle of this mess, while he's crawling on the ground, the communications guy takes out his Motorola. You know what a Motorola is?

For communications?

Boom, a blow to the head. He didn't mean anything bad. It was just after more than two hours of unbearable crying.

This was still at Gross?

No. At Givat Avot.

The police station?

Yes.

At some place by the side?

No, out in the yard where all the police cars . . . Where . . . Outside the interrogation room. That's it. I was with him then. So the communications guy took my picture. I didn't want it, this was fucked up. You just have no idea what to do. We were totally confused. And angry, too. Because you saw him throwing stones, you know what he did, you know it was dangerous. Again, you go through bad stuff, but the people doing it are like, I don't know . . .

How long was he at Gross until you took him to Givat Avot?

I don't remember whether it was an hour or a quarter of an hour. A while, I think. The bad part is that he was at the station for a long time. The worst thing about it is coming into contact with those people. Whenever someone does something bad, one of the Arabs, you take him to Givat Avot and he disappears. He's taken to some camp or somewhere for three or four days.

Do you know where?

I don't know. We were always told it was somewhere in the Occupied Territories.

Ofer base?

Maybe. I don't know. We'd bring them to the police station and forget about them. They'd come back after a while. They don't really go anywhere.

You said before that when you were at Gross, the deputy company commander shook the boy.

Right. We all did. He lost it.

What do you mean? Why?

Because at some point, they turn into such worms. I remember we just hated them. I hated them. I was such a racist there, as well, I was so angry at them for their filth, their misery, the whole fucking situation: You threw a stone, why did you do it? Why do I have to be here and you here, don't do this. He's on the floor, crying at you. His hands are tied. Eventually we untied his hands because he cried and begged. He was screaming and all wet from sweat and snot and tears. You just don't know what to do. We shook him out of desperation. It wasn't especially violent. I think we even began to laugh eventually, even now, when I think about it, you're in this situation and you're just lost.

You're saying that it wasn't just you and the communications guy, right? It was also the deputy company commander?

Of course. What do you mean? It wasn't like we shook him to ... It was to make him stop, you're driving us crazy, we kept yelling at him: Stop it already! Saying different things in Arabic to him, any word we knew.

15. The brigade commander explained, "You go up to the body, put the barrel between the teeth, and shoot"

Unit: Givati Brigade
Location: Gaza Strip
Year: 2008

There was a pattern. It started with Operation Hot Winter,* which until then was the largest operation ever, not the longest, but the biggest in scope and achievement. Before that there was Operation Fall Clouds sometime in 2006, around the time of the Lebanon war.† It was a forty-eight-hour operation, and afterward it turned out there was a battalion operation there for five months, the whole battalion plus a little less than a company ...

*A military campaign launched on February 29, 2008, in the Gaza Strip.
†Launched on November 1, 2006, also in the Gaza Strip.

How often?

Once a week. But that wasn't the whole battalion. During the five months there were maybe six battalion operations and everything else was a company operation, mostly searches and trying to bring out terrorists.

How deep did you go in?

Mostly not too deep, but also not just four houses in from the border. The deeper operations were, I'd say, a kilometer and a half to two kilometers in.

I want to ask about the preparations. For example, what about rules of engagement, civilians?

They said the objective was to search houses looking for weapons. Of course, part of the objective is also to see—there were operations where they deliberately fired for no reason, but the battalion commander said the shooting was to bring out terrorists so we could kill a few.

Where did you shoot?

There was a specific operation where I remember we had a force of grenade launchers, machine guns, and maybe even a .5 heavy machine gun trained on some houses. They didn't fire at the houses, but they fired randomly, around the houses. Not shooting to hit anything, but to try to bring out terrorists. In terms of preparation, I don't really remember whether they actually said "It's not black and white," and they didn't tell us to shoot at everyone, it's not like Operation Cast Lead,* where there was insane excitement.

How was the operation run? You finished the briefings . . .

There are operations on foot, there are heavy APCs, you arrive at the entry point, it doesn't matter if it's a company or a battalion, there's a marching order, you go, and at some point you take the target, every

---

*A three-week incursion into the Gaza Strip during the winter of 2008–09.

squad captures a specific house. You go in at night, get to a house, go into the house and verify that no one's armed, you never go in wet, there's also no wet cover, apart from a few specific operations where there was fire for show, to try and draw fire. We never used grenades, maybe only during Hot Winter.

The shooting for show, where was it aimed?

I don't know because I wasn't in that platoon. I know that the intention wasn't to hit anyone, but they did shoot toward the houses. I had a good friend who was in the battalion, and in the battalion commander's command force, not with him personally but around, and he heard him talking with someone on the radio saying, "Listen, pal, you've got no idea what's going on here," during the shooting for show. There was one operation where they were so worked up about firing grenades from launchers or a small grenade launcher they got from the paratrooper patrol or I don't know what, they brought it for the operation—the small launcher is lighter so it's better.

You went into the houses and then?

In most cases they searched the houses and then set up positions there. They searched for weapons and armed men, and then they'd set up snipers or sharpshooters, and sometimes they had to break the tiles to fill sandbags and they'd do 2/4 or 2/2*, depending on the number of men in the squad or the platoon. It was flexible until they packed up.

What did they do with the people who lived in the houses?

They'd put them together in one room, usually with their hands tied. I don't remember whether they were blindfolded, maybe only rarely, and they'd put a guard there. I don't remember if there was violence toward the people other than . . . there was no resistance on their part. I remember some rough things in places on the border, on the outskirts, totally rural areas where the administration there doesn't give a

*Hours on duty: 2/4 means two hours on, four hours off.

shit, they live in shacks, it stinks. There's nothing like that in the West Bank in terms of poverty.

Who would they handcuff?
Not women, I think.

Only men. Was there a certain age they'd handcuff?
I don't think the elderly. In Hot Winter there was one house with a whole tribe—we didn't cuff them there, we just put them in a room with a guard.

What about a twelve-year-old boy?
I don't think so. Maybe I exaggerated, and most of them weren't cuffed. There were operations where they'd go in with heavy APCs and come back on foot. There was one operation where we brought back a lot of people for interrogation with the Shin Bet, not particular suspects, just to get information and recruit collaborators, that's my guess. They'd load up men of a certain age on a large truck and it would go into Israel. Apparently the Shin Bet interrogated them.

Who chose them? Did a Shin Bet agent come with you?
For the most part, no. That happened maybe once, there was one particular operation I remember that we came back on foot with a few detainees. What's fucked up is that they came back blindfolded, it's not clear why, what secrets were they going to tell, it's not like they were in a Merkava Mark IV, right?* They were handcuffed together and it was tough walking there, even for us. Some of them lost their sandals on the way and they went barefoot in a place where it's not nice to walk barefoot. It was a nightmare. For me, too . . . In all these operations I just wanted to get there, the operations were hard, physically, and not only because they were physically hard, but because they were just hard. I felt bad for them.

*An Israeli-manufactured tank.

Palestinian detainees being transported in a "Safari," Ramallah, Operation Defensive Shield, 2002. The photographer was serving in Nahal Brigade, Battalion 50.

How many were there?

Not many, not a long convoy, but that was just my company. The operation I was talking about was a battalion operation, so maybe in other companies.

Was this something that surprised you?

No, it was the operation's objective, to bring detainees for interrogation.

Who gave the briefing?

A platoon commander.

During the briefing when they said you'd be coming back with detainees, what did they say?

You're detaining people for interrogation, I don't remember if they said the Shin Bet. Sometimes they defined that as a secondary objective. Bottom line, in the briefings they didn't talk about overall objectives, rather they'd explain what you have to do and they'd also explain things as it was going on. The operation was searches and "maybe there'll be some terrorists to kill," mostly it was weapons searches and if there was something for intelligence.

I wanted to ask if drawing fire was a method that worked.

I don't remember it working. There were a few operations like that. That was a change that happened after two months during that time, and they started doing that. There was a period of foot operations, and after that operations in the heavy APCs, and after that, toward the end, sometimes we did it one way and sometimes the other.

When you sat at the window of a house, did you need permission from someone to shoot?

It depends. If I see someone armed—no. I say no because I only remember things in general. If you see someone armed—then no, if I see someone looking suspicious because he's trying to hide or because he has binoculars or a cell phone—then yes. That's what I understood, at least.

After you'd come back would they tell you whether there had been any hits?

Yes, but in general, if there was something to say about the effect of the operation, then yes. After Hot Winter they made sure to say it was successful, a lot of terrorists were killed, and that it had a deterrent effect. But after [an] operation when we thought the terrorists had been killed and it turned out they'd just been wounded, it was surprising and frustrating. Surprising because, for example, one squad commander in my platoon had shot a terrorist who was walking with a Kalashnikov and a cell phone in the street and hadn't known he was thirty meters from the IDF. He shot him in the middle of his body and he fell, and then they threw two grenades at him to make sure he was dead, and afterward they said that the terrorists hadn't been killed. By the way, during this period, was it legal to verify a kill?

I have no idea. Why?

After the incident where they dismissed the platoon commander, we had a briefing from the brigade commander, who sat with the battalion commander in the room, and our platoon sat there while he questioned us to understand better what had happened. And then he gave clear orders about clashes and how they're supposed to end: "You go up to the body, put the barrel between the teeth, and shoot." Afterward, I heard that verifying a kill was illegal.

That's what I know, too.

I know they came up with a laundered phrase, "verify a neutralization."

16. They told the force to shoot anyone in the street

UNIT: ENGINEERING CORPS
LOCATION: RAFAH
YEAR: 2002–2003

During the operations in Gaza, anyone walking around in the street, shoot at the torso. In an operation in the Philadelphi corridor, anyone walking around at night, shoot at the torso.

How many operations were there?
Daily. In the Philadelphi corridor, every day.

When you're looking for tunnels, how do they manage to get around—I mean, they live there.
It's like this: You bring the force up to the third or fourth floor. Another force does the search. They know that when they're doing the search there'll be a lot of people trying to harm the forces. Generally it was assumed that they'd try to hurt the forces doing the searches. So they brought the force up, so they'd shoot at anyone in the street.

How much shooting was there?
Endless.

I'm ready, I'm up on the third floor. I shoot at whoever I see?
Yes.

But it's a street in Gaza, the most crowded place in the world.

No, no, I'm talking about the Philadelphi corridor.

It's a kind of rural area?

Not exactly rural, it's a road, it's like suburbs, it's not like the center. During operations in the Gaza neighborhoods it's the same thing. Shooting, during night operations—shooting.

Isn't there any kind of announcement saying, stay indoors?

No.

They actually shot people?

They actually shot at whoever was walking around in the street. It always ended with, "We killed six terrorists today." Whoever you shot in the street is "a terrorist."

That's what they say at the briefings?

The goal is to kill terrorists.

No, what are the rules of engagement?

Whoever's walking around at night, shoot to kill.

During the day, too?

They dealt with the daytime in the briefings: whoever's walking around during the day, look for something suspicious. But something suspicious is also . . . a cane.

17. Any kid you see with a stone, you can shoot

UNIT: PARATROOPERS
LOCATION: ETZION BRIGADE
YEAR: 2002

What finished it all—the brigade commander is there facing us during the briefing, we're in a *hudna,** it's a fragile situation, he talks about that, and then a minute later he briefs us, "Any kid you see with a stone, you can shoot at him." Like, shoot to kill. A stone!

Who gave the briefing?

The battalion commander or the brigade commander, I don't remember, the briefing went like this: "Now, the situation is very fragile, and a stone is a deadly weapon, you know what that means. I've seen someone injured by a stone." I think that our battalion commander, of the . . . he saw that the brigade commander was there. The Etzion Brigade, it was ——.

—— *gave an order that you can shoot at a child who's throwing a stone?*

Yes, because it's a deadly weapon, because they throw them in the road. It was during the *hudna.*

And there was no protest?

No. I told you, I was already one foot out, from my point of view, in my head. What annoyed me the most was that the guys on the staff were at the point where all they cared about was that they'd been told to wear regulation army boots for the briefing, because of the brigade commander. And they argued about it for hours, and one person went and yelled at the company commander, they yelled at each other for half an hour after the briefing. And no one questioned him . . . and of course I wanted to ask him, but I was in such despair over all these blockheads, and I knew that every time I asked there was opposition against

*Cease-fire.

me . . . the people who'd say, "Come on, more questions, more whatever, we want to play soccer." Or, "Shut up with your questions." It was there all the time, my group always thought the opposite, so I knew I wouldn't get an answer, as usual. To me, it was over the limit, it was really too much. The guys said, the soldiers said, as a joke: "Let's just shoot someone and end this stinking *hudna* and we'll stop with the ambushes and start going back to making arrests." And then this comes from the highest command, who seems just as sick of it, so he wants something to happen.

18. We collected all the men in the stadium

Unit: Nachshon Battalion
Location: Tul Karem
Year: 2002

I remember once they assigned the company some actions in Tul Karem. These actions drew a lot of criticism, even in the foreign press, because they collected all the men. What did they do? Every time they'd go into the villages, to the towns and whatever, they'd catch a lot, they'd get them. So what did they say? They went through, made an announcement, it was an order from above. The battalion was one of a few, one of many . . .

The order came from higher up than the battalion? Possibly the brigade commander?

Yes, at least the brigade commander. No, it was a serious IDF operation, it wasn't just the Nachshon Battalion there.

What sector?

In Tul Karem, the city. So basically, the order was for all the men to go to a giant soccer field, so then there would be like no men in the city, so it would be easier to do the searches, you get it? Less to worry about, because if you'd see a man he's suspicious, automatically suspicious. So it really got a lot . . . you can imagine.

How many men were there?

They brought in all the men from Tul Karem for some forty-eight hours. It was, it made—there was a pretty serious media storm just then. Like concentration camps, blah, blah, blah, you know. They collected them in some central lot.

They made an announcement.

Yes.

Who announced it, you?

No. I don't know. The white ones, I think, the white jeeps.

The District Coordination and Liaison.

In any case, afterward they assigned us a sector and we went from house to house looking for weapons. That was the mission. They told us during the briefings beforehand: "All the men have been informed that they have to be in some central location, so you're not expected to run into any men. If you do—they're suspect." They let us know what had happened so we'd understand the mission.

And did you see the lot?

No. But I remember that they said . . . it was like forty-eight hours that they were there, so there were lots of incidents. There wasn't even a bathroom.

Do you know who guarded it?

No. But I believe that during the in-depth debriefing . . . let's think about the date, at least which month, it was about a year and a half into my service, maybe a bit more, around September 2002, let's say. Let's say give or take three months, four months, probably more rather than less. In any case, so we go in . . . you know, at the beginning you're on like a high . . . you really feel the fear. You go into the first house, you check it and everything, you really check that no one's hiding, that you don't see any weapons, but it's still within what's reasonable. And then there's exhaustion and whatever. Then there's the stage where we went into houses and we'd put everyone left in the house, usually the mother and the children, maybe a grandmother or someone, in a room and we're all over the living room, say, all over it for maybe two, three hours.

Did you search the house?

They searched to make sure there really weren't any weapons, you know, everyone at his level. There's the kind who checked and pulled out all the clothes. But the houses didn't look the same as when we went inside.

You go house to house searching all of Tul Karem?

I'm telling you, it was a really serious operation, so everyone gets a sector. You know, you miss a house here and there, you don't go crazy, but basically you go house to house making sure there's no men and no weapons.

Were there men?

All kinds of old men. "Why are you here?" An old man, you know. And then there was one house where the woman had a picture on the refrigerator or something, of her man with a weapon.

A picture with a weapon?

Yes. What's this? and you know . . . I mean, people were crazy. Where is he, what is he, like that. She tried to explain, like, you know, it's a picture, it's pride, it's some Palestinian policeman. Just like we have. Why compare? Yeah, photographs, but it's like we had during the time of, you know . . . it's a militant thing, it's their national pride, you know, and ours, okay. So that's it, people were, like, crazy: "We're going to find weapons here." And to me it's clear they won't find anything, but never mind. I'm telling you, they turn the house upside down like a hurricane's been there. They left nothing the way it had been. Okay, they basically turned the other houses upside down as well, but in this one they also went crazy breaking things. And the sergeant obviously saw it, but at a certain point I say, Hello; I say to the sergeant, "Look what he's doing." And then some sort of tension started, like snitching, kind of, here and there. But really, I'm telling you, shelves with fragile stuff, it all went flying.

And you saw they had no weapons there?
No, it was clearly just vandalism.

There was no sense of doing a search?
No. There was some sense of doing a search, but at the same time it was also vandalism. You open a closet and on the way you see a shelf, so you send the whole thing flying. Yeah, that house took a beating. And as the day went on, the force's level of sensitivity dropped, and they've been holding [the family] for four, five hours. You know, it was a long action. People got really tired.

How long was it?
I think it was like twenty-four hours. The preparation was longer, but I think all the noise about collecting the men made a difference, because when we went in they said it was going to be three days. Because I remember we also ran into some—you know, no one dared to get involved, also there were no men, the roads were supposed to be empty—and there were two women from one of those international peace forces, what are they called?

There are a lot.
There are a lot, but this one's the best-known. Never mind, you know what I'm talking about. Basically, these two women come, and we're in the house and the family is shut up in a room there for hours, I think it may have even been that house with the weapon, where we saw the picture.

How many hours?
We were there at least three hours.

Was there a curfew in the street?
Yes, yes.

So they're shut up in a room. They're shut up in the house anyway.

Yes, you're right. They're shut up in a room in the house. So those two women were going crazy. So that every time there was someone else guarding the door to the house. I remember standing there and they come, these two crackpots—crackpot, I'm telling you, you get it?—and they say to me, they're screaming at me in English for hours. And I understand every word, I speak English at home. And I say, The last thing I can deal with right now is an argument with someone whose side I'm actually on. Like, everything here is insane. So I just ignore it, like it's insane, and one of them yells, "He understands English, he knows." I don't know, maybe she saw something in my eyes that I understood every word they were saying, and I'm just making a face like they're speaking Chinese. It was really hard. They really, they like feel it, they see what I see.

What do all you see?

Everything I told you, and it holds up a mirror to your face. It was really hard for me. And people are jumpy, "Those whores." We leave the house, and they start, they continue following us. And the [soldiers] yell at them, "Get out of here." Somehow they managed to scare the [women] enough so they leave. I remember just as they were leaving—I was last, I don't know, somehow I was last or something—I said to them, "You have to tell the world what you see."

How did they react?

I don't know, they sort of looked at me like, I don't know, I don't think they were impressed, and justifiably, if I'm objective. You know, me, if I was looking at someone like me from the side—I'm no great hero, on the contrary, I witness all these things. They made the effort, they came from the outside, they're the ones trying to save the world. Me, what am I doing? I'm there and I'm doing nothing. I enlisted in this army, I do all the missions they tell me to do. The fact that I think what they're doing is good doesn't turn me into . . . but I don't know what they thought. These are also things that are hard for me, personally, but that's what happened. And yeah I remember that I went there, I went home for the weekend, and on the radio they said there were operations in Tul Karem and they reported they found this and that and some fertilizer that they suspected could have been used . . .

As explosives.

Yeah. I remember saying, "What bullshit." And we were in the car I think with ——'s father, and ——'s father has moderate opinions, but he says: "What, just ordinary fertilizer, come on?" And I say from the back, "Who knows if even that was there." Then he says, "Come on." I suppose that if I were sitting at home I'd also say Come on and Whatever, but you know, after everything I saw, it was just . . . you know, the report on the radio in the end, it's unbelievable how in the end the report on the radio was, "In an operation in Tul Karem the IDF captured," like, you know, "twenty suspects, ten weapons, and fertilizer suspected for use in manufacturing [explosives], a ton and a half of fertilizer." So it's a success, because you hear it on the radio and you say, "Hey, look, like we went there, this is what we got, we did what we were supposed to do." And what we did was just the opposite. Because what did we do? We committed crimes. We destroyed homes. No house that we went into was the same when we left.

How many houses did you go through?

We went through whole streets. I'm telling you, every house, somehow someone came up with the idea that, wait, maybe they're hiding things in the water tanks on the roof, you know, they have those big black tanks on every house. So they turned over every tank.

Did the water leak?

They flipped it over, whoops. In our insanity.

Did you leave the residents without running water?

I don't know, they didn't think about that, they were looking for weapons. Maybe there's a weapon here under all this water. Anything went, there was no specific information on the house, but you had to check every house like it was Hamas headquarters.

19. Disrupting the residents' everyday life

UNIT: NAHAL BRIGADE
LOCATION: HEBRON
YEAR: 2005

Normally when you talk about disruption you're referring to terrorist activity, you disrupt terrorist activity. You break down what that means—why disruption, why don't you say thwarting or preventing? Like, what does disruption mean? You know, there's thwarting, preventing, disrupting, responding to terrorist activity, all of that. Yeah, you do a lot of things. So you see, what's disruption exactly? In general what we, the answers we gave ourselves, or the answers we got from the commanders higher up, is that it's kind of like creating no routine.

For whom?

Even in our own operations, so they wouldn't be able to follow us and do anything to us. One time, it's clear, it makes sense, to protect the patrol. But also with the . . . meaning we'd suddenly set up a checkpoint, like a checkpost,* for twenty-five minutes on some road, a road going up toward the Avraham Avinu neighborhood.† And then the minute you start doing stuff like this, the [Palestinians] start to think they can't plan anything because it'll get disrupted. If you go in the middle of the night and start doing mapping, then a guy who's wanted, say, or he's in charge of the Abu Sneina neighborhood, he's not going to get any sleep, or he decides to leave Abu Sneina, he decides to live in a neighborhood that's farther away. That's disruption. Disrupting everyday life for the people who live there. I don't remember, I don't think we had it as a written policy. No, maybe it was written policy in other places.

---

*A temporary surprise checkpoint.
†The Jewish neighborhood in Hebron.

20. Slapping, shoving, all kinds of stuff like that. Every day

UNIT: LAVI BATTALION
LOCATION: HEBRON DISTRICT
YEAR: 2002–2003

There was something that happened with a retarded kid, really retarded, who threw stones from some hill near Kvasim Junction. In the end they arrested him, with that same deputy company commander, and he said to one of my soldiers, "Okay, take him to the jeep." The soldier, who was relatively small, grabbed him by the shoulder. He was okay, that soldier, and the guy started struggling with him, and it was really hard for him, that little soldier, to control this, like, sixteen-year-old boy. So I threw him to the ground. During this scrap my weapon hit him in the mouth and it broke his tooth or something. He started bleeding and going crazy. I finally got control of him. All his cousins and uncles and his parents, I don't know what, they came, his whole clan, like four adults, grown men, and the deputy company commander threatened them, the next time he sees the kid there, he says: "I don't care whether he throws a stone or not, I'm going to kill him." And this kid, there's blood all over his face. And they say, "What, can't you see he's retarded, and his hand doesn't work"—his right hand, which was very, very strong, was okay, but the left hand was just, there was a kind of delay, it didn't function—"he's not able to throw stones," and on and on. The deputy company commander threatened the parents. Then we released the kid and he just grabbed a huge stone, like this, and almost hit the deputy company commander. The deputy company commander and the kid started fighting a bit and the kid got a pounding, and the whole time he's bleeding from his mouth from the cut he got from me. But the thing with the violence, I think, wasn't how harsh it was, it's how often it happened. It got to the point where there pretty much wasn't a day that went by without someone getting hit or a threat to hurt someone. Most of the time there was slapping, shoving, all kinds of stuff like that. And that was every day.

21. Pointless arrests

UNIT: NAHAL BRIGADE
LOCATION: RAMALLAH/HEBRON DISTRICT
YEAR: 2008–2009

We were tired of making some of the arrests. We had the feeling that they were pointless, for example, searching for people who cut apart fences, or people who threw stones or were inciters or who'd been identified at demonstrations against the wall. It felt pointless. If you had the feeling in Hebron that you're just arresting some poor loser, here it felt like we were doing nothing. There was one arrest, I don't remember which village it was, and things started heating up, and there was a mess and I remember the company commander pointed his gun and said they need to calm down, and then the Shin Bet came into the village, to a couple of houses belonging to the same big family.

What happened in the end?
They took who they needed and that was it.

What was the guys' age range?
Fifteen, sixteen up to twenty-three, twenty-four.

And you're saying that they'd cut fences, thrown stones, and had been seen at protests?
Yes.

Protests in Ni'lin?*
No, protests in the area. I remember one of my toughest experiences there—I often had to take detainees to Ofer base, and like I said, the army's right and left hands are two different things . . . I had to take this one guy to the battalion's base for a night until the vehicle arrived,

---

*To prevent expansion of the Separation Barrier, which will cut off a sizable part of the town.

the Safari. In the meantime I went to bed. The guy sat there cuffed and blindfolded. I told the guard not to do anything stupid, they gave him water, and we covered him with a sleeping bag because it was cold. I remember it was horrible, because Ofer only opens at a certain time and we waited, and the driver was sick, and it was horrible watching him like that, he had to pee, I was standing next to him with the gun.

How long was he like that, handcuffed and blindfolded?

A good few hours. Until they took him in and then it was over. No one could tell me what to do with him. A total mess. We waited at Ofer and he sat in the Safari and after the arrest I couldn't sleep for hours at night.

*Were there people who you just dried out?**

There's always tension, both in Hebron and in Rantis. The basic things—sitting in a room with a guard, the handcuffs, the blindfold, giving them food or water or a blanket—that we always do. There was no question. There were right-wing guys who thought it was too much and the leftists who . . . and you ask yourself that maybe we're being too kind. That's where the standards of good and bad start to deteriorate, and I think that's the hardest thing, that in Hebron, it was absolute, there's black and white, what's good and bad, but the day-to-day is so gray. Every person you arrest, his kid didn't do anything, and you get the feeling that you've destroyed his kid.

Guys you took in for detention?

The dilemma is every day, you go out on patrol, that's the basis of your presence there. I felt a dilemma. But in these places it's more about the limit of your decency. What it means to be humane is very unclear.

What I'm asking is, the ones where you felt a dilemma, were they people you brought into detention, or people you just dried out?

In Hebron it wasn't, again, I don't know, because there were also people in Hebron who stole metal, seven-year-old kids who wanted to steal metal, and the only thing they did was steal metal to sell because they

---

*The term refers to holding a detainee without formally bringing him into detention.

didn't have any money at home, so they crossed Shuhada street, which they're not allowed to cross. Shuhada separates the Jewish settlement from the casbah and they're allowed to be in Abu Sneina and the casbah, but not in between. So they'd catch them and there was nothing the police could do with them,* so you sit them down at the post for two hours. You've got no way to deal with it or solve it, so you dry them out. Maybe the way I see things is very distorted compared to how they are in the day-to-day. I don't know. My aunt is a psychologist and she told me that to understand it you have to be out of it completely, and I can't tell you what's good and what isn't, because I don't have the tools.

22. The guys pissed into the courtyard

UNIT: NAHAL BRIGADE
LOCATION: HEBRON
YEAR: 2002

There was this house we captured in Hebron . . . we took this house. You know the procedure: the family moves down a floor. Now, what did we do? We were . . . on the third floor, the guys set up a pipe, a pipe to pee, so they could pee outside. They put the pipe, we put the pipe exactly so that all the piss would flow into the courtyard of the house below us. There were a few chicken coops just there, it all poured out there. That was the joke every day, waiting for the father or one of the kids to go to the coop, and then everyone stands and pisses. Or like, I just remembered a friend who liked to brush his teeth and wash his mouth with the canteen, and then wait for someone to pass below so he could spit on them, spit outside.

It's part of . . .

It's part of the things you can do, yeah, it's just a thing you can do. No one's going to stop you from doing it, not even the commanders in the

---

*Israeli settlers in the Occupied Territories fall under the legal jurisdiction of Israel's police force; Palestinian residents do not.

field, because most of them are part of the consensus, not the exception. It's just something you're able to do. You can do it, so you decide that you will or that you won't. There's no judge and no judgment. No one's going to judge you for it.

23. Taking control of some family

Unit: Field Intelligence
Location: General
Year: 2004–2006

When I was an officer, in the beginning, I was very focused on whatever mission they gave me. They'd give me a mission and that's where I was, the whole time. And after, there was a stage where my soldiers were, I trusted them that they were on top of control of the mission, and I was very . . . I'd move aside, to where we'd collect the family, I'd sit with them.

With the family?

Yes, I'd talk to them, you know, talk about . . . I'd even give them some of our food. It's packaged exactly, you know, everyone gets his half a tuna sandwich, you can't carry too much because you're there for three days, and I'd bring them food because they had nothing.

For the family?

Yeah. They had nothing. And so you sit with a family and you're living with them. You're with them for three days, it's a lot of time. Not just an hour or two. Maybe the infantry spends a few hours, I don't know.

They're in the room the whole time, or you let them out sometimes?

That's it, that was the problem, what if there's no bathroom in the house? Normally a soldier goes with them one-on-one when they want to go to the bathroom. He goes with, and is there with them in the bathroom. The same deal when the mother wants to cook—so he goes with her to the kitchen. The truth is, it has to be an inside room so they can't get to the windows, to escape or yell out or I don't know what, so no one outside can hear anything.

Did you enter the house covertly, or did you set up a lookout even though you might have been seen?

No, it's covert. No one knows we're there.*

It's like taking hostages, basically.

Yes.

Three days.

It's as if the army says, like, that's it . . . it's the last resort. And okay—so the family's confined for a few days.

But they talk about it afterward.

Yeah, they tell people afterward, even though they won't know what we did. We went into their house and left, they don't know what we did in there. They go into one room, and we're in another room where we carry out our mission. They don't see and they don't know and they have nothing to do with it.

Did anyone ever complain, say they don't want you coming in?

Never . . . that doesn't happen. You go in.

If you came into my house, I'd . . .

Sure. But you go in with a whole team in the middle of the night with weapons, okay? And they don't know what . . . Our faces are camouflaged or something, so first of all, for a few hours they're in shock. Then the whole family goes into one room. There isn't . . . I never ran into resistance or anything like that.

---

*An example of a straw widow.

Identity check at the guard post below the Bet Romano settlement in Hebron. The Palestinian stores are permanently closed.

What did you do when the bathroom was outside?

So you had to . . . I don't know, they had to relieve themselves somewhere.

Inside? In the room?

So that's it, I don't remember our solution exactly. I'm sure that somehow we found a solution. But generally it's . . . even if we planned to be there for two days, maybe after a day you couldn't stand it any longer, because it was impossible, because of the bathroom or some kind of a problem. That's it, and then you see that there's something, you get it, and you start asking questions, you get some perspective. And then you go to the situation assessment, after you've been in all kinds of incidents like that, and then . . .

Later, once you were an officer, or just after a few days?

You're an officer, you go through all these situations with this poor family, you see they've got nothing, they're the most innocent people you can imagine, they barely know Hebrew, nothing. You know, sometimes you go to a town, they know a few words. But these people don't have . . . they're illiterate. They don't know anything, they have no connection to anything. So you say, you get some perspective, when you've been to some situation assessment and the brigade commander says: "Yeah, so you'll take over this house and this house, and this one and that one." And you say, You know, can't you think of something else? Maybe, I don't know, what on earth are you doing here? What's the army doing here?

It's not their job to think about why the army's here.

Yes, obviously. No, but you quickly . . . if they decide they're just demonstrating a presence, okay? So go on patrol or something, there are loads of military options. No one decided that you have to take over some family to demonstrate a presence.

Going into homes was demonstrating a presence?

Yes, of course.

24. A moving human shield

Unit: Civil Administration
Location: Bethlehem district
Year: 2002

I'm not going to give a run-through of the day-to-day, because if you've talked to soldiers who served in the field then you certainly know all

about the games—the village does have electricity, it doesn't have electricity, shooting at the water tanks, and hours at the checkpoints* and
other things like that. Every soldier who's served in the Territories
knows all about it and knows that it's become a kind of norm. But
there were two episodes that upset me, first, because to me they were
very serious, and second, because it was officers in the paratroops who
did them. One was Captain ——, and the other a first lieutenant, when
the captain was a company commander in the paratroops. Most of the
complaints reached us in the end, they came to us. I'm talking about a
complaint we got one day, at the entrance to Takua, where we weren't
stationed, which is why it happened, because we weren't at that entrance.
The soldiers went in without telling us, which is completely against
procedure. The complaint was just incredible: IDF soldiers had tied
a Palestinian to the hood of their jeep and drove through the village
like that. The complaint just didn't seem to make sense. We asked their
operations room, they said, "We'll look into it and get back to you." It
never happened. We said, "It never have happened." They said to us,
"Yes, there was something, you look into it." It didn't make sense, but a
complaint like that, you can't make it up. You can invent a complaint
about a delay at a checkpoint, but this was so outrageous that something must have happened, they couldn't just have made it up. My
commander, a lieutenant colonel, and another officer went out there.

Were you there?

I was at the District Coordination Office and I was part of the investigation, and I know the guy that did it and everything. In the end he
admitted it. They went there, and again we were told that it hadn't
happened. We started to investigate, started speaking to the soldiers.
Apparently, that captain had gone to Takua, which is a pretty hostile
village—they were throwing stones at the jeep. So he just stopped a
Palestinian guy who was passing, forty-something years old, and tied
him to the hood of the jeep, a guy just lying on the hood, and they
drove into the village. No one threw any more rocks.

*Detaining Palestinians at the checkpoints at whim.

A human shield.

Yes. But not just a human shield—first of all, a human shield is bad enough—this was a moving human shield. Tied to the hood of the jeep and they drove with him tied there. Drove with him through the village, it's horrific. That officer, by the way—a month before, we'd gone into the same village, Takua, he'd instructed his soldiers to stand on a hilltop, again, the same captain. I don't want to screw him personally, but all these incidents are written and documented, witnessed and documented at the DCL, and it made it to the papers, at least the story with the jeep. And he admitted it and was sentenced to two weeks' prison, and was dismissed from his command position.

Which battalion was it?

I don't want to just say any name. It was a battalion stationed in Betar Ilit, I don't remember which battalion exactly.

When was this?

In the middle of my service, something like that, March/April. But he was a captain in the paratroops, the incident made it to the media, to the papers. I'm almost sure it was Battalion 101, but I don't want to say it for the sake of saying something. I remember I worked with them the most, they were there most of the time. But in any case, that same guy, a month before, we went into Takua. He gathered everyone and said, "Guys, I'm putting three snipers on the hilltop, and I'm parking the jeep right smack in the middle of the village." You have to understand, they go out on patrol in Takua, it's legitimate. To locate vehicles and to demonstrate a presence. But what he tried to do was get the [Palestinians] to crowd around and start throwing rocks. He said, "I don't respond to rocks. When there's enough of a crowd, the soldiers on the hill will take out their legs." The Palestinians didn't know there were soldiers behind them, and the soldiers would just spray their legs. It was prevented only because I was there and another officer, and we prevented it. We reported it but it was smoothed over. It was just appalling. His one goal was to lure Palestinian children, just to cut off their legs. It was horrific. This is the same captain who led the incident we were talking about.

25. We were waving the gun, showing the boy what to do

UNIT: ARMORED CORPS
LOCATION: BAKA A-SHARQIYA
YEAR: 2000

I was on the front in Baka just as the Intifada began—really, one week you see a teeming village full of life, the whole place full of Israelis shopping for Shabbat, and then there's suddenly a kind of switch, the place turns into a ghost town, and no one dares leave their house ... We were generally at a checkpoint, and the main road of the village also leads to Mevo Dotan and Hermesh,* so we had to keep the road open so [the settlers] could come and go, and every now and then the Palestinians would leave burning tires near the checkpoint. They'd add anything they could get their hands on: tires, furniture, everything ... they'd make a blockade ... sometimes a few of them a few hundred meters from the checkpoint, not too big, and so we'd remove them. The logic behind this was that we wouldn't do it, because it's too dangerous for us, because we had no way to know whether there was an explosive inside, it was impossible to know whether a sniper was standing on one of the hills waiting for us ... So the logical thing to do was grab random people on the street and tell them that they had to do it. We grabbed all kinds of people, it depended on who was there at the moment. Sometimes it was older people, sometimes it was just people walking in the street ... One time we grabbed a kid, not a big kid, a ten- or twelve-year-old boy, something like that, and we explained what he had to do by pointing with the barrel of the gun, meaning we were waving the gun, showing him what to do. This created a situation ... there's this little boy, a patrol jeep, and three soldiers aiming their weapons at him, and he has to go and move the blockade, these blockades. And he's working and crying ... and removing the blockades, and we go and point our guns, and he goes to the next one, and like that ... then the patrol jeep commander with me decided that

*Israeli settlements.

maybe they'd done something like that farther down the road, which didn't make any sense, because that's how you leave the village, so there's no chance, and he says to me maybe there's something like that down the road, we'll take him with us. There's no place to put the boy inside the patrol jeep, so what he does is throw him in the back, my friend and I were in the back of the patrol jeep and the boy is on our legs and our equipment and the grenades, and he's crying the whole time, lying on us and on the equipment and our feet. I could feel through his pants that he'd peed out of fear . . . After we'd driven ten kilometers from the village and it was clear that they hadn't walked ten kilometers with a load of furniture to make a blockade, the commander decided it was enough, we could let him out. He stopped the jeep . . . pulled the kid out, threw him at the side of the road, the kid's crying again, and now he has wet pants and a ten-kilometer walk back, and we keep going to the settlements down the road.

26. You could do whatever you like and no one asked any questions

Unit: Paratroopers
Location: Nablus
Year: 2002

. . . There was another mission with an APC, imposing a curfew, driving around, going wherever you like. Wrecking their streets just like this . . .

What do you mean, wrecking their streets?

The APC drives on their streets and wrecks them.

What, cars and things?

Sometimes yes and sometimes no. Sometimes they'd drive over cars and sometimes . . .

Operational necessity?

No, no operational necessity.

No, I mean, if you want to go in some place and there's a car in the way, then that's operational necessity.

No, no, by mistake . . . you can't see that it's too narrow . . . and at that time we could do whatever we want. We'd shoot . . . we'd stand at the roadblock, at this abandoned house, and you could see people coming from a kilometer or five hundred to six hundred meters away. They can't hear you and you don't have the strength to yell at them to turn back, and you don't have the strength to talk to them and turn them around. So you try to push them back some other way, so that they don't get too close. So what do you do? Shoot nearby.

Live ammunition?

Live ammunition. Back then we only used live ammunition. We're in the city, you'd shoot at whatever you want. We'd shoot at street-lights . . . you'd shoot nearby . . . you'd shoot a warning shot, shoot in the air—you didn't need authorization from anyone higher than the commander in the field, nothing. They'd ask you about it over the radio, the company, the battalion. You'd say, "Hey, it's me, it's okay." No one ever asked why, no one asked anything. At some point we were inside Hummers, armored Hummers. We'd impose curfew on a city where no one really takes any notice of a curfew. So we crash into cars . . .

I don't understand.

You . . . Cars go by, and then the driver sees you, realizes he has to turn back, that he's not allowed to drive. So he goes in reverse, and you go faster, so you drive up over him. With your armored Hummer. You crash into it.

This happened to you, in your Hummer?

I was in a Hummer when it happened.

How many times?

With me, specifically—just once. And apart from the sergeant who was with me in the Hummer, no one knew about it.

Do you know if this happened a lot in the company?

If not exactly that, then pulling them out of the car and beating them up happened a lot, so they'd understand there's a curfew.

What do you mean, beating them up?

You know, a few slaps, a few kicks. "Come here, shut up! Why are you here, why . . ." and then you say, "*Y'allah*, get lost, go home!"

Do you know if the thing with the Hummer happened at any other time?

With the Hummer? No.

Who was there at that specific incident?

We were with an armored Hummer. Four people: the commander, the driver, me, and another guy. And I want to say that at the time I was just eight or nine months into my service . . . I had no awareness. It seemed okay, all this. With everything that's happening around you, it seemed okay, you're not aware at all . . . We came down the hill, and he got to the junction, started going in reverse, trying to get away from us.

Did the sergeant give the order?

Yeah. "Chase, chase him." And the driver, he had no doubts at all. A driver from the company, a real combat soldier. And then the car got stuck, because there's traffic in the city . . . we were facing him and we just kept driving forward.

The Hummer just went over the car?

It didn't crush the car. It went over the hood. And then we jumped out of the Hummer, we pulled the guy out. I don't think he lost his car. You catch the person, put him up against the wall, immediately start to . . . and then the driver from the car behind him comes over. He was a photographer. So he immediately started taking pictures. My sergeant got pissed off and all that, took his film and his ID.

What kind of photographer, foreign?

No, Arab. But yeah, he took his press card. And his film. Nobody knew, no one . . . There's no debriefing after the mission, you don't have . . . It was a time . . . like the Wild West. You could do whatever you like and no one asked any questions, no nothing.

And in that instance, you didn't say something to the sergeant like, You know, this thing with the car . . . it's wrong . . . and . . . ?

No, I didn't get that I was doing something wrong. I mean, you don't have the awareness. I . . . I don't know. It sounds idiotic, but you don't know that what you're doing is bad. Only later, maybe after two years, maybe after you're an officer and you start to grow up a bit, calm down. You start to realize what you did. I'm not saying I'm the one who . . . but I saw my friend putting them up against the wall, and these are thirty-, forty-year-olds, and not . . . I said, Come on, but it didn't set off a red light. I said, This situation stinks, and that's it. Going around the city, doing nothing, yelling. And sometimes we had the Border Police with us, in a jeep. Just because. They'd stop, see an open store, and beat the hell out of everyone. Just to make everyone stand up. It was incredible, I remember it. We stopped in front of a store that was open during curfew. The Border Police guys, right away, the commander opens his door and stands everyone in line . . . They say, "Why are you . . ." then whack, whack, two slaps, go home. Like that. Eleven people! Two slaps in the face.

27. They threw a grenade at him, then they put a bullet in his head

UNIT: PARATROOPERS
LOCATION: NABLUS
YEAR: 2002–2003

In Ramadan of 2003 or 2002, it was sometime during Ramadan, we went out to make an arrest. There were the usual rules of engagement about arresting a suspect and so on.

Who gave them?

The company commander, during the briefing. It's all just a question of how he's feeling. The sector brigade commander comes up with the orders for opening fire. He's got one or two battle procedures and he gives the orders for opening fire as he sees fit. Sometimes it's the . . . in the best case it's the brigade commander. When the situation's more urgent, it's the battalion commander. He decides. There is no clear procedure regarding orders to open fire.

But what were the orders on opening fire in this particular incident?

The rules of engagement for arrest of a suspect. The procedure for arresting a suspect is, "Stop, stop or I'll shoot," shooting in the air, blah, blah, blah . . . we never use it during actual operations. The procedure for arresting a suspect is the same as an expedited suspect arrest, which is, "*Waqf*—stop," boom. If he doesn't stop and put his hands up in the second when you yell *waqf*, then you shoot to kill.

Meaning, you don't shoot at his legs? You don't shoot in the air?

Stop, boom. And often the "stop" is just for protocol.

Boom, stop?

Something like that. Basically, we went in to make an arrest, it was during Ramadan. There was some confusion—one of the teams wasn't in the right position, which we only knew afterward, in the debriefing. We do an arrest with several teams that surround the house, and there's an operations team which comes to take the house. The operations team spotted a man in the alley, he had something in his hand. They yelled "*Waqf*." The man started running, and they started shooting at him, chasing him. The man escaped into the alley where the team had taken up the wrong position, and basically we had a situation of friendly fire, where one team chasing after the man and shooting at him was actually shooting toward another team. Now, this other team thought they were being shot, saw a figure, and shot at it, at this guy. They shot him. Again, they verified the kill with grenades.

Where were you when they shot at him?

I was on another team.

And you know about all this from the debriefing, and because they were part of your group and you talked about it afterward?

Yes. And I was just a few meters away. I didn't see it myself, I was watching the corner of the house, but the incident happened while I was there.

They shot at him by mistake because they thought—

They were being fired at. And they saw something in his hand and were afraid it was explosives. They shot at him, then verified the kill.

Who verified the kill?

Guys from the team, according to the verification procedure they know—they threw a grenade and then put a bullet in his head. Turns out the guy was holding a drum. What did we learn later? That there's a custom during Ramadan, at four in the morning people go out and start drumming to wake everyone up for breakfast, before the fast. We didn't know. If we'd known, if someone had, you get it? It's not just that we didn't know, ordinary soldiers, but no one else in the platoon knew either. No one in the IDF bothered to tell us that during Ramadan at such and such an hour people go around holding something, with a drum in their hands, and maybe you need to tone down the rules of engagement, maybe you need to be more careful. No one bothered to tell us, and because of that this man died. Because of our ignorance.

28. The commander said, "I want bodies full of bullets"

UNIT: GOLANI BRIGADE
LOCATION: GENERAL
YEAR: 2003–2004

We had a commander in the unit who would just say in these words, and it's awful, he used to tell us, "I want bodies. That's what I want."

Do you remember a specific case when he said that?

I remember ten cases when he said it, ten . . . From his first speech to us, and in these words, he said, "I want bodies full of bullet holes." It was just awful. Later I met him out of the army, at the home of a friend who'd been wounded. He said, "Yes, we killed twenty-eight people. They're not people at all, they're terrorists, it's okay." Forget that there have been mistakes, too, let's put that aside, we'll talk about mistakes later, though not so much in that area, but let's put that aside. That's what he wanted. That's what he said we had to do. Before we went out on an important mission he'd say, "I want bodies full of bullets." And if we came back with someone we'd killed, he was happy. That's how it was.

How did he express it?

By saying "good job," when we came back from an operation and we'd killed someone.

29. The division commander said, "You're ranked by the number of people you kill"

Unit: Paratroopers
Location: Nablus
Year: 2007

Okay. What kind of missions did you do during that period?

During that period, it would change. I think it's important to say, I remember when I was enlisted in a patrol unit, then the thinking was—I always heard friends say this—that what the patrol unit does, the difference between a patrol unit and a battalion is that the patrol unit makes arrests. It goes to arrest people and whatever, and I said, sure, sounds interesting, let's go for it, I don't want to stand at a checkpoint, we'll make arrests. At some point during my service there was suddenly an unconscious change and the units got more extreme. What do I mean, that the unit wasn't ranked anymore by the number of its arrests? We had a talk with a division commander when we got to the

Shomron Central Brigade. He said, "You're not ranked by arrests—you're ranked by the number of people you kill."

Who said that to you?

The division commander. Above the brigade commander, the most important man.

Which division commander, of the West Bank?

The division commander of . . . I don't even know how it's divided. Probably the West Bank.

Do you remember which division commander it was?

No . . . it was when I was a sergeant, after we finished training. It was in 2007. He said unequivocally, "That's how you're ranked. With Xs. Every night I want you to be out for contact, and that's how you'll be ranked." That's how the company commanders were ranked as well. At some point I realized that someone who wants to succeed has to bring him dead people. He—no point in bringing him arrests. "Arrests are routine, the battalions are making arrests. You're the spearhead, the army has invested years in you, now I want you to bring me dead terrorists." And that's what pushed us, I believe. What we'd do was go out night after night, drawing fire, go into alleys that we knew were dangerous. There were arrests, there were all kinds of arrests. But the high point of the night was drawing fire, creating a situation where they fired at us. There were "bad" Arabs, the ones who didn't shoot at us. Mostly, we'd go out every night, we got some mission, we'd try to exploit everyone's abilities, go into a house, of course all these homes belonged to people who weren't connected to anything, you see, now even I'm saying it. Innocent people. "Go into the house, do this, we'll try to draw . . ." We were a new team on the patrol unit. They really tried . . . he really, really wanted us to . . . the snipers to kill. He was on fire with it. "We'll do it all, you'll be at the opening and we'll make sure to draw armed men up to the roofs." That was the goal. It's a situation, totally insane, you're in it, it's hard to explain. You're looking through the binoculars and searching for someone to kill. That's what you want to do. And you want to kill him. But do you want to kill him? But that's your job. And you're still looking through the binoculars and you're starting to get confused. Do I want to? Don't I want to? Maybe I actually want them to miss. I remember there was one night when my soldiers were on the scope, there was someone armed, and I'm praying that they'll miss. And I'm standing next to them, saying, "Come on," but praying that they'll miss. That they'll miss and not kill him. I didn't want them to kill a man.

Did they miss?

They missed. He was injured. But they missed . . .

And when you went around looking for fire, did you get fire?

Yeah.

And then what would happen?

First of all, it depends on what point we were at. The time when we're inside the house is very short.

By the way, in terms of returning fire, when you talk about identifying the source of fire, you mean that you see someone armed on a roof or in an apartment window, or does identifying the source of fire mean shooting at the house when you know that someone fired from one of the windows? How precise is it?

No, I don't think there was a situation where there was fire from the window of a house and they sprayed it. We wouldn't do things like that. But what did happen was that they'd do everything to try to draw fire. The situation was that, the goal was . . . you know, you go into their neighborhood. Your goal is to bring them out, to make them come outside so you can kill them. And you did it any way you could, to get them outside. If you saw a flash, there was a discussion, is a flash enough? Yes. A flash is enough if it's from a window. There are all kinds of subtleties, I don't remember anymore, if you identify a figure then you're allowed, if you see a flash and then a figure, you're allowed—everything to make what's forbidden permissible. Basically, we'd do anything to draw fire. For the most part we wouldn't be out on a specific mission and get shot at by chance. It happened a lot of times that we'd go out on a search, and if we got shot at on the way to the mission, we'd drop everything and look for the fire, because here, we've got someone with a gun, why go look for someone else? The previous company commander might have been no saint but he was locked on a target, we'd go to do something. Again, maybe there was some conceptual change in the army, I don't know what it's like now. He was locked into the mission, so if there was peripheral shooting, fine, you had to ignore it and go on with the mission. When I finished with him he was ... that's what drew him. He'd get drawn by fire, and he'd do everything to respond to that fire.

30. We only killed four children

Unit: Paratroopers
Location: Nablus
Year: 2003–2004

We were based at the regional brigade, and we'd go into the city each time for ambushes.

When you say "each time" you mean ...
Something like four or five times a week. Arrests, straw widows, diversion tactics.

How many Xs does the company have?
Hmm . . . eleven armed, I think. And something like four or five kids.

Four or five kids?
At some point they told us that since we'd only taken down four kids, they were giving our company missions because we were known for not hitting civilians.

Who told you that?

The company commander said it was the brigade commander. We were given certain jobs because we knew how to be selective and we didn't harm innocent people.

And these were "only" four children . . .

Only four children . . .

And the four children were killed when?

Between December and May.

Between December and May—four children.

It's a company of sixty men who know how to distinguish between . . . there was one operation, Calm Waters, it lasted two and a half weeks, and the whole brigade went into Balata. Each time they were there for a few days. Went in, came out. I think that just during our time there,

Ramallah, 2002. The elderly man lying on the sidewalk did not hear or did not understand the order to clear the street. He was killed by solders from the Golani Brigade. Photographer: Sagi Blumberg

as part of the brigade, we took down a lot of civilians. We'd read the papers afterward and I'd see that an old man had been killed. We weren't aware of it at all. They wouldn't tell us that a force nearby had taken someone down. "An old man and four children were killed in Balata because they were in a battle zone." Now, imagine you're there, you know what a battle zone is.

What's a battle zone?

I don't know. According to the papers, Balata's a battle zone. There weren't that many incidents there. But it's a battle zone . . . I don't know . . . soldiers shoot, so it turns into a battle zone.

31. They'd deliberately wreck the house

Unit: Engineering Corps
Location: Bethlehem district
Year: 2001

The truth is that the Shimshon Brigade did the worst of the things I saw. That house where they destroyed a wall, they went like crazy looting it . . .

What do you mean, "looting"?
They, say, they shat on the . . . they shat on the couches, they stole.

They shat on the couches?
Shat on the couches before they left, just shat on the couches. They stole suits, they lifted all of the suits in the closet.

You saw that?
I was there. I left the house with them.

They just put a suit in a backpack?
No, they just, like, threw the suits in the APC.

Okay.

They'd leave behind, like deliberately, a house that was totally wrecked. They'd turn the house upside down, like when, when the family's locked in a room . . . they'd just turn their house upside down . . . And also how they . . . their arrest procedures were very, very violent . . .

What do you mean? Give me a specific example.

We ran into some . . . we were separate forces for a while, we'd come from one place, and they'd be stuck with, with the tank in some alley, they couldn't get out . . . So they were with the tank, and there were some four cars in front of them, blocking them, and a porch. Like the whole entrance to a house, an old Arab house, and they drove up with the . . . they drove the tank over the cars. Of course, they could have got out by reversing, but . . . they decided they had to turn around, they drove over four cars with the tank, they just went up, they turned around, and took off the whole entrance to the house with the back of the tank. They took down half a house, like with the tank, and left. And say, also that . . . I got there and they'd detained people, like there were, we'd round people up and all the men had to come to . . . before we'd break into the Mukata'a,* the commercial area, they'd announce that all the men had to go somewhere where they'd all be checked, and then we went into the Mukata'a, and then they were allowed back. And when they got all those men, they just . . . they'd make them undress to . . . undress down to nothing. Anyone who hesitated a bit, they'd start beating him, pushing him, hitting him, shooting in the air . . . things like that. And then they released them. These are people who came, who were told they had to come and they came of their own volition. And by the way, when we went into that Mukata'a, it was supposed to be, the way the Shimshon commander had characterized the mission in the briefing, he said, "Some of you won't come back," just like that. "Some won't come back, there's going to be some insane fighting." When we went in they didn't fire at us once, but those Shimshon guys were firing all over the place in fear. With the . . . acting like they were in their APCs.

*The administrative offices of the Palestinian Authority.

32. We go into the homes of innocent people. Every day, all the time

UNIT: FIELD INTELLIGENCE
LOCATION: GENERAL
YEAR: 2004–2006

The thing that shocked me, that really gave me a shock, was that you, every day you go out on a mission where you go into houses and it's just . . . and to families . . . and then we got to this family who didn't . . . they didn't even have a bathroom—it was a shock. That's why it's . . . it's something that really weighs on me. Because I felt that I . . . So this guy, he collects eggs, he sells eggs, that's his job. No one else, his wife doesn't work, she's in the house with the kids. That day he'd planned to take the chickens out . . . I had someone on the team who spoke Arabic, so we were able to communicate a bit. So you hold your head, you say, "That's it, I stopped him from making a living that day." That's it. That's what, and then I said, like, I get it, everything that's happened, because that's what we do: We go into the homes of innocent people. Every day, all the time.

Some would say that they're not innocent, that they might be hiding something.

Of course. No, some would also say, it's good to do it even if they're innocent, the sanctity of the mission is everything, okay? Meaning, there's no problem here, they'll tell you there's no ethical problem with what you're doing. You're not tainting the purity of arms,* you're not beating them up. If they resist, you have license to let them have it, to react or whatever, so there's no problem in terms of punishment. So it's all okay, it's for the good of the mission, it justifies the means, and that's it. But in the field, when you look at the whole period, then it's not always, most of the missions aren't thought through. There were a

---

*The purity of arms (Morality in Warfare) is one of the values stated in the IDF's official doctrine of ethics: "The soldier shall not employ his weaponry and power in order to harm noncombatants or prisoners of war and shall do all he can to avoid harming their lives, body, honor, and property."

lot where there wasn't much point to them, or we were sent out when the intelligence was so thin that maybe it would've been better to let it go. Basically, bottom line, in the end the family got screwed and that's it, that's what happened on that mission. And it didn't happen . . . that was most of the time. Let's say 95 percent of the cases, the whole point was to hurt the family and go back.

Intentionally?

That's what happened in practice. And then you start thinking. Okay, but you can't really know. I can say from experience, we saw which missions were a success—the ones that had really, really clear, focused intelligence, and the work was done using the whole intelligence network, meaning the Shin Bet and so on. Only then was it successful. But maybe there are, the army always has all kinds of . . . meaning, even if you're not aware, there are other ramifications. There's the army's presence, there's always the thing about presence, and it has ramifications for the army's goal or for its big missions.

33. Stun grenades in central places

UNIT: SHALDAG, SPECIAL AIR-GROUND TEAM
LOCATION: GENERAL
YEAR: 2002–2004

I want to point out that actually for me the worst times are the routine times, the things I have the priviledge of doing on a daily basis and becoming immune to them. And it is these things, the ones we do every day, that affect me the most.

Give me an example.

I can tell you that targeted, complicated, difficult assignments involving killing, I can tell you they seem much more reasonable because you know who the people are. But it's the missions I've carried out because something happened in my sector and they needed backup, so our unit was called to help out, and we went and did the routine actions—that's where I came across the really hard things . . . particularly the denial of freedom, denial of the most basic human rights for no reason, because these people aren't terrorists, that's what got to me the most. There are loads of examples. So many that I don't . . . examples of helping on violent patrols.

What's a violent patrol?

A violent patrol is one where you do it so that they'll know you're there, to demonstrate a presence. You suddenly yell to everyone to go indoors. You're demonstrating a presence.

In response to something?

No . . . either in response to something, or you're afraid that someone's coming out—I hope they're afraid that someone's coming out— and then you do it.

What do you mean, "you hope"? You weren't a wimpy little officer, you were an army captain for three years.

I didn't know whether someone specific was supposed to be in that village, but it's possible . . .

It's possible that the regional brigade commander knew?

Could be. I wouldn't know that kind of thing. Could be that the regional brigade commander knew and sent out a violent patrol.

What do you do on a violent patrol? Okay, you yell. Are you really violent? Do you beat people up? Throw stun grenades? Shoot in the air?

Throw stun grenades, yes.

Where do you throw them?

In central places.

You mean, you come to a shopping center, yell at everyone to go home, and if they run, great, if not, and if you think they're not fast enough, you throw stun grenades?

Yes, yes.

In the middle of the day?

The middle of the day.

Sometimes with no connection to what's happening in the sector?

I'd hope it's connected, but . . .

Not that you know of.

Not that I know of.

34. Going in festive with stun grenades

UNIT: NAHAL BRIGADE
LOCATION: HEBRON
YEAR: 2003

You're a platoon sergeant?

Yes.

You're supposed to know about the missions and the objective, why you're doing them.

Exactly. In Hebron our missions were mostly to protect the Jewish settlement. Those were our missions, either guarding the settlers on their way to pray in the Cave of the Patriarchs, or just everyday walking around the city there. Looking back, when you think about it, about [the Palestinians'] lives there, you've turned them into a nightmare, if you're doing intelligence warfare.

Intelligence warfare?

Exactly. Making a noise.

What's intelligence warfare?

It's letting them know that the army's there. Even where there is no army, giving them the feeling that it's there. Whether it's making noise at night, throwing stun grenades, or if it's going into some area in the middle of the night, into a house in the middle of the night, going in festive, like with a stun grenade, searching, you search the house and you leave.

How do you choose the house?

How do you choose the house? It could be any house, it could be a house near the post, you do it to frighten the residents there a bit. Maybe you think the residents pose a potential danger because they're close to the post. Basically, they're innocent people. There it is, every day there are foot patrols where you just walk around town, go into houses, any house, no reason, just because. No, there's no report on something specific in that house. You go in, look around, leave. And the moment you go in, you go in and relax there because there's no other place to relax. You can't sit on a bench outside and relax.

This is at night? During the day?

Could be at night, or during the day.

Can you describe a specific time that you remember?

A specific time? You go into a home with the goal of maybe finding some kind of something suspicious, you don't even know what exactly. You put everyone into one room. Usually they put their money in a closet, they hide it. They don't have, they don't put it in the bank or anywhere else. They put it in closets, hide it there. Now, to prevent looting and whatever, we'd usually put the whole family in the room with the money, so they won't come afterward and say we stole it. That's it, we start searching the rooms. Turn it upside down, searching, poking around just because . . . the guys also take stuff.

Do you remember any looting?

When I commanded a mission I wouldn't let it happen. Although there were soldiers who said, "Let's take this, let's take that." But I wouldn't have it.

But were there things you saw in the company? Equipment? Small things?

Equipment, small things. Walking canes, all kinds of flags, you know, the Islamic movement, all kinds of pictures. I didn't see really serious looting in the company. But again, I heard a lot of stories that there was looting, and I wasn't surprised.

Let's get back to the search. Everyone's in one room and you search. How is the house left?

You leave it . . . you try to leave it as we left it. You know, soldiers stink, they come, sit on the couch, get it dirty, still it's . . . still. Again, I don't know what happened on other patrols, I'm talking about myself. We tried to put the house back the way it was. But it might be that during some observation action, you suddenly go up, land on some innocent family, you drop into their lives and move into their home.

For how long?

How long? It could be a month, two months, two weeks.

Soldiers from Nahal Brigade, Battalion 50, in a Palestinian house watching the World Cup during a search operation.

And during that time, where's the family?

The family? I don't know, not in the house. I don't know, they make some arrangement with them, I don't know what they do with them exactly. We come to the house when it's empty. Who knows what they do with them, I don't.

You never asked?

No. At the time, it's of no interest. And that's it, you're just there, you turn the house into, like, a post. Camouflage nets and everything. You try not to use the bathroom and whatever. Not use the bathroom?

So you do use it or you don't?

Use it, of course. A patrol can be four hours long, it can be eight hours. Of course, when I was a commander, I made the decisions. Usually, you go out around the area near the post, and you try not to walk around in the same area every time, and you just go from house to house. Again, you don't know what you're looking for. Going into the house is more of a warning. That's it, the whole procedure that we talked about of going into houses. You finish, you leave, if you want, you stay for a rest for a half hour, hour, and then you go on. That's it. However long the shift is, that's what you do.

35. They came, set the explosives, blew up the house

UNIT: CENTRAL COMMAND
LOCATION: BETHLEHEM DISTRICT
YEAR: 2002–2003

Were there orders to take photographs from a certain angle? Not to photograph other things?

There weren't orders not to photograph something, nothing like that. The opposite, the point was to not ignore things, to photograph everything, and if there were things that weren't okay, to bring them to the attention of those responsible. Of course we didn't distribute anything outside, and in cases where the army would benefit, they used it, like opening up checkpoints or easing the restrictions on transferring goods and things like that. The unit consisted of me as the sole photographer. There were supposed to be six, but something happened, I think it was with the IDF spokesman, something political in the army stopped the other five from coming. They started with six the year before I arrived. Slowly the numbers dropped. When I came I replaced someone who was released. There were some clerks and editors who were responsible for processing the material I brought, and the officers. I was the photographer. I'd go out with the units mostly at night to document operations.

Who decided where you went?

The officers. The officer was a major and there was a deputy officer below him. The thing that sticks out the most in my memory from that period, they started the operation—I think it was called "Change of Address," or something like that. What happened was that they blew up houses of people suspected of being involved with terror.

Who used that phrase? You?

That's what they called the operation. That's what they called that kind of thing. Operation "Change of Address"—an operation to blow up a house. At first, it was people who carried out terrorist activity. Then it was, "He's his uncle," "He's the brother of someone who knows him" . . . all kinds of distant connections like that. It was also something that became much more acceptable over time. That sums it up, basically. At the very beginning, when it started, it was done in pretty much the same way. The forces went in. A different battalion each time. Securing the surrounding area, removing people. If there were men, they were arrested. There was always a Shin Bet agent there with the forces, I think, and someone from the Civil Administration, and someone connected to the government, who was responsible. For the few houses that were blown up, there had to be explicit permission from the Defense Ministry. I forgot the exact position. Permission by telephone at three, three-thirty in the morning. They'd call, get the okay. Sometimes we'd evacuate the house fifteen minutes beforehand, depends on how nice the officer was—sometimes five minutes, sometimes half an hour. And, we're not talking about tin shacks. These were houses, with everything that a house has, couches, electronic appliances, refrigerators, picture albums, everything. In most cases the order was about fifteen minutes, again, children, women . . . From the moment the officer gets there they have fifteen minutes to evacuate . . . And during that time the soldiers from the Engineering Corps have already begun laying the explosives in all kinds of places, while the residents are evacuating. They close in, form a ring around the house to prevent injuries, and then the moment they get the okay, that stage might be delayed for an hour or two until they get permission, for political reasons apparently, and then they demolish the house. From the moment after they demolish the house, there's a final search to make sure there's nothing unusual, and then they evacuate the area within five minutes. There were a lot of operations like that. As time passed, after a few months, they stopped making calls to the legal adviser, or whoever it was. Things started happening, there was a response from the media, it became more and more frequent, and at a certain point the okay wasn't needed anymore—they just came, set the explosives, blew up the house, and we left.

How many incidents were there like that?

Dozens, a lot. From villages . . . to Bethlehem, Beit Jala, everywhere.

What was the procedure for evacuating the adjacent houses? Or did you only evacuate the one house?

I remember a few cases where other people's houses were really close, right next to them. But even that never prevented blowing up a house. I think the Engineering Corps tried to take down only the particular house, as much as possible, the orders were to prevent destruction of other houses because then there'd be lawsuits against the army because of surrounding damage, and that was one of my jobs, to photograph the area afterward, but this was rare, because we'd get out of there really quickly.

What kind of pictures do you bring back from something like that?

Photos of the entrance, the entrance to the house, the whole conversation between the officer and the soldiers, evacuation of the residents, evacuation of equipment from the house.

On video?

Video and stills. The placement of the explosives. After that, you stand back at a safe distance. The demolition, the explosion itself. Just wherever I see something happening, I film it.

And what do you do with the footage? Say, with the explosions?

Things like that end up in the computers in the offices. They choose six pictures. A picture of the explosion, a picture of . . . each picture has a title: "officer of the force," "the officer prepares the residents for evacuation," "the officer allows the residents to remove their belongings from the house." Never mind that it's a tenth of their belongings.

Straw widow, Gaza, 2008.

Has a family ever asked for more time?

There were times like that, I don't remember exactly, it really depended on the officers. Sometimes the officers gave the order and weren't seen again. After fifteen minutes they control everything over the radio. Or sometimes the officers were present, there was one case where four soldiers carried an elderly woman on their shoulders in a chair, it was kind of funny, they took her out of the house.

She couldn't walk, or she didn't want to?

She probably couldn't.

36. We killed police who weren't armed

Unit: Engineering Corps
Location: Ramallah district
Year: 2001

At that time there was that terrorist attack on six people on route 443. Six soldiers from the Engineering Corps, some terrorist came from one of the checkpoints, and by some stroke of dumb luck he killed them all. He came at them inside wherever and shot them all, killed all six. The same night we were in one of the villages with nothing to do. They ran us over to their base, crowded us into some room, there wasn't much for us to do. All of a sudden our staff officer comes from some two-minute briefing, says, "Listen, this is the briefing . . . we're doing . . . it's a revenge operation. We're going to eliminate six Palestinian policemen at a checkpoint. It's in revenge for the six they took from us." That's the story I want to get at. It was on 443: if you, you cross toward Area A there are . . . there are, like, four transfer posts, and the Palestinian police oversee them. They sent us, along with the paratrooper patrol company, or the paratrooper auxiliary company and someone else, to just, like, eliminate all the Palestinian police there. Right? And the briefing was maybe two minutes. It was defined as, like, revenge, and at the time when I hesitated, like I asked, "What did they do? Who are they?" They said they're Palestinian police. I said, "What did they do?" They said, "There's suspicion that the terrorist who killed the six came through that checkpoint." There's suspicion, but they don't know for sure. It could be one of those posts, but they said, "It doesn't matter, they took six of ours, we're going to take six back."

They said it like that?

Like that. Revenge operation. The day after, it was in the papers as a "revenge operation." They didn't hide it. It was like reported as a revenge operation and it was . . . insanely praised as fitting "blood revenge." And we went down to . . . it was a very, very long trek, we went there by foot at four in the morning, there's no one there at night, they like . . . that checkpoint is closed at night, there's some building where they live . . .

They go to the checkpoint during the day?

During the day they're at the checkpoint.

And you waited in an ambush?

We waited in an ambush until . . . until they arrived. And the idea was—the idea was that we would just kill them all, like they'd arrive and we'd take them out, whether they had weapons or not . . . like—this is a Palestinian policeman? Shoot him. And we sat there, and it's nighttime and more nighttime . . . it's freezing . . . I'm trembling all over with fear, that's the truth, but from cold. I was the radioman. There were three men with viewfinders, and they were supposed to fire first, and then we'd charge in from the side. And they arrive. And we catch them doing some search, they're like five meters from me, standing five meters from me, there were only three and another one far away, and we go up, I get on the radio to get the okay and no one answers me. I get an answer from some . . .

An operations sergeant?

Some, like, girl answers. And there's no okay, and still no okay, and they can't find the battalion officer, they can't find the battalion officer, and my unit officer takes the radio. Now they're right next to us. He yells, he says, like, yelling, "We've engaged, engaged, engaged." No engaged, no nothing. The guys fired a few shots and hit nothing.

The moment they heard the yelling they opened fire?

We hadn't "engaged, engaged, engaged." At the same time, I gave the order to the guys to open fire, but he like yelled to the battalion officer, yelled "engaged," when we hadn't actually engaged them, like we didn't have the okay to fire . . .

They were close to you? He decided it was . . . he did it at his own discretion?

He did it at his own discretion.

He decided . . . ?

Yes. Like we didn't have the okay to go out to . . . we basically didn't have the okay to act. There's a list of permissions that you have to get. There's permission to go to the place, and then there's permission to stay there, I think, and then permission to open fire, and we didn't have it . . . so we yelled "engaged!" . . . like he yelled "engaged!" . . . those guys, the three soldiers fired, they screwed up and didn't hit anything. They were supposed to hit the streetlamps, which they didn't manage to do and also they . . . also were supposed to hit the [Palestinian police] . . . to shoot at them. They didn't hit a thing. We got up, fired off a round, we hit two people, like, two people died . . . but no, they didn't die, I'm sorry, they were wounded. We hit one in the leg, I think, and one in the shoulder or something like that. They ran, and we went after them . . . we kept going and going. I had a rifle sight. I put a bullet in one of their heads while he was running and another one was crawling behind . . . we all stood up, we ran . . . it was . . . The truth? I really enjoyed it. It was really fun because it was the first time you were like "Forward charge" for real, like I did in training and we were amazing . . . we functioned above and beyond, and he kept running . . . we continued going forward. He went into some store-room, something made of corrugated tin. Four guys outside, we shot it up to hell . . . there was a gas tank there, the whole tank blew up, everything burned, burned, burned. Meanwhile me and the . . .

That's where he ran to, that's where the guy who was crawling went?

That's where the guy who . . . in the meantime we had killed one. Another one was going up in flames inside the thing, and another one was running. We ran after him, he ran into, like, a cemetery, he went into a cemetery or something. I think it was a cemetery, yeah, it was a cemetery, he ran into the cemetery. We stood on the wall, we fired at him and killed him.

Were they armed?

Wait. During this whole time they didn't fire back at us. They didn't fire back. No, they didn't . . . we weren't engaged, they didn't fire at us at any point. We started shooting from a distance, we didn't hit anything, we got up to charge, we hit one and he ran, I took him down with another bullet. Another one ran into the thing, which we set on fire, and we chased after another one.

To the cemetery?

To the cemetery. And another one who shot at me, and another one who like, disappeared, we didn't find him, and then . . .

So there were four?

There were four. Now that we're talking about how many they were, even in the debriefing it wasn't absolutely clear that there were four. Like it could be there were only three and it could be there were four. We couldn't, no, we couldn't identify them . . . like all of the testimonies conflicted, because someone said that he definitely identified three, one that said . . . and someone else said he definitely identified two here, and like from all the connections we identified four, but there wasn't really any verification, and of the twelve, eleven people in our group no one can really tell you how many there were. We don't know exactly. And then I get to . . . like they sent me to . . .

Wait, you're in the cemetery—was the guy killed?

No. We stood on the wall, we fired at him, he fell, and that's how it ended. Now, the guy I killed, the one I took down, I shot a bullet at him, he was lying on the ground, we only saw . . . like we only saw him from this angle, something was concealing him, and there were three or four of us who'd just put bullets in him, perforated him . . . we just kept shooting at the body.

To verify the kill?

Not to verify the kill, but out of the high of our excitement. We perforated his . . . we like totally perforated him, and then after I got back from the . . . like we retreated from the cemetery, and I went to see, not to verify the kill, but to take his weapon, and then I got to him, and he was like hacked to pieces. His body was hacked up, with a bullet here, and another three there, and another one here, and on his leg from here down was nothing . . . like, it was just, there was nothing . . . we perforated him completely. And I tried and managed to turn him over . . . he was a fifty-five-year-old, if not a sixty-year-old guy, very old, and he didn't have a weapon, like after the fact we understood, the same with the one in the cemetery, none of them had a weapon.

Were they in uniform?

They were in Palestinian police uniforms. They were in Palestinian police uniforms without weapons.

Okay.

Then we walked some more, we threw another grenade into the burning thing, we packed up, and then from every direction, like the whole population started coming and our snipers continued firing in their direction, and then they stopped . . . they didn't hit anyone, but there was a ton of fire and we packed up.

Did you go through an anti-terrorism combat course or something?

We did, yes.

And in that course do they teach you how to verify a kill?

Yes, of course. They teach you about verifying a kill everywhere. You always verify a kill, like, put another bullet in the head even if the guy is dead.

You know that the IDF denies it?

What's with you? Of course. Of course they do.

Was part of the course, "Now charge, 'bang . . . bang . . .' verify the kill"?

When we were packing up. Verifying the kill, of course.

Okay.

Yeah. Why, you don't? No?

37. Aim for the eyes to take out an eye

UNIT: ARTILLERY
LOCATION: QALQILYA
YEAR: 2000

One of the things, it's something that really shook me . . . because they didn't train us for going into the Territories, so they gave us a very quick overview. So they explained to us a bit about, I don't know what they're called, riot control agents.

RCA.

Okay. I don't know. You understand from this that I wasn't such a great fighter. On paper I'm in combat, but I wasn't brainwashed or anything. They just taught us things. In any case, they taught us about rubber bullets, and they showed us how it comes in what's called a "tampon," which is a kind of plastic bag that contains the bullets. So they said, "You need to separate them, meaning you tear open the package and put them in one by one so you cause damage." And they actually explained it to us, in this really pornographic way, "Aim for the eyes so you take out an eye, or at the stomach so it goes into the stomach."

Who explained this to you?

The company commander at headquarters.

To the whole company?

Yes, and he says these things, yeah, and laughs. He says "Split them up," and shows how you split them up, how you put them in. He says, "They're not effective in threes." To me it was really terrible, because it's clear they were made that way so they're aimed at a crowd and not directly at someone, although that's bad enough. They really explained how you turn it into like live ammunition. And he explained how they can't prove it. If someone gets hurt it's like by a rubber bullet. "No one will do anything, you've got nothing to worry about."

And how did the soldiers react?

They laughed. No one was really shaken up, except for me.

Did you talk about it with anyone?

Actually, yes. The truth is that I wanted to go to the battalion commander, but before that I spoke with my friend, who was the company commander's driver. He said, "There's no point in talking to him." The commander himself, my friend went out with him to the field—he said, he splits up the rubber bullets all the time, and he instructs everyone to do it. Okay, so in the end I turned to B'Tselem.

What did B'Tselem say?

They also took my testimony. They asked me a ton of questions, they asked me for names. I have no idea whether they dealt with it because it was close to my discharge. In the end, it's not something that like, today, like no one knows what it is. There was that thing called the Tenet report or something, about Israel's activities in the Territories, so my story went in. I got a letter about it.

38. A patrol to beat up Arabs

UNIT: KFIR BRIGADE
LOCATION: HEBRON
YEAR: 2006–2007

There are loads of incidents. All kinds of crap that we'd do. We'd beat up Arabs all the time, nothing special. Just to pass the time.

Do you remember an incident when you opened fire on Palestinians?

Do you know how many times it happened, when there'd be disturbances and we'd open fire?

Live ammunition?

When you needed to, yes, when you had to, when there was enough coming at us—then yes, at the knee, the knees.

You've said that you'd think about how to heat things up all the time.

Of course.

What does that mean?

You know, we wanted things to be interesting, so we'd look for ways to rile the Arabs up a bit, so we'd shoot a lot of rubber bullets, that it'd be interesting, and the time in Hebron would pass a bit quicker.

Who came up with the ways?

You think there weren't enough people? Soldiers, officers.

While talking with the company commander?

Company commander, are you kidding? No way, I tell you, it wouldn't leave the platoon. The platoon is like a state secret, that's what we'd say. No one knew.

So you'd just be talking with the platoon commander?

You're kidding. The platoon commander didn't know either.

So who did?

Officers and a sergeant.

Where would you be talking?

In the room. There's the senior room, and the junior room? In the senior room.

So what would you say, "On patrol today we'll do this and that"?

Yes.

You'd plan ahead?

Of course.

So what did you do?

All kinds of crap. We'd do a lot of stuff, we'd say: Why a patrol? A patrol to beat up Arabs. Children, Arabs, all kinds of crap.

Who would initiate those patrols?

All kinds of people. The patrol commander wasn't supposed to know.

Sergeants and squad officers?

Yes, they had no connection.

They'd say, "Now we're going out to . . ."?

We'd know where we were going, we'd have a briefing beforehand. We'd go out on patrol.

The squad commander came and said, "Now we're going out on patrol"?

They'd know we were going out on patrol. Also, listen, you don't do it with every squad commander, you know who you can do it with.

A force doesn't go out on patrol of its own volition.

Everyone knows there's a patrol. That's the job, to patrol, to secure. We just, like, carried it on, you know.

What does the company commander say to you when you go out?

What does he say? He also knows it's going to happen. He'd also take, he'd choose the people to go out with him. Let's say, I told you about ——, he'd never go out with him, there's no way in the world he'd let him go out with him.

What would happen?

We'd go out on patrol, here's an example, some kid would just look at us like this, and we didn't like the look of it—so he'd immediately get hit.

Who'd hit him?

The squad commander, the soldiers.

39. We went into the house for filming for television

Unit: Nahal Brigade
Location: Hebron
Year: 2002

We got an order, some team went to an IDF benefit, and they told us to go into a house in Hebron. We'd been in that house two weeks before, same owners, same procedure. We didn't really understand why we had to do it.

You went to search, or to stay there?

The same procedure, to take down the family . . . that night, all of a sudden they tell us a TV crew's coming, they want to film you—it was Hanukkah—eating doughnuts. Slowly we started to realize that they sent us into the house to film us for television. Really. They sent us into the house to film us for television. Also, afterward, we left in the morning or the afternoon, there were warnings or something. And they sent us in to film us for television. That night we were on the Channel 2 news for twenty seconds, that's it. They prepared everyone, they brought us doughnuts to show that we were happy and strong.

40. Watching soccer in Nablus

UNIT: MAGLAN SPECIAL FORCES
LOCATION: NABLUS
YEAR: 2004

In Nablus, there was another incident with my original team. I wasn't there but they told me about it afterward.

The guys from your team?

Yes. They go into a house, part of what's called "personal pressure," the whole idea is that you go in . . . you rest inside the house. Meaning, you move the family to some room and you rest, you make a kind of war room in some room, in the living room or I don't know . . . whatever room you come across. But there was one time when they came, they went in, and they wanted to watch something on TV. So they took the family and put them in another room. The family was sitting near the TV, but the soldiers wanted to watch something, they took the family, moved them into a different room so they could watch something. There was an explicit rule not to do something like that, not even to sit on the chairs. When I went around, I normally went around with the deputy company commander, wherever he went around, he made sure the soldiers didn't . . . the team above me, they sat on the sofas and moved the family. But this was an incident the team talked about a lot. That it was pretty ridiculous.

What did they say about it?

That they came and moved the family. You get it, it's a bit ridiculous. You want to watch something on TV, you're in the middle of an operation, so you take the family, you sit in the living room so you can watch. There's no target.

What was it?

What was it? I don't know, soccer, something with soccer. It's not that important why. That's true of most of the things I encountered during my service. Not so much big things, more little things that created a certain feeling, a certain atmosphere.

What?

First, that it doesn't matter what you do, you always come out okay. Meaning, I could slap people, hit them, shoot someone in the leg. I can't see any situation where I'd be responsible, because I could always say it was self-defense. Second, the lives of ordinary civilians matter less than the needs of the army. Meaning, either they're not important, or they're less important compared to the military objective, or to the force, if I tell you that soldiers come and move people out of their living room so that they can watch TV, which is totally against the rules.

Did anything happen to the soldiers afterward?

No. It's also . . . I think it's something pretty common, even with us. Even though where I was, at least, they made sure not to sit on the whatever . . . it was in the briefings, not to sit on the sofas and not to go into their . . . meaning, do just what you have to do, like, in the houses, and nothing beyond that, not drinking coffee, but there were things like that. People come, drink coffee, like the family offers it, so they drink coffee with them.

What do you mean?

They come, they go into the house, you know, the families are used to it, they no longer get worked up by something like that, so they even get to the point where they offer it. Once I saw something like that. They come, offer coffee. There are guys who drink it. It always seemed strange to me to come into someone's house, you come and drink coffee like you're a guest. Even if he offers it, it's still a bit funny.

41. The World Cup finals in a refugee camp

Unit: Nahal Brigade
Location: Ramallah
Year: 2002

We get an order to go into the Al-Amari refugee camp, I think. There was an order that now we're going every week to a refugee camp to "go over it." "Going over it" means you search everything. With kibbutznik cynicism we called it an *Aktion*.* We'd come in, send all the men to the school—from age fifteen to fifty . . . there were always all kinds of numbers. Whoever has a mustache goes to the school . . . they stay there all day. And with the women and children we go from house to house with maps. You go through each house and search everything. We're good kids, so we come, open the closets, look, move things around, put things back, like that, all day. That particular day was the World Cup final, and we're finished, also because it was the final, and because it was extremely hot. So we go, make our rounds, as usual we don't find anything, like in all those operations. Our officer was always into . . . we'd go in, like, a team of five to blow up every door. This was covered up. It wasn't really, it was to train us to blow things up. So we'd learn a bit. Also, we did it out of enthusiasm for this game: any door that was a bit difficult, even though we had a crowbar, hammer, all kinds of equipment, we had to blow it up. Even if we only spent half a minute on the door. We argued with him, we tried to tell him, "There's no need, we'll have it open in two minutes, there's no problem here." It got to yelling, "Don't blow it up," "Do, blow it up," "Shut up, don't bother me while I'm working."

What did you blow up the door with?

With those sticks with the wicks. That time, it was already afternoon, the heat was bad, you really want to stop, you want to be done. Again this recurring pattern—it comes from the officer. He starts turning

*The German term used for Nazi operations.

things upside down, going into rooms, he's had it. He starts turning things upside down. We got into this absurd situation where we're cleaning up after him and putting things back in place. With me, for example, it usually came from the officers. All this "crossing the line a bit" and the "just a bit for the hell of it," mostly, it came from the officers. It was just disgusting that whole day. We found ourselves watching the finals—everyone took a break and settled in all kinds of houses—we found ourselves watching the finals with this unfortunate woman and girl, we sat in their living room in the refugee camp. All the teams sat in different houses. We sat and watched the finals in the living room. I was knocked out because of all the stairs, I wasn't even . . . I didn't even look at the screen, I was wiped out. They're talking on the radio, great, goal, this, that, the scene was totally crazy. Thinking about it—a friend of mine said afterward, I was less aware of it—the World Cup is like a holiday. And during the final you send . . . how many men are in a refugee camp? A thousand? You send them all to the school, and they're punished, whatever the situation is. Like now they're making a cease-fire for the Olympics. A bit of sensitivity. It doesn't matter, it's just something small.

42. You can seize a house for years

UNIT: CIVIL ADMINISTRATION
LOCATION: HEBRON
YEAR: 2003

What about the army taking over Palestinian homes?

For posts. Okay, seizing a house for posts, again, this idea also changed, you're not talking about straw widows and things like that, right? You're talking about seizing a house . . . This practice changed again in 2003, there were unpleasant incidents in those houses, where soldiers messed them up on purpose, you say, "Fuck this house, I'm out of here in two weeks and I don't give a shit." At a certain point we started doing thirty-day rotations between a few houses, a few posts, to make it a bit more pleasant.

Detainees, Hebron, 2003.

Soldiers?

Yes, we'd switch posts every thirty days. You go to the adjacent house. We'd do thirty-thirty or a bit more, we'd ask for an extension. I remember a case, for example, where someone got married, so we changed the house, because he married someone from the family. There were all kinds of things like that.

But there are still posts on the roofs of houses.

On the houses. Are there still ones inside the houses?

There's one, at the bank intersection.

Okay, if it's temporary. On the roofs of houses is a totally different story; if it's on the house, and if you have a separate staircase, it's totally legal and if it's an ordered seizure, it's half-yearly, you renew it every half a year with no problem. You can seize it for years . . .

Who decides these things?

The brigade commander decides these things. There are very clear criteria. When the brigade commander says he's seizing a house, you tell him it's an "allocated room." There's an order of operations for this. How do you check if it's legal? Even before you pass it to the legal adviser you're like a kind of mini legal adviser. You get it? There are times when you say, "No way, don't even bring it up. Don't talk to me, switch houses."

Does it depend on the house or on the demand?

It depends on the house. He has to mark the house. He has to explain to me why that house in particular. He has to explain to me, the operations branch officer, not the brigade commander, why this house, and if, for example, there's an adjacent house belonging to a pair of bachelors, then why he is seizing a house belonging to a family, and that the security need is specifically tied to that house. He has to come with a lot of explanation. But he gets permission from the legal adviser and he takes out a warrant.

Nablus, 2003. This house was seized for use as an IDF lookout post and a base for operations. The camouflage net and the APC parked below demonstrated the army's presence.

Do you deal with evacuating the family?

No, yes . . . it'll come back to me . . . again, at the beginning of the Inti-fada it wasn't like that, and these are procedures which were formulated gradually because there weren't any before. Note that basically, the evac-uation is violent, there were violent evacuations—not during my time in Hebron, because we did them all and we went in with them. Apart from the times when they'd seize a house without telling us. They'd just throw people's things outside, so the whole thing of concentrating everything in a certain room, the furniture, we'd accompany it.

Where's the family? Did you take into account where the family would live?

If there's a house where there's a clear security need, it's the tallest house, then no one cares where the family's going. No one thinks about it. If there's a real security reason, if it's a family with a lot of kids, I don't know, or if they live in a small house, or they've got no other place to live and there's a parallel security need, then okay, I have no problem.

43. It brings out the madness in you

Unit: Golani Brigade
Location: Ramallah
Year: 2002

After we entered a building and found nothing inside, it was the Pales-tinian logistics building, there were just some parkas and stuff, and after all the stress of the night, when a soldier from Egoz was killed and we heard all the screaming on the radio, we hung around . . . we were in the building for a week or a few days, and after resting for a day you start looking around for things. I remember that at a certain point we began to break stuff. It's really, really fun to smash things, frankly, I think it's a fantasy most people have, throwing a television set out the window if they could. But here, you're twenty years old and you have your chance to do just that, so you start to smash things. I felt myself, me and a few others, in this kind of moment of frenzy, breaking tables and doors, tossing loads and loads of documents in every room, stuff like that. The madness inside breaks out, just because you can, I'd say.

You can do it, so why not?

Exactly. You can go ahead and smash stuff. It's a lot like when you see guys on MTV smashing their guitars on stage. There are a loads of clips of someone going into his room and smashing things. It's a kind of logical fantasy, but there you have the power to act it out, and these are not your own things anyway, and you're at war.

How much stuff did you smash?

In the Mukata'a we went all the way.

What do you mean?

I mean whatever we could smash, we smashed because we were sure they were going to get the place back, so we said we didn't want to leave it intact. It was a kind of personal decision. Without leaving it up to the politicians or anything. But I remember that in the house searches as well, when you go from house to house, there's this thing about sometimes breaking televisions. Sometimes you hear some story that once someone found an explosive belt inside a television, and sometimes it's just to hurl the television, to toss the drawers out instead of just opening them and looking inside, stuff like that.

44. You just put it all in your backpack

UNIT: GIVATI BRIGADE
LOCATION: GAZA STRIP
YEAR: 2002–2004

Did you happen to see any looting?

Yes, plenty.

What do you mean, plenty?

Whenever you'd get to a house, like straw widows, you'd settle in for a few days and probably leave the place totally trashed. Yeah, there was looting after Operation Rainbow, Mosquito Sting, all kinds of big operations we were in. I once took prayer beads myself. But yes, there was looting. A friend of mine took this large baseball bat, prayer beads, cigarettes. How do Arabs make cigarettes? They don't buy them, they roll them. They have this tobacco and rolling papers. Yeah, there's looting, sure.

Any looting of valuables?

Yes. A friend of mine took a Discman. Listen, they live there, they have stuff, it's not the third world, you know. There's plenty of stuff to loot. They have really nice houses, they're living the good life. Yeah, you know, you just put it all in your backpack.

Like what?

All these kinds of figurines from the living room, CD players, cigarettes, daggers, a baseball bat, prayer beads.

Was it something the commanders and officers knew about? Is it a known phenomenon?

I can't answer that, I don't know. I assume that somewhere they do know, but they didn't ask. You know, we saw nothing, we heard nothing. No one checked the soldiers for stuff, although they did come back with their backpacks bursting. But they didn't ask. The question didn't come up. But yes, there was looting, sure.

PART TWO

Separation: Control, Expropriation, and Annexation

An Overview

At first glance, separating Israelis and Palestinians seems designed to protect Israel's citizens and give the Palestinians greater independence. But the testimonies collected in this part suggest that the various Israeli mechanisms of separation serve mainly to assert control over the Palestinian population, leading to the expropriation of their land and its effective annexation.

Most of the barriers that restrict Palestinian movement in the West Bank are not positioned on the 1967 borders dividing Israel from the Territories, but are located within the Occupied Territories themselves, and they allow Israel to maintain almost total control over Palestinian movement. The elements of separation that have been put into place over the last ten years have not reduced Palestinian dependency on Israel but deepened it. Despite the ostensible disengagement from the Gaza Strip in 2006—undoubtedly, one of the clearest examples of separation—Israel has maintained control over the population of Gaza, and, indirectly, of the West Bank as well. Israel treats the West Bank and the Gaza Strip as two distinct social and political entities: for most of the past decade, Israel has forbidden transit between the two, implementing, in effect, an additional policy of separating Palestinians from Palestinians.

The internal separation of Palestinians in fact began in the 1990s, when according to the Oslo Accords the Territories were divided into three zones: the territory in Area A was transferred to the administrative and law enforcement authority of the Palestinian Authority; Area B was subject to the security control of Israel and the administrative control of the Palestinians; Area C, the majority of the West Bank, including the settlements, came under Israel's exclusive control. In practice, however, Israel has effective control even over Area A, ostensibly Palestinian-controlled territory, through checkpoints, offensive operations, and frequent military incursions into Palestinian cities and villages.

As part of the policy of separation, Israel has established a vast network of checkpoints and physical barriers throughout the Territories, some permanent, others portable and temporary. The various barriers and obstructions separate Palestinian residents of the Territories from Israeli citizens—Jewish and Palestinian—who live within the Green Line. They also separate them from Israeli settlers in the Territories, and from Palestinians who live in different towns and villages. Alongside these physical barriers, Israel operates a convoluted bureaucratic system that regulates Palestinian movement in the Territories by issuing permits. The testimonies in this part reveal how Israel has tightened its control over Palestinian lives through the threefold system of barriers, obstacles, and permits. Israel maintains a "permit regime" that has the authority and the power to restrict and even prevent the movement of Palestinians in territory controlled by the army and other Israeli authorities.

The main symbol of separation in recent years has been the Separation Barrier, the construction of which began in the West Bank in 2002. The Separation Barrier is comprised partly of a wall, partly of a sophisticated system of fences and ditches. Certain segments of the barrier are located close to the Green Line, but others penetrate deep into the West Bank. The Palestinian territories that are enclosed by the barrier on one side and by the Green Line on the other are called the "seam zone." Palestinians living in the seam zone have their movement restricted by a complicated system of permits, licenses, and passage through gates and fences. In many cases, the Separation

Barrier encloses concentrations of Israeli settlements, forming a broad land belt around them. Thus the barrier greatly restricts, and even prevents, Palestinians' access to their land adjacent to settlements, especially to large areas of agricultural land, which the barrier "attaches" to the settlements. In other words, the Separation Barrier doesn't only separate populations, but also people from one another, from their land, and from their livelihood. The Separation Barrier contributes directly to dispossession of Palestinian land, which increasingly becomes part of the Israeli settlements.

The system of "bypass roads" constitutes an additional means of separation. The areas next to the settlements are closed to Palestinian entry by roads that are for "Israelis only." Construction of the bypass roads also began in the 1990s to shorten and facilitate Israelis' access to the settlements, and to enable settlers to bypass Palestinian settlements and cities. But in the last decade, Israel has placed restrictions on Palestinian use of West Bank roads, and in many cases has even completely forbidden Palestinian movement on roads close to settlements and on roads that connect settlements. By means of temporary or permanent physical obstructions of the entrances and exits to Palestinian towns and villages, Israel prevents Palestinian use of many roads, thus reinforcing another system of separation between different parts of the West Bank.

During periods of the last decade, Israel has implemented a policy in the West Bank termed "isolation," in which the Palestinian population in one region cannot travel to another without special transit permits granted by the army. While the Israeli government has maintained that this "isolation" is intended to prevent the movement of Palestinian terrorists from city to city, the soldiers' testimonies suggest that this policy has helped deepen Israeli control on the ground. For example, Israel has cut off the northern part of the West Bank, where Jenin and Nablus are located, from Palestinian towns and villages in the south. At times Nablus was entirely isolated, and the army prevented all passage to and from the town, even to surrounding villages. The policy of isolation has had severe consequences on the Palestinian economy, as well as on the social and familial fabric of Palestinian life. For long periods it inhibited family and commercial ties, as well as relations between Palestinians living in cities, villages, and separate regions.

Finally, the testimonies in this part reveal that the principle of separation in the Territories distinguishes between Israeli Jews and Palestinians who are citizens of Israel. Testimonies from soldiers who served at checkpoints reveal the difference in soldiers' attitudes toward Jewish citizens as opposed to those toward Palestinian citizens, who must undergo rigorous and continuous inspections. Additionally, even though the law forbids the entry of all Israelis into Area A, Palestinian citizens of Israel are generally permitted to enter these zones, whereas the law is mostly enforced with respect to Jews. Moreover, some settlements have an explicit policy forbidding Israeli Palestinians to set foot on the premises. In some cases, the army cooperates with this policy. It seems that the army views these settlements as exclusively Jewish, and so forbids the presence of Palestinians, whether or not they are Israeli citizens.

The soldiers' testimonies in this part show that "separation" is a policy that extends Israeli control of Palestinians, helps the army dispossess Palestinians of their lands, and leads to effective annexation of the Territories and de facto expansion of Israel's sovereignty.

Since 2008, there has been some discussion regarding easing the internal restrictions on Palestinian movement, through limiting the checkpoints, for example. These testimonies reveal, however, that this shift in on-the-ground policy does not reflect a change in paradigm, and that policy is still determined by an assumption of total control of civilian movement.

The Occupied Territories, Checkpoints and Barriers

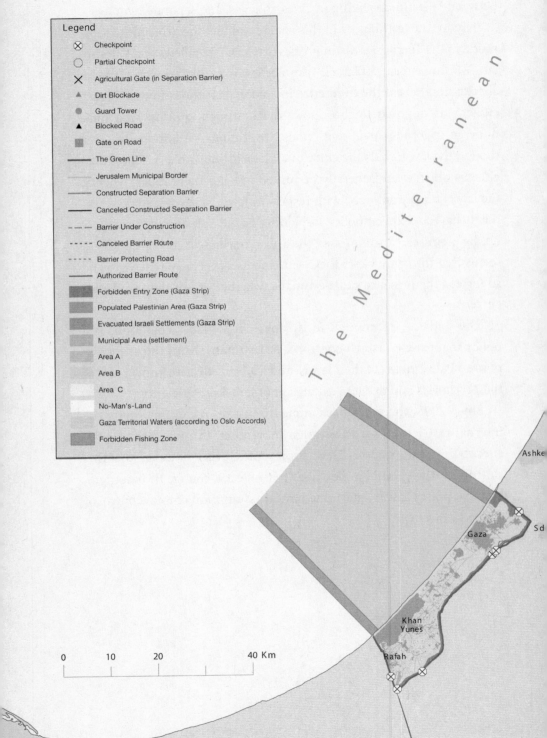

Legend

⊗ Checkpoint

◯ Partial Checkpoint

✕ Agricultural Gate (in Separation Barrier)

▲ Dirt Blockade

● Guard Tower

▲ Blocked Road

■ Gate on Road

── The Green Line

── Jerusalem Municipal Border

── Constructed Separation Barrier

── Canceled Constructed Separation Barrier

─ ─ Barrier Under Construction

- - - Canceled Barrier Route

- - - Barrier Protecting Road

── Authorized Barrier Route

■ Forbidden Entry Zone (Gaza Strip)

■ Populated Palestinian Area (Gaza Strip)

■ Evacuated Israeli Settlements (Gaza Strip)

■ Municipal Area (settlement)

■ Area A

■ Area B

■ Area C

■ No-Man's-Land

■ Gaza Territorial Waters (according to Oslo Accords)

■ Forbidden Fishing Zone

The Mediterranean

Ashke

Gaza

Sd

Khan
Yunes

Rafah

0   10   20   40 Km
├───┼───┼───┼───┤

Map by Shai Efrati

45. I didn't know there were roads just for Jews

Unit: Artillery [Reserves]
Location: Jordan Valley
Year: 2002

The whole thing with the Jewish roads is a pretty upsetting experience. There's no design, no general policy. You drive on a road, and you have no instructions about where to set up the checkpoint. In principle, it's forbidden for Palestinians to drive on the road.

Which road are you talking about?

The Allon road, a long road.

Parallel to the valley, right?

Yes. Palestinians are forbidden to drive there. If you see a Palestinian vehicle, you're supposed to stop him, check his ID. You radio all the numbers, they check to see if he's wanted. I go over the report, we tell him he's not allowed to drive on the road, that he needs to turn around, and he turns around. You stop at a random point on the road. Here's a hypothetical situation—usually there's just one jeep on the road, but say there are two. You tell him to turn around, and then the other jeep catches him.

Did it ever happen that someone said to you, "They told me to turn around"?

I don't remember, because I was just the driver. The driver's role is to stay inside the jeep. That's why I agreed to go, it was part of the discussion I had with the company commander beforehand, he said that I'd be the driver and I wouldn't have to do operations. I drive and they do everything else, they set up the checkpoint. Even if something happens, you stay in the jeep. There was also an APC team . . . they'd do all kinds of operations, ambushes . . . the commander said that I wouldn't even come close, I'd just drive. I don't know what they talked about, I can only guess that there wasn't much logic involved. Then there were also surprise checkpoints. You pick a spot, an intersection or something, you park the jeep on the side of the road, you put up a stop sign and spikes, and the road is blocked.

They block the Allon road?

At the spot where the soldier's standing. At different points on the road, it might be open. When you get to the spot, you wait. Generally, the troops' attitude is really bad: you're standing there, a twenty-year-old soldier, and you see people waiting, sometimes even a sheikh, sixty-year-old men waiting, stuck. I'm reading this book right now, *Lords of the Land: The War over Israel's Settlements in the Occupied Territories*, and that's exactly what it's like. The lords of the land say, "Don't let this guy cross, let him wait until we decide what we're going to do." When we go to eat, they fold up the checkpoint, and everyone leaves.

How long does the checkpoint stay up?

First of all, they can't drive on the road, so the only reason for the checkpoint is to show that we're in charge, that someone controls the road, that they can't just do whatever they want. Another thing, we were the second reserve battalion there in a row. And you know how reservists are . . . they usually look the other way, they don't stop every car.

Did you stop every car?

No.

You did it however you wanted?

Yes. In principle, we're ordered to use our discretion and demonstrate a presence. If you see a car, for example, a taxi with women, you say, "There's no terrorist here." If you see young men, you stop them. If the commander's moderate, he'll let them go, but if the commander's bored and his politics are a bit more extreme, he'll stop them. I couldn't figure out the logic behind it.

A checkpoint on the way out of Jericho at the District Coordination and Liaison, 2003, Armored Corps.

How long were you in the jeep and on patrol?

A shift, most likely eight hours. I don't remember.

What were the actual orders? You had a briefing and then what? Was there a briefing before you went out?

There's no special mission. You have different patrol shifts. The patrols go around the different settlements—one of the settlements is definitely illegal because there were three caravans there, and the parent settlement, which is legal, had our soldiers guarding the other one. You drive through the settlements, you make sure everything's okay, you go around and do patrols all the time. The idea is that if something happens, the jeep is in the area, close by.

Who told you the rules for the sector? Is there a briefing before you go out each time?

It was five years ago, and if there was, it was definitely pretty minimal . . . it was definitely a jeep commander, not a company commander or something, going over the orders to open fire, if there were incidents. It was during the Intifada. He'd talk about incidents in the sector or in the next sector over, what had happened in the days before.

When you arrived, was there an order in place forbidding Palestinians from using that road?
Yes.

Were there closures only on the Allon road?
That was the only main road we were on.

Were they allowed to drive on the side roads?
Yeah, that's like the justification for it. The main thing I wrote to you about was the day they told us we were going to guard a tractor. The tractor moved a bunch of dirt, and the dirt blocked the whole way from the road to the villages.

A army tractor?
No, a civilian tractor. We guarded it.

You did it just like that?
No. Where did the order come from? I don't know. It was coordinated with us, we were the military part of things. Blocking everything. Even though they were forbidden, the Palestinians drove on the road. You drive on it, and you see that every side road is blocked with a mound of dirt, and no one can cross. You ask, "What happens if someone has to use it?" because the road connects Ramallah to Nablus. They say, "Don't worry, there are side roads, they drive through the villages." They have to use the side roads, and instead of taking twenty minutes it takes at least an hour.

Which side roads?
Side roads to the settlements.

So Palestinians couldn't drive on those roads? Do you remember which village this was?

Right after I got home after reserve duty, there was an article in *Ha'aretz* by Amira Hass called "Now Even Water Is Under Closure." It described exactly how they block access to the villages. I'm not sure if it was about our sector or farther north, but right in that same area. She wrote that water tanks weren't allowed in, they don't have running water, they just leave them and their flocks without water, the goats are dying from thirst and the people there are at risk, too, and the price of a water tank went up five times. We saw a settler working in the quarry with Palestinians, you know, a right-wing settler and everything, who said that something isn't right here . . . you can't deprive people of water and not be surprised when it comes back to you like a boomerang. He was also talking about the whole thing with the closures, he said there isn't a day when his workers don't call him and tell him they're stuck somewhere on the road, even though they have permits. Anyone living or working there has to get a specific detailed permit.

Based on his record, or his work or location?

I don't know, but he has to have it. If he hasn't got it, he's worthless. I told you before, a lot of times they stop people for no reason, so they don't even make it to the checkpoints.

The soldiers don't check them and then move them along?

Nothing.

They just stop them?

Nothing moves. The guy just stands there. He can wait there for half an hour for no reason.

How long was your reserve duty?

A month.

Patrols, ambushes, arrests?

No, I didn't do that. They did. They had a team and I don't know what they did there. What made me feel really shitty at the checkpoints was the road they weren't allowed to use, it's trivial but it's terrible. There's a checkpoint and it's just for one specific group. How do you decide? They have their license plates and they have to stop, people with Palestinian license plates stop. There are two lanes—one for the cars that stop, and the other's empty, every once in a while [there's] a jeep or a settler driving fast. It's clear to him that the checkpoint's not for him. He doesn't even slow down, only when he gets to the checkpoint itself, but he goes around the cars, he waves or he passes the cars and goes on. It doesn't make sense operationally, because a terrorist can steal a car with yellow plates* and say "See you later," because there's basically no order to stop him. And ethically it looks disgusting, the heat of August and there's a row of cars stopped in the sun . . .

How long are they there for?

Up to a half hour.

And then they have to turn around?

No, after that, they're done with the checkpoint. There's absolutely no logic—that's the whole idea, I think it's just to make it hard for them, so they won't want to travel on that road—(a) delay them, get them off of the road; (b) physically block the road; (c) create these checkpoints, dirt embankments—but in terms of operational logic, clearly, there's no point. It's not going to stop a terrorist with an IQ higher than 40, that's not what's going to stop terrorists—it's just to make the civilians miserable.

If I went to the reservists' first briefing, what would I hear?

For most of us it was the first reserve duty after the Intifada had broken out, so the first thing you think about is the danger, will they plant explosives on the road? During the briefing, the battalion commander

*Israeli.

said we have nothing to worry about, it's forbidden for locals to use the road, you'll barely see any Palestinians there. Right away, it was a red flag, because I wasn't aware there were roads just for Jews. I asked him if [the Palestinians] know about it. "Yes, they know. If someone doesn't know—he sees the army jeep and turns around, they get it themselves."

Is that really how it worked?

Yes. If we stopped at an intersection, then of course. Or they'd stop and wait, the trucks, for example, would just wait, because there are quarries there. In the briefing they told us to stop the trucks because of the quarries. The trucks couldn't turn around, they were just idling on the road. That's another thing I brought up, the passivity. You're there and you show your power. People just took it—it was at the height of the Intifada.

I just got back from the Jordan Valley—people there are also very passive. So, you just sit in your chair, tell them to come over and they do, then you stop them before they get too close? No one argues?

Once in a while. If it was the afternoon and the heat got to them, then they'd start to yell and wave their permits, and there was always a soldier who'd say, "Don't get too close . . ."

Was there ever any violence?

No. I'm sure they were too nervous. You know what could happen, you're standing in your *jalabiya* in front of four guys with guns, you know where the line is. I'm telling you, even yelling was rare. Ninety percent of the time people were totally obedient. The yelling was really rare.

46. The checkpoint wrecks lives

UNIT: NAHAL BRIGADE
LOCATION: RAMALLAH
YEAR: 2002

The Qalandiya checkpoint literally wrecks lives. We used to call it that, the "life-wrecker," me and another officer. Families were completely broken apart. Neighboring villages suddenly had this barrier running right down the middle. Mothers, fathers, totally separated. Company —— of the 932nd (Battalion of the Nahal Brigade) was there, a platoon of yeshiva students. These guys are sick, totally crazy, hate Arabs, willing to risk jail for the chance to do something to Arabs. They've got no God, they wear a yarmulke but they've got no God when they're in the army. Eight-hour shifts at the checkpoint. There are two sides at the checkpoint, with a sergeant and a squad commander. During the day there's an officer there, at night there's a sergeant and a squad commander. The officer stands on one side, and there's just the squad commander on the other. And there are also soldiers and another squad commander patrolling around, making sure no one sneaks through. It was the Wild West, the area around the checkpoint. What do I mean, Wild West? Setting tear gas, booby traps where the fence is broken, where there are holes and anyone can sneak through. I'm not talking about terrorists—I'm talking about women and children who go through every day. Kids who don't want to be late for school, women going to doctors' appointments use that hole. So where there's a loose brick, right at the hole, you put a tear gas canister with no safety pin, so it's released the moment someone steps on it. There was endless shooting in the air. And not just in the air, but also what's called preventive fire. Aim at a stone near the person and fire.

A firing wall.

A firing wall. Exactly. We used rubber bullets, stun grenades, tear gas. Really the Wild West. No one knows, no one hears anything. No supervision.

There was no hierarchy of a commander giving orders?

Nothing.

Every soldier does whatever he wants?

Yeah. It's the yeshiva students' favorite spot, that Wild West, because they know that they can do whatever they want, beat people up as much as they want, just go wild. I remember many times when we'd detain people just for the hell of it, because someone started pushing at the checkpoint, or someone tried to go around it. Handcuff him, sit him by the concrete slabs, dry him out there the whole day. On principle, "Don't mess with my checkpoint."

It was up to each soldier's judgment?

That whole checkpoint is the Wild West. Everyone does whatever he wants.

47. The city's hermetically sealed

Unit: Paratroopers
Location: Nablus
Year: 2003

This story's about runaways in Elon Moreh. There were runaways. There were people everywhere and loads of pathways, dirt paths.

Illegal aliens?

They're not illegal aliens because those are near the seam, and there it's far from the seam. The thing about Nablus is that it's under siege. The IDF's tactic with Nablus is to split it off from the surrounding villages. Meaning there's absolutely no movement at all—at all—no one going in or out of Nablus. You've got to understand what that means: a guy in Nablus between sixteen and thirty-five years old hasn't left Nablus in the last four years, not even to go to a neighboring village. He can only be in that city. And because of that, there's a very large smuggling culture. And the majority of the things smuggled into the city, because it's hermetically sealed, go through the check-points. Whoever wants to get things in without going through the checkpoints, which is faster, makes all kinds of dirt paths nearby. There's a valley there that's totally churned up with paths, millions of them, and every day it's a game of cat and mouse. You close the paths, bring a bull-dozer to block them, and they open the paths again. On that deployment in Elon Moreh we had to separate the valley and Nablus. So there are trucks that come from the valley and want to go into Nablus, and there are people who want to get out of Nablus, and people who want to go to work and go to university, and they escape, sometimes on foot, and you can't stop them all because there's no wall around Nablus. There are a million ways to get out. There's a patrol there called the run-away patrol, they chase after people all day, trying to stop things, and it's really funny, because you stop someone . . .

When they catch a runaway, what do they do?

So that's it; either you detain them, or tell them to return to Nablus, and if you catch the same one a few times, then you can take him to the temporary prison camp, the improvised prison camp the company set up, where we brought detainees from the checkpoint, and they stay there handcuffed for a day or two. That happened as well. The tricki-est time for the company-in-training was . . . again, the company-in-training normally follows accepted practice, because most of the time the commanders are there with the soldiers and they follow the ethical code. But the trickiest time was when we were given some kind of vague permission from the deputy battalion commander, like half-permission, to shoot car tires, for example.

In the valley where the runaways were, or in general?

In the valley. When you're catching a car, after you catch it, you flatten the tires. It was allowed, and I didn't like it. There were other com-manders who didn't like it, and not everyone did it.

The deputy battalion commander instructed you to do this?

He, like, gave some kind of permission to the company commander. After about two weeks they said that permission hadn't been given, and they stopped doing it. But for two weeks the soldiers went wild. They shot the tires, they'd take a knife and slash the truck tires . . . it got to the point of pulling the plugs from the cars. Violence to the cars. Where they drew the line was, don't break the windows. Don't vandalize the car, just take it out of commission.

And what made them stop?

An order from the battalion commander. The fact is, it was illegal, the whole thing with shooting the tires.

And how did they deal with the fact that they'd done it?

They didn't, you don't deal with things in the army, you don't talk about it, you just move on. It was allowed, now it's not, end of story. That's how things work in the army, like every time there's some kind of breach, someone closes their eyes, exploits an ethical breach, does something, okay, it's smoothed over, it's over. It never happened, forget it, it goes no further. They treat it like nothing. The fact that a few people shot up the whole car, riddled it with holes and destroyed it, no one cares. They're just things that happened. It happened in the valley. The place with the runaways was very tricky, you play cat and mouse every day, it's exhausting, you feel like an idiot. You're chasing after innocent people. They just want to work. It's very hard for soldiers there to do it, the job sucks. It really sucks. It was, you live through it, and it's shit. That's all. It was a really rough time, 8/8 three months between the two checkpoints and the valley, eating dust, living in the APC. A disgusting place. It's like a wilderness. That was it. After that I was finished. I'd had enough, with that five-month period, they really broke me, 8/8. So I decided I was going to the auxiliary company just to be a regular soldier. It didn't feel right to be a commander in that situation.

48. What is it if not a ghetto?

Unit: Paratroopers
Location: Qalqilya
Year: 2004

As an instruction officer I'd go around the tactical headquarters with the battalion commander. It was actually very interesting. The battalion commander would ask a lot of questions, talk with people. It was my first—and I think also his first, certainly my first—time dealing with the separation fence. We'd go around at night in a jeep, to get to know the sector, and he'd ask questions, see that there really are villagers who can't cross, and it's their livelihood. He'd stop, he'd see a family sitting in their yard. "Tell me, how do you get to such and such a place?" And they'd say, "You can't get to such and such." "What do you mean, you can't get there? You obviously need to, so how do you do it?" "No, you can't do it." He'd talk to the residents a lot. Or they'd close down the route on them, some village's main thoroughfare. Just like that, cut off by the fence.

How did you react?

In this case, it's not so much the army, it's policy, it's the physical reality of the fence. Again, it's seeing how terrible it is. Especially in Qalqilya—around Qalqilya it's closed on all sides, and there's only one gate. Enclosed by a wall and a fence. Say what you like, what is it if not a ghetto? It's closed off. There's one gate, maybe more. When I was there they decided, I guess something happened, they decided on no more gates, that they'd be closed. There's just one gate where they go in and out of the town, Qalqilya. Okay, it's not Nablus, but it's still a big town. One of the smaller ones, but it's still a town, with a lot of people.

49. The commander said to block the road

UNIT: ENGINEERING CORPS
LOCATION: GENERAL
YEAR: 2002

Who gives the order to close a road?

It could be the lowest-ranking sergeant. He takes you . . . a few times you can just go ahead, they take you out in the morning, you go around all the roads. Everything is open . . .

Wherever there's a closed road, there's a mound of dirt. Is that what you do more or less? You put up a mound of dirt?

A mound of dirt. If there's stones nearby, then stones. If there's a wrecked car, you use the car.

Do you ever open a closed area?

Yeah, usually before the army's going in, and then you go where the place is closed off with concrete blocks. They're relatively easy to move.

The concrete blocks are easier to move?

Yes. It's easy for us. I once destroyed . . . because of a mistake in the order, I once destroyed an IDF checkpoint of concrete blocks. It's simple. I just pushed away at least twenty blocks with the bulldozer—didn't feel a thing. I just kept moving forward.

Does the Border Police officer give the order to set up a blockade?

Yes.

He actually tells you, "Block this road, it's disrupting my checkpoint"?

Yeah, he'd say something like that, but he gets the order from higher up. He's the one who tells me just because he's part of the force on guard. That time I had an NCO working with me, either he was an officer or a pretty senior NCO in that area. He really enjoyed the whole

Checkpoint, Jericho, the District Coordination and Liaison, 2003, Armored Corps.

thing. After the first blockade with the bulldozer he'd go up on the hoe and ride with me, which is supposed to be forbidden.

What do you mean?
You mean, why?

Yes.
Because he just liked to do it.

What? Ride on the hoe? When you'd move the dirt mounds?
No, no. When I'd go from blockade to blockade he'd ride on the hoe instead of riding in his own jeep.

50. A sterile road

UNIT: NAHAL BRIGADE
LOCATION: HEBRON
YEAR: 2005

This is something I remember well. In Hebron . . . we were in Tel Rumeida and we were on guard there. You know what it's like, there's Tel Rumeida, linked to Mitkanim and the Cave of the Patriarchs, and that whole route is sterile.

What do you mean, "sterile"?

Great, "What do I mean, 'sterile'?" You see the injustice? "Sterile" means that all the stores on that street, which all used to be open, almost all of them, except maybe one or two, are now closed. Ten stores, closed, all along the street. It means that all of the houses there, someone used to live in them, or doesn't live in them anymore, or they're blocked off, so they can't live there anymore. Palestinians can't use that street. Or just a few of them. There are a couple with work permits, but they don't work in the stores, because the stores are closed. There's one store still open. Only certain people have permission, and it's very specific. So like it's an atrocious injustice, you see that it's closed, just so there can be [Jewish] places there, like the Bet Romano Yeshiva, and next to it there's another house, I don't remember, some house.

Hadassah.

Maybe. Tel Rumeida, such an injustice. You see, they just closed it. There are also neighborhoods beyond Bet Romano, there's one, like a courtyard, where a Palestinian guy blew himself up. Next to Gross Square.

Avraham Avinu.

Avraham Avinu. There, as well—I had to guard there—there, too, it's like one house on top of another house, because Hebron is crazy, like the casbah, and the houses are right on top of each other, we had a

"Mapping," Nablus, 2008.

patrol where we just jumped over the rooftops. We did the patrol itself on the roofs, not in the street, because they were like real paths. So they closed all the Palestinian stores down below so they couldn't plant explosives there or break through from there. Okay, it makes sense, complete sense that you'd want to keep a close watch—it makes sense. Killing when there's clear and present danger. The problem is, you start thinking about whether they need to be here, do they really? And you see it, you see the poverty, and the checkpoints, and the enormous struggle of a whole city or a whole neighborhood just to live, all because of a few hundred [settlers]. You see it clearly. It was also . . . you see the insane social disparity, the wealth next to the poverty, and you see the terrible hatred.

51. Hebron, a stinging slap

UNIT: NAHAL BRIGADE
LOCATION: HEBRON
YEAR: 2004

It's the most frustrating thing about Hebron. If we were in Gaza for two weeks . . . right before we were in Hebron we were in Gaza, so there was an operation, and a soldier from the battalion was killed, and you really felt like you were there because it's the kind of situation where you need to be a soldier. Hebron was the exact opposite of that, a stinging slap. You're there to uphold a certain status. One of the most frustrating things in Hebron is that the settlers don't care, they do whatever they want, even if they're just a meter away from you. The first week there were a lot of us, there's a road, the Tnuva road, which leads from the Avraham Avinu neighborhood to the cave. Now, it was right during the time of, I don't remember if it was a Jewish holiday, there was some holiday, Jewish or Muslim, I don't remember. I think it was during some Muslim holiday. So they put up partitions in the middle of the road, the Palestinians crossed on one side and the Jews on the other. Now, the number of Palestinians crossing the road was significantly— not just two or three times more, but ten times more than the number of Jews who crossed then. I'm talking about hundreds, every morning, every prayer time. And they went on their side. If just one, there was one Palestinian woman who did it on purpose, and all her friends started yelling at her. I came and said to her, "Madam, you cross and it'll . . ." I had my weapon. At some point she got quiet and went back.

Who yelled at her, Palestinians?

They said, "Yes, yes, stop, stop, come back." They didn't want her making trouble. And then the same day, there's a family of something like ten or fifteen Jews and they walk in the road, like freestyle. And I go over and say, "Listen, sir, we partitioned the road for a reason, it's just for now, I'm asking you to wait." He says, "Who do you think you are?"

That's how he talked to you?

Yeah, "Who do you think you are? This is my road, this is my town. I do whatever I want." I said, "I'm here to protect you, please, if you don't mind." "No, I'll do whatever I want. You're giving in to them, you're too easy on them, you aren't tough enough, you aren't enough whatever." It was as if, from that moment on I . . . there was a time where I said I'm cutting myself off from them, like this whole thing about yes taking their coffee or not taking their coffee. I said, "I don't want them feeling any legitimacy because I'm there, or feeling good about it." From that moment me and the settlers were at loggerheads, until the end of my service. I refused to take anything they wanted to give me, or any help. I said I didn't want it. They annoyed me. There were a few examples. That one, and a situation where a Palestinian father, again, it's all on the Palestinian side of the road, he was walking with his son at his side, and then four settler children showed up. They picked up a rock, threw it at the Palestinian boy. I yell at them, and the father comes over and says, "Here, see, we aren't doing anything," and he's frustrated, "Look what they're doing to us." And me, other than lower my head in shame, there's nothing I can do. Because I can't lift a hand against settler children. I can't threaten them with my weapon. If the situation was the reverse, I don't know what would have happened.

What would happen?

If an Arab boy picked up a rock against a Jewish boy, then we'd probably have to handcuff him, blindfold him, send him wherever, follow the orders.

Those are the orders?

It's in the rules of engagement, situations and responses.

The suspect-arrest procedure?

Right, procedure for arresting a suspect. If a boy picks up a rock. Forget it, if a Palestinian boy went, started not doing what I told him, like the Jewish guy who said, "Who do you think you are," and whatever, I'd have to start shooting in the air, then at his feet, all kinds of things like that. There were incidents like that in Hebron, all kinds. The company that relieved us told us. There was some crazy boy, not crazy, a bit retarded, he didn't understand what they were screaming at him. In the end he got a bullet in his leg. It was the 931st Nahal Battalion.

52. The protesters were getting beaten, the officers were cracking sunflower seeds

UNIT: ARMORED CORPS

LOCATION: RAMALLAH DISTRICT

YEAR: 2007

On my second deployment in the Territories, I was in Makabim, with the front command staff the whole time.

Whose?

Investigative operations officer. You don't stand at the checkpoint unless something happens. You go out to Bil'in every Friday. I'll never forget it. I went to Bil'in, we went to the fence, I was all excited, action, protesters. All you care about when you're in the army is action. Those were my first days, I was all right. We see the fence on the right and the olive groves. On the left I see olive groves, and something doesn't make sense. How do people get across? So I ask my commander, totally naïve, thinking he's a major in the Israeli army, he must know: "How do they get across?" "They get special permits, they have to go to the gate." "Whenever they want?" "No, there are times." "And why didn't the fence go up around the groves?" "What are you asking questions for? Come on, there's a protest." These were usually the answers. They're basically saying, "Don't think."

There are orders.

Yes. Either it's "This will just make things tougher for you," or "Look on the bright side, it's all in a good cause." We got to Bil'in. There was a protest at the fence, so we went to protect the fence. We warn them, "If you get too close, we'll use force." They get a bit closer. There's shoving, stones, punching, tear gas, rubber bullets. It's gradual. I'm standing above the demonstration, above the Border Police guys. My commander is sitting with the BP commander and another officer, I don't know where he came from, some lieutenant colonel, and they're laughing, and meanwhile people are being beaten up. I see them from behind. Try to imagine it: I see my officers with their backs to me, laughing, falling about, and below I see the Border Police beating people up, guys being choked, one guy bleeding. And I think, "This is just like the books I read." Okay, there's a difference. I wouldn't want you to quote me, although that's what I felt. It came into my head, it's not my fault, that's what came into my head. I feel bad about that.

It doesn't have to go in.

Whenever people get shot, I have this image in my head, I must've seen it in a movie, of Nazis shooting Jews in pits, and officers standing at the side, laughing. It's not the same thing and there's no connection, but people are getting beaten, there's blood, and they're laughing, cracking sunflower seeds, and I say, "You are such evil people." I look at them and they're saying, "Look at the blow that guy just took!" . . .

What's happening down below? Did the demonstration start peacefully?

Yes, they come with banners, the Border Police says, "If you get too close we'll use force, this is a closed military zone." They get closer, the police shove them.

What triggers the shooting?

As soon as there are stones, we're allowed to fire rubber bullets at the leaders.

Did you shoot as well?

No. They always asked me if I wanted to shoot. But I said, "What for? There's all of the other guys."

Border Police?

Border Police, Armored Corps, Artillery Corps, they rotate.

What's the first means of response?

First of all they push them, and there are clubs, or used to be. Today it's lots of tear gas and stun grenades, and sometimes rubber bullets . . . now they don't cross the fence, but they used to. Now they stand on the other side of the fence.

So first there's physical violence, hand-to-hand [fighting], clubbing, and then what's the first phase of shooting?

First clubs, then stun grenades and tear gas together.

Did you see tear gas canisters being fired out of launchers?

Yes. I have a film here that I took while I was standing with the soldiers. You can't see it that well.

Do you recall the orders you were given there as a soldier?

Yes, on the radio. Risk is risk, what can happen from throwing stones? Forget it, not important. A fifteen-year-old was shot in the leg with a rubber bullet . . .

Do you get instructions on the radio about other things, too, like how and when to fire?

Yes.

What kind of instructions?

There are lookouts watching through their screens, saying over the radio, "There's a guy there behind the tree, on the left," and then they fire at him with rubber ammo.

And what happens when it goes beyond rubber?

I didn't see that, the orders there were specifically not to . . .

All the activists with cameras.

We were told to try to avoid being filmed. I remember one Asian journalist was arrested and my commander yelled at him and I felt really ashamed. A journalist . . . My commander terrified him, and I was shocked. That's all it was, soldiers swearing at leftists, "Because of you guys I'm stuck here on Friday instead of going home."

What were the orders about launchers for tear gas and stun grenades?

I heard the orders every Friday. They were not to fire without confirmation, not rubber or tear gas, then the confirmation came right at the beginning, and you could fire freely.

So there's an initial confirmation that allows you to open fire?

One time, all the Armored Corps soldiers were lined up, and the commander told the guys throwing stun grenades to do it all at once. There was an insane blast, and then the tear gas started. Usually they're directed, but you know, when four soldiers shoot together, he can't direct each of them where to aim. The idea is that the commander tells the soldiers where to shoot.

In theory, are you supposed to fire at a certain angle?

They make sure to say that, too. The rules are fine. The problem is when someone fires straight ahead . . .

Did you see that happen?

Yes.

What was the reaction?

No one noticed and it didn't hit anyone. I don't know if he did it on purpose, it was continuous. He didn't aim, but he did fire. Once when I came back with the Border Police, one of them said, "I nearly killed someone out there," and someone replied, "Pal, don't mess up . . ." And everyone laughs. No one's serious about the fact that someone almost died. The commander said, "Pal, don't mess up." These are good Border Police compared to what I've seen. At the demonstrations at Bil'in, I realized how it's all so unnecessary, I saw that it's a land grab. After that I watched the film about Bil'in and saw my commander in it.

You saw it as a soldier?

Yes. I began to talk to people, and once we were on patrol during the week and there were some guys in the olive groves and I talked to them, and I was told not to. Every now and then my commander did try to help them out, but the direction was clear.

53. They'd close the stores as collective punishment

UNIT: NAHAL BRIGADE
LOCATION: RAMALLAH DISTRICT
YEAR: 2008–2009

Cutting the fence, throwing rocks, and so on, that was constant, every day. That was our main activity, there was no hostile terrorist action. It's important to say that it was young men, twenty years old and up. Every now and then there were more serious protests, but from what I remember there were no weapons, it was slingshots and stuff like that. These were guys who went to Ni'lin on Fridays.

What did you mainly do there?

During that time I was in the operations room a bit, and we had two vehicle patrols at the fence or deeper in, and a bit in the villages.

How did it work with the fence? Was it forbidden to be within a certain distance of it?

Yeah, there was a distance where getting any closer was considered suspicious, or where the lookouts would identify kids, at a particular time, after school was out or at night when they'd cut the fence. This was every day.

What do you do? Let's say the lookout sees a boy getting close.

We show that we're there, so that they'll move away, we try to make them see us, and if they get close or start cutting [the fence] or throw stones, then it goes downhill. I don't remember the command to open fire, but it didn't include live ammunition. The worst was the Ruger.* Many times we went into the village to move them back there. Sometimes we used tear gas.

In the village?

Yes. I think we almost never used the Ruger. Maybe when we were on the Israeli side of the fence they'd shoot toward the village, where it was more open, but stun grenades, tear gas, rubber bullets, in that order.

Were there orders about how to use the gas and rubber bullets?

We needed the officer's permission, maybe even the company officer. Stun grenades and tear gas—with permission of the officer in the field, if I'm not mistaken, because it was immediate, and rubber bullets was with the company commander's permission, and perhaps at a certain point with the battalion commander's permission, because there were anomalous incidents with rubber bullets in other places. Also shooting at people's legs.

Were there instances where people were injured?

I think so. There were no injuries from tear gas but . . . from rubber bullets, yes, they hit people.

Are you talking about guys at the fence, or about protests in the village or at the entrance to the village?

Either in the village, or forty meters away from the fence, or both.

And when they disperse the protest inside the village?

I wasn't there, so I don't want to say. I was almost never at any disturbances. It was a very strange time, I was almost never present at those events.

---

*The Ruger 10/22 suppressed sniper rifle, which is classified as "lethal."

What did the guys say who came back from Ni'lin?

That it's total chaos, loads of tear gas, stun grenades, at some point there were Rugers. For a short while in Ni'lin there were a few guys who shot Rugers, they positioned sharpshooters in the area and they were supposed to shoot at the knees and below. But they told me, I wasn't there. It didn't happen every Friday.

Were there agricultural gates along the fence?

I think so. I think we got there after the olive harvest, so there wasn't much engagement.

Weren't there soldiers posted at your part of the fence to open and close the gate?

No. But there are two settlements there, I don't remember their names, and the road was used by Arabs and Jews, and rocks were thrown at the Jewish cars, the road goes through the villages, it serves both Palestinians and Israelis, there were a lot of incidents of rock throwing.

Did you respond?

We'd go, check things out, sometimes there were scouts. There's no way to find a boy who threw a rock at two in the morning. There were periods during our time there when they'd close the road or the stores as collective punishment.

In which villages?

Qibya, Budrus, in that area, I don't remember. Not necessarily there, but in the area.

How many stores were closed?

It changed.

And they reopened afterward?

After a few hours or days.

54. "You really think I'm going to wait behind an Arab?"

UNIT: KFIR INFANTRY BRIGADE
LOCATION: TUL KAREM
YEAR: 2008

There was one checkpoint that was divided into three lanes. In Sha'ar Ephraim. There's a settlement, a checkpoint, and then Israeli territory. In the middle, there's a Palestinian village, so they just split the check-point into three lanes. Three lanes, and the brigade commander ordered that Jews should only wait at the checkpoint for ten minutes. Because of that we had to have a special lane for them, and everyone else, the Palestinians and Israeli Arabs, had to wait in the other two lanes. I remember that settlers would come, go around the Arabs, and just did it naturally. I went over to a settler and said, "Why are you going around, there's a line here, sir." He said, "You really think I'm going to wait behind an Arab?" He began to raise his voice at me. "You're going to hear from your brigade commander." I said, "He's an Israeli citizen just like you, you have the same ID, there is no reason that you . . ."

55. I'm ashamed of what I did there

UNIT: COMBAT ENGINEERING CORPS—NUCLEAR, BIOLOGICAL,
    CHEMICAL
LOCATION: ELKANA
YEAR: 2005

When I was commander at the company-in-training and then got to operations, we were at a checkpoint, I don't remember the name.

Where?

It was in Elkana, at a fence that separates the Jewish and Palestinian houses, and there's still one Palestinian house on the Jewish side—they made a mistake with the fence there, and because of that there's a checkpoint. Their whole access was . . . There were families on the other side so they had to cross there, so the army put up a checkpoint. There were rules for who could cross, I don't remember what exactly, it's forbidden to cross if they don't have this document or that permit, a work permit. There was someone coming back from the other side, and he pretended that he didn't understand why he couldn't go in. He had a bag in his hand, and he was asking why, why, and he knew very well why. After two hours he came back and said he was the other guy's twin, I don't remember if he had a permit, I don't think he did. He really annoyed us . . . I don't like talking about it . . . He really annoyed us, and we decided to punish him, so we put him in a corner, with his bags and everything, blindfolded and handcuffed him and he sat there for four or five hours. Just like that, like, it's something I'm ashamed of. I'm ashamed. I don't know . . .

Why?

Because it's, my god, a totally different world there with totally different rules. In this world, that story is unacceptable, at least for me . . . there it's so natural. The rules are so different. No one understands this unless they've been there. If I tell one of my girlfriends . . . it's a little story out of many shocking stories, it's a little thing that makes me feel uncomfortable. If I told a friend who didn't go into the army whose ideology is—I don't know how she'd react.

Did you tell anyone?
No.

Did you feel ashamed at the time?
No.

How many people were there?
Three.

What did they think about it afterward? Or today?
I don't talk to them today.

But did you talk about it afterward, about whether it was okay or not? That maybe he deserved better?

I remember that at some point, one of my soldiers said he'd bring him water or he'd go and release him. Yes, they felt a bit . . . But we really didn't talk about things like that, what happens—happens.

When did you start thinking about the incident?

When I was released, only afterward, also, some time after.

How did it suddenly come up?

All of a sudden, a picture. This powerful image I get whenever people talk about what they did in the army. I saw a documentary on Channel 8 about women soldiers. A lot of images came up during the movie. Images that I never thought about at all.

Were there other incidents like that? Similar?

All kinds, yes.

You don't remember?

I have images in my head, but I don't remember details. I really repressed that period. It's not like I suffered there or that I'm traumatized, but I finished the army and I started a totally different life. I'm telling you, the most banal things, I don't remember terms for them. I know what you're talking about, but you have to remind me.

56. You don't know what you're doing there

Unit: Nahal Brigade
Location: Hebron
Year: 2004–2006

In Hebron, which of the roads are sterile?

David road. That's a sterile road. In our area, David's the only sterile one, I think.

What about the wholesale market?

That, too. But I think that's the Tnuva road, too, no?

The wholesale market is in Avraham Avinu.

So okay, that, too, totally sterile.

The gate there?

Totally sterile.

Were there problems at the wholesale market?

There were break-ins, and once these two girls tried to set fire to something.

What do you mean, "break-ins"?

They tried to break in with crowbars. After all, everything there is abandoned. Once I remember these two girls set fire to something, I don't remember what exactly. I thought: Two girls, what the fuck? What do they want? And there was this thing, we talked about it, where Jews walk through there, they don't give a shit, even where they're not supposed to be. So there was one time they walked through, I think, Jews weren't allowed to go by foot from Shlomo post to David road toward the school and toward the Pharmacy junction, only by vehicle. I'm pretty sure. So once they just walked through. We tried to stop them, and in the end, we heard on the radio, "It's okay, let them go." What could we do? We tried to keep them back, it didn't work.

Officially there's no ban on them walking.

I don't know. I have no idea. Could be.

Are there official prohibitions for Arabs?

Of course.

They tell you in the briefing?

If you see an Arab on David road, it's the suspect-arrest procedure. Always.

The wholesale market, Hebron, 2003, vandalized by settlers.

You know that's illegal?

Really? No. Why?

David road was open all the time, but in fact the army closed it.

Too bad no one told the soldiers. I didn't know that. I don't know, listen, so I broke the law. I didn't know about that. I know that back then, when we were there, and I was deputy company sergeant major, the Supreme Court ruled that they could use the David road, the whole way. I remember it was a real mess, it made life really hard for the army. We didn't understand the ruling, it was really pointless. Like I said, as soldiers all we wanted was no rioting, violence. And that just created violence. It's not as if the Arabs couldn't get to the cave. Again, obviously it messes up their lives, they're stuck with it. But if you look at the scales and say, Okay, what would you prefer? That they have to walk another five minutes, or have riots?

You're sure there would have been clashes?

Positive. Sure thing. You know ——, the sergeant? I remember he once told me that in his time, there'd been the David road patrol. There was this market, on the Arab part of the road, that is. He was at post 38, he told me, everything there had been more . . . less of a mess. I simply couldn't imagine it. I said, How can that be? Because now, any Arab who'd show up there, no way, it's like they've got intelligence, the settlers would be all over him, immediately.

Did that happen?

Yeah, sure. Plenty of times, plenty, all that hitting. That's what happens there, it's very quiet in terms of activity, no stone throwing. Occasionally, but not . . . I've been in other areas where stone throwing goes on all the time, every day. Over there, there's none of that, not too many serious outbursts. A few punches here and there, and then separate them, end of story. There's a kind of status quo. But when there's a real clash, it's like you're in a movie. Wow, it's a mess. That's what's so amazing in Hebron. It's not a posting where lots of stuff happens, not much in the way of terrorist activity and stuff like that, but you get really screwed up there mentally because you don't know what you're doing there. You simply don't know why.

57. The soldiers played a prank, the workers' permits disappeared

UNIT: NACHSHON BATTALION
LOCATION: YAKIR
YEAR: 2001

I felt that something was going on here that wasn't right . . . One time we were with the battalion at Yakir, and we went to buy something in the settlement, we went and sat around there. There was a guy from the reserves who was doing settlement guard duty. So we got talking. It was me and another two guys, and we were just talking. Then he came out of the post, and the guys took these passes for Palestinians, the kind with a picture. Like an ID, but a pass that lets Palestinians use the roads in the West Bank.

From the District Coordination and Liaison?

Yeah. Now, these cards, what's amazing, which you know from being at the checkpoints, is how hard it is to get them. Because people are always showing you cards that have expired, and they tell you stories about how they've been trying to get them renewed. So you know that it's almost impossible to get a card that's still valid. So we were surprised to see that the guys who work on the settlement still have valid cards. There were Arab workers in Yakir. So they leave their cards at the gate and go to work in the settlement. So what did these two guys with me do? They took the cards and put them in their pockets. A guy without his card, you can imagine what . . .

Why did they put them in their pocket?

No reason, just spite. Just because. The guard went out for a smoke and they played a prank, they hid them. Nothing's going to happen to him of course. Like what? It's just some guy's travel pass. They'll come after working all day and start . . .

These weren't ID cards?

Travel passes that allow you to go on the Jewish roads in the West Bank, and I don't know what else exactly. At our checkpoint, say, anyone who showed us that card, nothing changed. You still couldn't cross and that's it. But apparently there were places where it helped.

They just took them? Did they give them back later?

No. They just took them. It wasn't like, they'd never seen those Palestinians, ever. They just took the cards. So I said, "Give them back." Basically, there was like . . . they weren't the nicest guys in the company . . . there was like this thing . . . I said, "If you don't give them back, I'll tell the guard when he comes back that you took the cards." So they started with the threats, "We'll fuck you up" and whatever, you know. You know what? I'm ashamed to say it. I don't even remember how it ended. I don't know, really. It was like when I was, what? Half a year, a year in the army. I don't remember how it ended. I just remember it like . . . I really remember that it was the first time I got it that an eighteen-year-old boy with a bit of malice can fuck up someone's life. The next day the guy can't get to work, and you know that he went through seven circles of hell to get that card. You've been there, in Kedumim, the District Coordination and Liaison, you know what goes on there. And you know that you've never seen a card like this that's valid, because they're so hard to get. And they, these guys, just liked the cover that the cards came in. Instead of a wallet, it was like a trend to go around with the ID covers . . . there's orange ones and green ones. So when you see the older soldiers walking around with them, it means they took them. What did they do with them? They used them for something, because you need something hard to fix your equipment, so they'd . . . they used the hard bit of the cover for something. Yeah. Listen, I was so great with my equipment, I'd let someone else do it for me. Anyway, if someone pulled out a card like that which had expired, then you could take it, I think, confiscate it. Because you could say, "If you're using this card, then you're trying to pull a fast one on the soldiers. You can only cross with this and this." So they'd take the card, and they'd use the cover for their equipment . . .

Did they take those things a lot?

Yes.

58. A bone in their throats

UNIT: ARTILLERY
LOCATION: SHAKED
YEAR: 2002

I was in charge of the Shaked checkpoint near Jenin for four months.

You were a squad commander?

Because I was a veteran in my battery. There was a shortage of commanders, so the veteran soldiers were assigned to command the checkpoint.

In general, was most of your engagement in the Territories at the checkpoints?

Yes. Of course there were operations, but since I was a checkpoint commander, I hardly ever took part in them, all I know is from hearsay.

What kind of training did you get to command a checkpoint? What's the preparation?

It's a pretty short briefing about the designated area given by the battalion and the company commanders. What the threats are, the mode of action, and a kind of five-minute practice we performed in the Golan Heights so we could see what a checkpoint is supposed to look like, what we're supposed to do, before we go out on the front. A short lecture from the battalion commander that the Palestinians aren't our enemy, that we're there to carry out ongoing security activity, that we're there to prevent terrorism, a talk about the purity of arms and its importance. All in all it was pretty useless. Both operationally and from a humanitarian perspective, things were left pretty much to our own discretion. What ended up happening was that each soldier in fact determined what his checkpoint would look like from a humane point of view.

Please describe the Shaked checkpoint.

Actually, Shaked checkpoint no longer exists, because the Separation Barrier now runs right through there. In principle, it's supposed to be a point of crossing in and out of the Occupied Territories, but it's situated pretty deep inside the Territories because of a pretty large bloc of settlements near the 1967 line. The checkpoint was set up to separate the Jewish population in the area from most of the Palestinian population. The problem with the checkpoint is that the people who used it regularly didn't have permits, none of them. This was a time when the Territories were under near total closure, no entry or exit of workers, but the village located east of the checkpoint, Tora-something, a large part of it belongs to the Kabha clan—a very big clan, most of them live inside Israel. Villages like Ein a-Sahle, Arrabe, some villages in Wadi Ara, all come from the same clan, so a lot of the residents have blue [Israeli] IDs through marriage or other family connections. So they have permits to cross the checkpoint. In terms of the security check, they had the standing of Israeli citizens, that's one thing. But they're Arabs, so their cars had to be literally taken apart. Another problem was that a few tiny villages west of the checkpoint didn't really have entry permits into Israel, but . . . school, shopping, family—it was all on the other side of the checkpoint, to the east of it, toward Jenin, Nazlat Zeid, Ya'abad, the larger communities in the area. So on a daily basis we had to deal with the same group of people. You got to know them personally, their personal stories, what each one was going to do on the other side of the checkpoint, when he'd cross, and when he'd come back. So that's how it worked: overall we only checked people who were allowed to pass, and we also checked a lot of Israeli Arabs' trucks coming from the Territories that needed to get out at the end of the workday. This was basically the function of the checkpoint.

How many people crossed each day?

It's not comparable to the Tunnels checkpoint, a-Ram, or other points of entry in and out of the Territories. Maybe because of the reality at the time I was there, during Operation Defensive Shield, when the Territories were under total closure, there were very few people allowed passage—only permit holders. The main village west of the checkpoint is Umm al Reihan, with about fifteen families living there, and nearly all of them crossed on a daily basis—children, young people going to school, adults on their way to work, a few women.

Crossing into Israel?

Crossing into the Occupied Territories, eastward, mainly to Ya'abad and Jenin.

These people are considered Israeli citizens?

No. Umm al Reihan is west of the checkpoint, but its residents have Palestinian IDs. Today I don't know what they do, because there's a fence, a wall running between them and their lives. I haven't been back, but I understand that because of the wall it's a mess.

You monitored the passage of . . .

Palestinians living west of the checkpoint and Israelis living east of the checkpoint. That was the chaos there.

And there were no Palestinians living east of the checkpoint who crossed over to the west?

There were, but only those who had blue IDs. This was what the everyday reality was like. For the most part, there were no huge crimes against humanity committed at this checkpoint. Just the fact of its existence was very, very problematic. It was like a bone in the throat of a population that had done nothing out of the ordinary other than going to school and going back home.

59. They aim their weapons at students

UNIT: ARMORED CORPS
LOCATION: RAMALLAH DISTRICT
YEAR: 2006

We provided support for the Halamish front, until the Nahal troops arrived. It was the first time I was exposed to a checkpoint. We were four guys, three privates and a young commander, who'd also never been at a checkpoint. You stand there, in the middle of the night, between a village called . . . it was north of Ramallah—Anata, I think. Atara? A checkpoint north of Ramallah, which all the students went through . . . to Birzeit and whatever. The first time we were there, we were all scared. No one knew anything. You're in the middle of the Territories. We had no idea what we were doing. Our commander, he totally had no idea what he was doing. And that's it. It passed quietly. I didn't really understand why we were checking them, because they were crossing from a Palestinian side to a Palestinian side. They're not going into Israel.

What's the briefing like? What do they tell you to do?

Nothing. There are people that . . . men between the ages of eighteen and forty can't cross the checkpoint.

Why?

I don't know, we're privates. It's not supposed to be our concern.

That's how they said it?

That's what they said.

From the Palestinian side to the Palestinian side.

Yes. Into Ramallah. North of Ramallah, toward the city. It's a road that goes above a Jewish road. It's a road that Palestinians also use. I didn't really understand what . . . I asked, they said, "There's nothing to do. You have to find them." You know . . . It's a bit, I started questioning things . . . nothing serious, but I always had to ask. I said, "Guys, we're here interfering in their lives." I was considerate. "Say good morning, thank you." They'd say, What's the point. You know, I'd say, "Try, they wait here in line for a long time." So at night, there was a religious guy with me who was in an army preparatory program in the Territories. He'd come up to me afterward and say, "Every Arab who crossed, I said to him 'Good morning, safe travels.'" I decided, that's it, see, I'm changing things in the Territories. By the way, before the army, I wanted to enlist in the Border Police. I asked for the Border Police. I said, "I'm gonna make some changes here."

In the Border Police?

Yeah, I was lucky they didn't send me, in retrospect I would have been really miserable. Or maybe I was a little crazy.

Why, don't you feel like you changed some things in the Armored Corps?

Yes . . . but I was only successful with people who were ready to listen. Anyway . . . that's the checkpoint at Halamish. In the morning, we were there from the evening until the next morning. By the way, that same night, they tried to run us over.

What? Who tried to run you over?

A Palestinian. We were standing at the checkpoint on the road. When the man came toward the checkpoint, he started accelerating. He accelerated, kept accelerating, and there were clear orders—you don't shoot at a vehicle after it's stopped. The moment it stops being life-threatening, it's forbidden to shoot. He kept accelerating, and the soldier and I look to the sides, we shot in the air, and a patrol went out.

They didn't find him?

I assume they didn't. And then afterward, they said, "You see what your Arabs are doing?" And then I thought to myself, "They're half right, what are they doing? They're trying to kill us." And then my questions started, like, what are we doing to them here, it doesn't ever justify killing. Anyway . . . in the morning, it began the pressure of the checkpoint . . . both the company commander and the deputy company commander are there. They put me at a small guard post nearby, not at the actual checkpoint . . . I point my weapon, I'm inside, the weapon is visible, the barrel, and I stand there in case something happens. And I see a lot of students, good-looking girls, going to university and I'm pointing my weapon at them . . . The hell with it, I'm standing there with tears in my eyes, what am I doing, pointing my gun at them? And I see my company commander and the deputy with their weapons, waving them in the air like phalangists, agitated, saying, "You, come here!" People are anxious and everyone's yelling, and it's one big mess, the Palestinians are pushing and want to go around, they're late to work. It's total chaos, and I'm standing there in the guard post, aiming my weapon at everyone. You know what image comes to mind for a Jewish soldier pointing a gun at a bunch of citizens? It popped into my head and flipped a switch. I'm not comparing, not for a second, I just understand. The comparison isn't legitimate, but the fear is . . . you know, that, too, began somewhere. What frightens me isn't that we'd really do things like that, I'm jumping ahead to conclusions—but that they no longer have the same worth as other human beings.

The Palestinians?

Yes.

Did you feel that as well when you were there?

Less so, but it grows with time. I don't know, in school they're given the same worth as other human beings, also at home, and also in the army according to the rules, generally, but when you interfere in people's lives like that, and you're in control, and you can decide when he eats and when he does whatever, he slowly loses his worth. After two years, they don't have any worth. They're dolls. That moment was the beginning of the turning point in my thinking. I'd been pointing my gun at students. It's so completely obvious to everyone, and it's also not at all obvious. I went, and spoke to my platoon commander, I said that today . . . I liked him, I also knew that he was also really to the left . . . I asked him to speak to everyone, so they'd understand that they're not ruling over anyone, so they'd understand they should treat them with respect. His tone was really distant and I couldn't figure out if he was with me or against me. The company commander was religious, and he listened to me and spoke nicely and agreed with me and everything, he was a settler, by the way. It was okay, they spoke with the soldiers. Two weeks ago I met with a soldier, and he told me that our company commander really did go to talk with him, because he was a soldier with a lot of influence in the company, so he should talk with the guys and tell them not to do anything. I felt great: there's a response from the system.

60. Guard duty in the Palestinian village

UNIT: NACHSHON BATTALION
LOCATION: DEIR BALLUT
YEAR: 2001

Our front was in a settlement called Alei Zahav, in the Yakir sector. The battalion was in Yakir, and we got Alei Zahav, Magen 50. The checkpoint is in a very pretty village, on the west side of Deir Ballut.

What's pretty about it?

There's a path leading to it. Everything's flat, but the path twists, like it's Oz, with no connection to the rest of the surroundings. The checkpoint prevents the passage of Palestinian vehicles on the new road that links Alei Zahav and Peduel to the trans-Samaria road. So the checkpoint is there to stop Palestinian vehicles from crossing the nice road they built there. Once the road used to go through the villages there. It's called an "only road" in military terminology. It crossed through the villages there, a-Dikh, and Brukin, which are facing Alei Zahav. But because of stone throwing, they made a bypass road, and Palestinian vehicles are forbidden to drive on the bypass road, of course. The checkpoint is there to stop Palestinian vehicles from coming.

Were they prohibited from going from the beginning?

When we got there, it was prohibited. The company hadn't changed that. Aside from not allowing Palestinian vehicles, they also checked all the vehicles that passed. It was basically a gate to Deir Ballut, because from that road . . .

That's the only road to Deir Ballut?

Yes, that's the road to Deir Ballut, which leads to the other villages. There's a left turn, if they come from Deir Ballut, you can go toward Refet and then Bidiya, Misha, and everything, or there's a right turn towards Rantis. At first they wouldn't allow the right turn, later they did. Basically, you really had the feeling that you . . . At a certain point we knew everyone from the village. It's a very small village. Just like there's a guard at the entrance to a settlement, there was a guard for the people in the village for when they traveled out of the village, the inspection itself, if you stop and think about it, is pointless, since they can only get to neighboring Palestinian villages. There's no Jewish traffic on that road, and there isn't really any access from it. So it really shows how you just put a checkpoint there for no reason, every day. To prevent hostile terrorist activity. Like during the briefing before going to the checkpoint, they say, it's to prevent hostile terrorist activity on the only road, which is the Jewish road. And they really do prevent Palestinian vehicles from driving on it, and they check Palestinian vehicles to prevent hostile terrorists from trickling into the sector.

Was anyone caught there?

No, there's nothing there. There's nothing to catch, no one would have any reason to cross. There's nothing. It's totally a Palestinian checkpoint, there's nowhere to run. If someones makes it through, he could drive on the road as much as he wants. He'll run into another checkpoint or another concrete block, he won't meet up with anyone, he won't find any Jews. All the Jews he'll run into are soldiers. Like, there aren't any there. In any event, it's a completely pointless checkpoint, which is why they gave it to a regular company in the Nachshon battalion, which is small, not so well-known. It was only set up in '98, they didn't give it a particularly a hot sector, certainly not to a company that had been up at the front. So the checkpoint quickly developed this sense of, like, I know that when I was at the checkpoint, I'd usually just let the vehicles pass. Because again, the inspection was pretty unnecessary. There was even a dirt road that went around the checkpoint.

And you let them go around the checkpoint?

You could see if there were cars driving there, and whoever cared about their car and had nothing to hide would come to the checkpoint. But still . . . you know, they're bloody-minded, they'd probably check the guy who came to the checkpoint and didn't use the dirt

The closed casbah, Hebron, Nahal Brigade, Battalion 50.

road—because the dirt road, people driving on it, it showed you the absurdity of the whole thing.

61. Every Friday: a closed military zone

UNIT: KFIR INFANTRY BRIGADE
LOCATION: SOUTH HEBRON
YEAR: 2004–2005

So how do you remember your time in Susiya?

In Susiya there were a few things. There's an area between the settlement and the post, the post isn't too far from the settlement itself, but there's a road of two kilometers or so that had a few [Palestinian] families living there in tents, that's the first thing. There were a lot of clashes with left-wing activists in the area. All kinds of complaints about Jews bothering them while they're harvesting the olives and things like that. It was a period when the army declared the area near Susiya a closed military zone more or less every Friday.

So how did the settlers get home?

Of course they didn't close the settlement or the access road to the settlement. I'm talking about the area between the post and the settlement, which is a distance of about two kilometers. That's where a few Palestinian families lived, and that's what started the whole mess. Because the Jews were suspicious of the Palestinians' proximity on the one hand, and on the other the Palestinians complained that the settlers kept bothering them with their farming and wouldn't let them get to their grazing areas with their sheep. The left-wingers came to support the Palestinians and went with them to the grazing areas, while the Jews called the army to get the Palestinians away from there, because they were getting too close to the settlement.

Then what happened?

What normally happened is that we'd move the people away. Each encounter was different, more or less extreme. The less extreme times were when we stayed there, separating the area close to the settlement, where the Palestinian shepherds and left-wing activists were, and keeping them apart. Those were the minor events. The more serious ones involved a patrol moving the Palestinians from a certain area, and once or twice we arrested left-wing activists because they were in a closed military zone, which is forbidden. Beyond that . . . I remember one afternoon there was an argument with one of the . . . We were in the company commander's car and we saw a Palestinian shepherd in an area close to our access road, where he wasn't supposed to be, and we stopped to talk to him. I don't remember what was said and how it started, but more or less he refused to leave. The men from his family showed up, some kind of violent struggle broke out . . .

What does that mean?

In simple language, basically at some point someone said a few words they shouldn't have said, and they started throwing punches.

One of the Palestinians said a few things they shouldn't have said?

It started with his basic refusal to leave, because it really had been a few months, we knew him, he knew us, he knew exactly where he was allowed to be and where he wasn't, and for some reason, that day he decided to take a stand and say, "This is my grazing area and I'm allowed to be here." I remember that his family turned up very quickly, and a bit later, after that, left-wing activists came to the area.

Wait, what happened during the confrontation?

At first just our company commander's jeep was there, later another Hummer patrol arrived, meaning there were about seven or eight people altogether, four to five people on the other side, and there was a violent clash. If I remember correctly, it made it to the media. There were no serious injuries or anything like that on either side, but there were punches. There's no other way to describe it.

And later?

Afterward, those guys ran off, at some point they ran away to their tents. We had more forces show up. They ran to their tents. The one guy, the one who started the whole thing, the shepherd who kind of stood up for himself, the police came and decided we were going to their tents to look for him. One of the guys, I think he was a policeman from Hebron, and if I remember correctly, he saw this guy near a tent fifty to seventy meters from us, and the company commander and the policeman decided to chase after him. They took off most of their equipment and started running after him very fast. There was a funny thing, sort of unrelated. A policeman pulled his gun, there was a dog, probably one of the dogs that hung around the area there with one of the families, the dog was barking, which seemed to threaten the . . . the dog started running toward the policeman, the policeman shot near the dog to scare it. That's it. In the end, the guy had managed to get away, and the chase continued more or less all night. The clash on the access road kept going pretty intensely, constant, between the left-wing activists, the army, and the settlers. It happened almost every week. There was almost no direct contact between the settlers and the Palestinians. Normally what they did was they'd see the Palestinians come too close to the settlement for their liking, or in an area they declared was too close—the moment they got too close they would call us.

The time when there was that confrontation, it's generally unthinkable for a Palestinian to hit a soldier, but you're talking about a situation where they actually hit you?

Yes, there were definitely some punches thrown, I remember. The first actually came from the Palestinians, and it all went downhill from there, everyone trying to help back up their friends. We weren't too worried, not to the point of using our weapons, shooting in the air or something like that, it wouldn't have helped. So everyone's first response was as soon as one of the Palestinians raised his hand, our guys came to help. The Palestinians did the same thing, and then we started to call for backup because, as you said, it's unacceptable and you can't let it go. The response was very . . . I don't know if I should say harsh, but yes, people came as fast as possible in order to suppress the thing.

62. They closed the road for a month

Unit: Kfir Infantry Battalion
Location: Emmanuel
Year: 2005

How long was the road closed to Palestinian traffic?
Sometimes it could be for as long as a month.

A month?
Yes. I don't want to just pull out a number, but it could be a long time.

What were the reasons?
Attacks on the road.

There were attacks for a month?
No, there's an attack so they block the road for a month.

Where was the attack?

I can't tell you, I don't remember what the story was ... It was when I was just starting as a platoon commander, when I came to the front as platoon commander, and was sent out with my soldiers.

Was this your first time as platoon commander on a long deployment?

Yes. The first time I was a platoon commander on the front. It was the Otniel line, in the South Hebron Hills. A week before the whole company went up to the line, I went there for some briefing. That day there was an attack on Bet Haggai, a Palestinian fired shots from a vehicle.

From Sheep Junction?

No, not from Sheep Junction, a little farther south, junction 200.

Do you remember when this was?

Around June 2005. They shot, they basically shot from a moving vehicle, a drive-by shooting at hitchhikers. Two seventeen-year-old boys who were standing at the hitchhiking stop were killed. They wanted to go from Bet Haggai into our sector, a little before Hebron, in the direction of Otniel. The car drove past, turned back at a roundabout, came back, shot at them, turned around again, and drove away. They weren't able to catch the vehicle. Because of what happened, they said, "Okay, Palestinian vehicles are no longer allowed to drive on the road, cars with green or white license plates aren't allowed on the road, it's just for Israeli traffic."

Then the blockade of all the villages began?

Yes. Then what happens basically is front-end loaders and so on come and block all the dirt paths that run from the villages to the main road. They block the paths. Your objective is to basically set up a lot of checkposts that are meant to prevent people from getting on the main road. It happened in a few other instances, where they put explosives on the road, all kinds of things like that. Now, this is a north–south road, a route the army considers essential in the Territories. Meaning, if there's no Israeli traffic on that route, if Israelis are afraid to use it day-to-day, then the army's objective has basically failed, that is, the goal to create a normal life.

How long was the road closed after that incident?

I can't tell you exactly.

Did that happen at other times?

Yes, there were a few other times the road was blocked. Whenever there were explosives on the road, basically, every time there was a security threat, the road was blocked. Every time they, like, tried to attack the road or someone traveling on it.

Every time you found explosives, the road was closed for a month?

No, not for a month. It depended on the decision of . . . generally less than a month. A month is the longest that I remember. It was around a month. I think it was a month, I don't remember exactly. Generally it's a few days, a week, two weeks, something like that. But yes, it happens a lot in that sector. At least in the summer of 2005 it did.

63. We played at Tom and Jerry

Unit: Lavi Battalion
Location: Hebron area
Year: 2005

There was this whole thing with the trucks carrying marble. There are quarries in the Bani Na'im area and all the factories are in Hebron, South Hebron. All of the drivers, none of them have a permit to use the road, so they drive on the Mamila road and bypass the barriers. It drove the battalion commander and the brigade commander crazy. The battalion commander stands in front of you, "What are the Palestinian vehicles doing on the road?" He'd go crazy. And you can't stop them. It got to the point where we'd take keys, IDs—which is illegal, by the way. Taking someone's keys is also illegal. And you can't just stop the traffic. Most of the people are just ordinary people who want to make a living, right? There was some meeting, the brigade commander came to speak with the staff, and I said to the brigade commander, "You're giving me an order that I can't carry out. If you don't want traffic here, give me one magazine, live ammunition, permission to destroy two trucks and shoot someone in the leg, that's the price." He said, "What? How could you do something like that, it's unethical." I said, "Yeah, that's right, it's unethical, but that's what we need to do if you don't want traffic. Give me the means, you're giving me an order without the means to carry it out, and that's the price." That's after I'd been there, I don't know, eight months, I understood what was going on, right? He said, "You can't do that." I said, "Okay, then don't give me the order, or don't get annoyed when you see trucks on the road." At least he seemed shocked, like, I wasn't seriously suggesting it, right? I don't want to shoot anyone, I wanted to shake him up a bit, that's what you'd need to do if you really, really wanted to, you'd have to use force, a relatively large amount of force. And he said, "Okay, we won't use force." There still was the order, but okay.

It ended there?

Listen, the whole thing with Palestinian traffic on the road around Hebron is a game of cat and mouse, really. It's like a Tom and Jerry cartoon. Someone leaves from here, then you go, and he goes like this. It got to the point where we were trying to keep the trucks out of commission. As far as I know it didn't go as far as destroying property. Why? Because you can stop a truck, you can take the person's keys, you can take his ID, you can remove all the air from the tires, you don't have to puncture them, you can just take out the air, right? You can even take the person.

Where?

Sometimes to the base . . . handcuffs, blindfold, you leave him at the gate to dry out.

A truck driver transporting marble on route 60?

Yes, sometimes it's marble, different things. You know, anyone who bypasses the barriers and drives on the road without a permit, and so on—in short, a Palestinian. Sometimes you bring the guy just to the gate, put him in the booth and he stays there, for an hour, sometimes half an hour, sometimes a day, from morning to night, it doesn't matter—even if you take the guy, you go back to where you stopped the truck at the side of the road, an hour later, sometimes just five minutes later, and there's no truck. It's gone. Every time. It doesn't matter—you take the keys, lock the truck, let out the air from the front tires, they have some kind of compressor, right? You let out all the air from the compressor, you don't cut the wires . . . the cabin is locked and the motor is off . . . —you come back, ten minutes, half an hour, an hour, and the truck's gone. Amazing, just amazing. Listen, a man in hardship who needs to make a living, he'll go to great lengths. Until it . . . if he's afraid they'll just burn the truck or shoot at it, then he'll stop driving. The risk is too great. But take his ID? Okay, take the ID, who cares. Take his keys? Okay, he has another set of keys at home. Or sometimes you can start it with a screwdriver, those old Mercedes, a screwdriver, or a nail, same thing. He's very motivated.

64. We got conflicting orders

Unit: Nahal Brigade
Location: Bethlehem
Year: 2005

There was a story that was crazy, we realized we had conflicting orders from the DCL. It was incredible. There was one DCL in Hebron and one in Bethlehem. It was just incredible. So some guys came with one set of orders, and another lot of guys came with different orders. And you got an order, and the orders for the checkpoint, for example, came from the Jericho DCL, so people from Bethlehem couldn't get back home. All kinds of stuff like that.

Did you understand the orders?

No, we understand nothing. We had to figure it all out for ourselves. We had the feeling that something stank, and then we realized there were two DCLs and they contradicted each other. It was incredible.

65. It's like totally arbitrary

Unit: Paratroopers
Location: Hebron area
Year: 2001

Each time they'd open and close the road with a front loader and build a dirt mound. And every time they opened it we'd have to guard the crossing. There's hundreds or thousands of cars coming through, thousands of pedestrians. You stand there, three or four soldiers and an APC. There isn't even anything to do, one person at least has to guard the APC, it's also a huge area because it's like there's a checkpoint on both sides of the road, and on each side there's like a line of cars four to five kilometers long. And then what's important for operations is that the road shouldn't be blocked, there shouldn't be a traffic jam.

On the Jewish road?

Yes, yes. So you let them through, they start driving, and there isn't enough room for two cars at the same time, like in both directions. So right away there's a traffic jam, and you start directing traffic because you have to end it somehow.

And what happens at the checkpoint? You inspect everyone?

No. There's a surge of people. Thousands of people.

Then what's the checkpoint for?

The checkpoint is to limit their movement at night or during the hours when there's curfew. You might inspect something suspicious. Some cars are allowed to go through if they come from route 60, trucks, with yellow license plates, of course—cars with other license plates don't drive there. Each time the order changes, who can go through and who can't. So a line builds up again, because truck drivers don't know they're not allowed to cross because two hours ago, or yesterday, or two days ago, they were allowed, so there's another traffic jam. How many times a day can the orders change? It's like totally arbitrary, which at a certain point I . . . I definitely remember one incident, there was some restriction on trucks with yellow plates, that such and such, and they can't go through anymore, and the traffic started to build up. I said, I'm not letting them through. Up until now they could, but I don't care—I'm not putting the road and my soldiers in danger.

66. Incoherent information

Unit: Otef Jerusalem [Reserves]
Location: Ramallah district
Year: 2004

Something that really, really bothered me—and I can't even begin to imagine what it's like to go through it for three years, the guys there from the military police have no one to relieve them because this is their whole service—it's the lack of order. I happen to know, I have a friend who was there before, he was the checkpoint commander before they brought in the military police. They were a group, in the Armored Corps, it was like a front, they had well-organized briefings and they knew, "Today there's passage from Jenin, today there's no passage from here, today there is passage from there, warnings from this place and that . . ." When I was there, on the other hand, none of the soldiers could give . . . he'd get chewed up. You're in this absurd situation, where they don't tell you anything in the briefing. It's a briefing . . . just to check it off the list: this sector, and that and whatever, and you go up to the checkpoint. Then the rumors start that there's been a warning about this or that, I don't remember who, but let's say Intelligence says it's this, and the DCL says it's that. So everyone's sure of something different, not that it really interests them, I'm talking about the soldiers who are at the checkpoint. Suppose you were coming, I'm just throwing this out, from Bethlehem, and you wanted to go through. Maybe in this line there's a soldier who'll do the inspection and let you through, and in this other line the soldier won't let you through, because he heard one thing, and the other soldier heard something else. They're sitting right next to each other, but there's no communication. And you feel like every . . . you have to argue with someone, explain that he can't go through, but what are you arguing about, really? Meaning, what's your authority if the guy next to you is contradicting you completely? You feel like everything you're supposed to be fighting for, you want to feel some sense of national purpose or some goal because you're there, but basically, it's built on air. Because nothing's based on any kind of warning you can depend on. All the information's a mishmash, and this totally drove me crazy. It was out of control. I tried, I said, Okay, if I'm already here, I'll try and understand, I'll go around with a notebook and update the soldiers, but it was just impossible to get anything, any kind of coherent information. It really disturbed me, and I can only imagine it disturbed the soldiers there, too.

67. The orders weren't clear

Unit: Nahal Brigade
Location: Tapuach
Year: 2007

What did you do in Tapuach besides the checkpoint?

I was in the settlement without a fence for a week, twelve hours at the gate with a friend. It was fun.

The road you described that was just for Israelis, do you remember which one it was?

There are two roads. For Palestinians the road leads to the villages, it's blocked and they can't use it. They used it to get to a different village. It created a lot of trouble because they used that road, so they paved a road that Palestinians weren't allowed to use. They have to walk three hundred or four hundred meters, and whoever isn't strong enough, they'd come with cars to get them. There was no organized checkpoint there, so it was impossible to stop the cars. The orders were unclear, it wasn't black and white.

What did you do? Turn them around?

Yeah, but so what? Even the brigade wasn't sure what to do.

So what did you actually do in that situation?

At first we turned all the cars back in the direction they came from. It was dangerous to turn them back like that, like with a truck.

68. It's all up to individual interpretation

UNIT: NAHAL BRIGADE
LOCATION: RAMALLAH
YEAR: 2001–2002

We were talking about who wanted to go into Ramallah.

Suppose someone comes with a child, a grandmother, whoever, shows me documents, says he needs to get to the hospital in Ramallah, he has a doctor's appointment. The procedure, as far as I understand it, as someone who sat through the briefing, is that people like that can go through. I let the guy through, and after a few minutes the next checkpoint's on the radio, they say, "What the hell, why did you let him through?" But there's a procedure, and he can go. They don't want to let him through. I don't know why.

They'd say, "I don't want to," or "You didn't understand the briefing"?

No, it's all very much up to individual interpretation. The briefing didn't go into detail. They tell you, "Okay, if there are humanitarian cases, they can go through." What exactly are humanitarian cases? It's very much up to the interpretation of the person in charge of the checkpoint at that moment. The guys at the next checkpoint, they started calling me "UN guy" all the time, because I'd let people through who they thought shouldn't go through. They'd say, "What the hell?" They, like, it's really not organized who can go and who can't. It was totally . . . It could be based on what's going on with the guy in charge of the checkpoint, with his girlfriend back home, or how long he's been on the base. Really, it's up to the guy's personal issues at that moment. It's not, it's not like someone comes and tells you what to do, no one's coordinating it, not the operations room. There's no procedure where you get on the radio to the operations room, and ask, "Okay, there's a guy right here . . . Can he go? Not go?" Sometimes you do that. Sometimes whoever was in the field decided. It was all a very big mess.

69. The great wisdom of the IDF

UNIT: ARMORED CORPS
LOCATION: JORDAN VALLEY
YEAR: 2001–2002

Company A was at a checkpoint called Noam, on the way to Jericho. I think it separates the Jordan Valley road and Jericho. It was winter, the beginning of 2001, and it was a pretty rough winter as far as I remember, raining and cold. There are the bases, which are basically a few buildings, where the unit that runs the checkpoint is located, and outside there's an open shelter, which is basically the checkpoint. The checkpoint was very . . . I think it was improvised, I don't remember, it wasn't like the checkpoints today, which are like airport terminals.

That's only certain checkpoints.

Yes. No, but I think this one was set up shortly before we got there. And I sat there with an officer, the Company A platoon commander, who was really a fine person, considering it was Battalion 433. And we sat there, and they covered the shelter with plastic sheets because it rained a lot. And it was nighttime and aside from us no one else was awake, it was the middle of the night. And really, when I think about it now, it's really scary that you're sitting in the middle of nowhere, the wind is gusting around you, and the plastic that's covering you makes it hard to hear and see what's going on around you. And basically you're waiting for a car to come, and how would you know? Because you see, you see the headlights. And we sit there, two of us, and the orders are—yeah, the great wisdom of the IDF—the order that day was to not let cars through if there are only men in them. The car had to have either a child or a woman in it to be able to pass. Yeah, of course it's a specific order, very specific.

Did you ask . . .

Why? Even if I'd asked, the other guy was an officer, that's his duty. When I asked why, the answer was, "Those are the orders, what are you gonna do?" You're not supposed to ask why in the army, and when you do . . .

But there can be pretty strange orders.

True, there are some strange orders, and your duty as a soldier is to carry them out and not ask why.

Would you look for the logic?

There's no logic. If you look for logic in the army you go crazy. They'd lock you up.

So what would happen? You'd stop cars?

No, there were almost no cars, it was the middle of the night, it was raining. But there was one car, I remember, it was a Subaru with two Palestinian men in their forties, I guess. They were very nice. They stopped, they asked to go through. And the officer, a guy with a head on his shoulders, didn't say what every other person in the army would have said, which is, "No, you can't." Instead he said, "You need a woman or a child." They argued a bit, and he said, "Those are the orders, what can I do, either a woman or a child." They turned around, went into Jericho. Ten minutes later, they came with a boy in the backseat, and he says, "Please, go ahead." He's smiling at them and they smiled back, everyone understood that the situation's just idiotic and ridiculous. Yeah, you know, it's just further proof that the IDF's job is to make the Palestinians' lives miserable. Because if you think about it, there's really no operational need. What's the difference if the same men in the same car bring a child? They grab some kid, pay him a shekel and a half, tell him, "Come with us for an hour or two." Yeah, so there it is. It just seemed ridiculous, not shocking. Today it seems shocking.

70. Aren't there people who just want to work?

UNIT: PARATROOPERS
LOCATION: HEBRON
YEAR: 2001

It was the first checkpoint in my life. At first they tell you, "They only cross with permission from Civil Administration." Okay, you're there, here's the first person. You ask, "Have you got permission from Civil Administration?" "No." "Then what have you got?" "Student ID." You say, "Wait, in principle he's not allowed through, but so what, let's ask." You get on the radio, you ask the guy in the company operations room. Who's in the company operations room? ——, the company clerk. You ask the company clerk, "Listen, someone with a student ID, do they go through or not?" She doesn't know. She calls the brigade operations room, they must know. Who's in the brigade operations room? The operations sergeant. Does the operations sergeant know? She doesn't know. She has to ask the officer. So she asks ——, the operations officer. The operations officer doesn't know, but because he's the operations officer he can't let on that he doesn't know, so he says, "Yes, someone with a student ID can pass." Okay, fine, you can let someone with a student ID go through . . . Someone else comes, you ask, "Have you got permission from Civil Administration?" "No, but I've got a teacher's license." Wait, if you let someone through with a student ID, then what, shouldn't you be able to go with a teacher's license? But I don't know, so I ask. I ask ——, again, —— doesn't know. —— calls ——. Just then ——, the operations officer who was in some meeting, shows up, so —— says, "Okay, if you let someone through with a student ID, then someone with a teacher's license can pass." Of course, you don't know all this, it's only after the fact, when you do your turn in the operations room, that you get it. So you accept it, you say, okay, some people can pass, some can't. Who decides? The operations sergeants decide who can cross and who can't. And that's when you're still young and you listen to them. Slowly you realize that no one who comes to the checkpoint is going to say, "Listen, I just want to cross. I just want to cross because, I don't know, I want to cross the checkpoint, I want to go over there." Either he's sick, or he's a student, or he's a teacher, or he's from the Red Cross, or he's from UNWRA. They pull out papers, scribbles, until you realize, the penny drops. It hit me after a month, isn't it a bit weird? Aren't there any ordinary people in the Territories? Aren't there people who just want to cross? No, everyone's either sick, or this, or that.

71. Some products it's forbidden to bring into the West Bank

Unit: Military Police
Location: Qalqilya
Year: 2006–2008

What's the checkpoint in Qalqilya called?

There's a lot: The Eyal crossing, the Eliyahu crossing, that's the fruit checkpoint, the Zufim barrier—that's a funny story. In principle, it's an agricultural checkpoint for Palestinians only, but the residents of Zufim who live close by think they have privileges, so they complain to the officer in charge of residents in the area, it's in the brigade's jurisdiction. Because of the complaints, they decide that the Zufim residents can also cross there.

Did that affect the Palestinians' ability to cross there or the way the checkpoint was run?

I think that an agricultural gate is an agricultural gate—Bolem 7 is an agricultural gate, Jews don't go through there, so why should the people from Zufim cross here? Though it wasn't just Zufim residents, it was anyone who had a permit, I don't remember exactly. Anyway, it's a pretty funny checkpoint. On the one hand, in the beginning we didn't check anyone coming from the Israeli side of the fence to the Palestinian side, but then there was the crossing administration, which was basically established to oversee the transfer of all kinds of goods.

Customs, for example, deals with certain goods like textiles and furniture, and it's the same for agricultural goods. The crossing administration dealt more with dangerous substances. The way it was done was that the military police had the authority at the checkpoint and helped them, because they didn't have certification. The number of people working at the checkpoint always changed. In terms of the goods going into the Territories, there was concern that they'd start making Qassam rockets in Judea and Samaria. I remember standing at the checkpoint at the entrance to Tul Karem. An Israeli Arab came with two and a half iron pipes and received a summons, because theoretically, if you bring in dual-purpose goods—so, you used to be able to bring in iron, but you can use it to make . . .

There's a prohibition on bringing things like that into the West Bank?

If I'm not mistaken, it's prohibited to do business in the Territories. When they buy vegetables or meat, for example, Israeli Arabs are limited to three kilograms of meat or three containers of olive oil, during the olive harvest it's five, but it's always limited. An Israeli Arab can't go back in with twenty bottles of oil.

And what about bringing things into the West Bank?

Things like secondhand stuff aren't allowed into the West Bank unless it's approved by the administration. From what I remember, they checked you only if you were going from the Palestinian side to the Israeli. Mostly, if you went from the Israeli side to the Palestinian, there wasn't much of an inspection, but it also changed with the priorities.

You're saying that if they caught someone bringing in iron it's a summons and a fine, even if it's from Israel to the West Bank?

The way it works is that I'm the authority, and if the person doesn't cooperate—let's say that all I want to do is check his papers. If someone has certain goods and he doesn't have papers, then I can't know where the goods are going. I can't say that he has a bill of lading for where he's going. I get the bill of lading and see if it exactly matches what he has. You learn to identify whether the bill of lading is valid or forged. Mostly, if it's from the Israeli side, it's either goods you can transfer or not, or maybe that person was summoned for having an iron pipe or two, and he can't cross. You don't need a bill of lading or a receipt if the guy at the crossing administration defined the item as dual-purpose or dangerous—you just don't let him through.

Is there a list of products forbidden to bring into the West Bank?
Yes.

What are dual-purpose or dangerous items?
Dual-purpose is something like iron—it's brought in by weight and only with the platoon's permission, all kinds of trucks, say from the Palestinian side to the Israeli side, that you let through. If, say, there's a truck filled with iron, and it doesn't have permission from the platoon—you turn it back . . . I once saw the list of substances, materials that you come across and you start to feel bad, because you just don't know what to make of them. I can't list them for you, but I trust

Detainees, Nablus, 2003. Photographer: Sagi Blumberg

the list because the people who put it together were in the military police and now work in the administration. They know which materials are allowed and which aren't. If it's dual-purpose, a piece of scrap iron or something, even just a small amount, it can't cross, especially from the Israeli side.

Fertilizer and things like that?

That, too. Probably if you have fertilizer, acetone—it's for explosives.

And these are things you say you can't bring in, not even in small amounts.

There are certain cases where they make sure it's enforced. The guy from the administration uses his discretion, and I back him up.

There's room for discretion. Is there a situation where you can get permission to bring dual-purpose materials into the Territories? Say someone's building a house and needs metal beams, what does he do?

When it comes to construction, they manage just fine, and they don't need to bring anything from Israel.

Where do they get them from?

I don't know, but they do construction there. I dealt a lot with trucks transferring earth, concrete, etcetera. As long as they have documentation that lists what they've got in the truck—mostly, it's Arab Israeli construction companies.

Did every checkpoint have a list of what was and wasn't allowed, or just at the terminals?

It's different at every checkpoint. If you're near Bet Iba, and there's an asbestos quarry close by, I imagine that a truck can cross there, but not from the Israeli side. If it came from the Israeli side, it would need to go through all the steps. There are also restrictions on Jews, not just on Israeli Arabs.

Do you distinguish between Israeli Arab and Jewish drivers and what they can transfer?

Each checkpoint has its own procedures. At Eliyahu there's a lane just for the Shomron residents and the red lane is just for Israeli Arabs and Israelis. The next lane is only for Palestinians. They can also transport goods, but we cooperate with the Border Police on inspections, and they can only bring goods in if they have a permit saying it's for a business, then it's okay. It's all according to the permit.

Who produces the permit?

The District Coordination and Liaison office.

What's Operation Three Circles?

The crossing administration normally does the inspection, but where we came in was when the military police would guard them, sometimes it would be a combat soldier and you'd guard him. The focus is on entry from the Israeli side to the Palestinian. There are checkpoints with no one, so the guy from the administration does the inspection alone, but he has authority or someone with him has the authority. Let's say the military police have more authority at the checkpoint than the civilian police. Apart from the ordinary duties of the police, there are all kinds of places where a military policeman's there to inspect items entering Israel. Like I said, because of concern about transferring Qassam rockets.

Basically, Operation Three Circles meant that someone from the administration does the inspection on the Israeli side.

Some checkpoints there's only one person from the administration there, and it's a problem because the checkpoint has two directions. Some places there are more. But even then, he needs someone with him at the checkpoint who has authority. That's why they'd normally be on the side where goods go into the Palestinian side. Again, when we're talking about goods it's usually things coming over in Israeli vehicles. If it comes from the Palestinian side in an Israeli vehicle, then there's normally an inspection and the guy from the administration is on the side of the checkpoint where the Palestinian vehicles come . . . for Palestinians you check the whole crate, but in general you inspect 20 percent of a large truck, like those Volkswagens.

72. Don't let ambulances through the checkpoint

UNIT: NAHAL BRIGADE
LOCATION: BETHLEHEM
YEAR: 2005

There was another procedure where Palestinian ambulances couldn't pass the checkpoint. They had to come to one side of the checkpoint, and another ambulance came from the other side, and they had to hand the patient over.

Back to back?

No. The Palestinian ambulance was parked behind the concrete blocks, and the patient had to walk some twenty meters to the other ambulance, or be carried on a gurney. Now, I don't know if you've ever seen a ninety-year-old woman cross a checkpoint with an IV in her arm, but it's not a pretty sight. Certainly no fun for the Palestinian woman. The even crazier part is that we were instructed to inspect both ambulances. Here's an ambulance, it's classified a humanitarian vehicle, you let the old woman through because obviously she has the right permits, and she's old—with old people, children, it doesn't matter— and she goes through all nice and dandy, and then you inspect both ambulances. This whole time the patient has to wait. Never to the point of putting the patient's life at risk, and when there were really bad cases we didn't really inspect the ambulances, even though we're supposed to, but in the meantime, the person suffers. I mean, there's nothing to do about it, but they stand there and suffer. And the accusing look in the eye of a ninety-year-old woman, who most likely did nothing wrong, is something that stays with you.

73. Going to the Jordan Valley? You need special permission

UNIT: NAHAL BRIGADE
LOCATION: JORDAN VALLEY
YEAR: 2006

At the checkpoint, the way it goes is that anyone living in the valley—a Palestinian who lives there—can go through without a work permit, doesn't matter why.

He can cross the checkpoints in the valley?

At our checkpoint specifically, the one in Gitit. I also think he can cross at other checkpoints. Everyone else needs a work permit. If they don't have a work permit, they can't cross. You get the permit at the District Coordination and Liaison office.

Where is the DCL?

There's a DCL in Nablus, and a DCL in Jericho. I think they get it from the DCL in Jericho.

Can they get to the DCL?

They can get to the DCL, sure. Oh wait, no, I'm sorry, they don't have to, the people from . . . I'm not even sure which DCL they're supposed to go to, Jericho or Nablus. There's a DCL in Jericho and a DCL in Nablus, and they're connected to one of them.

Do most people have permits from Nablus or Jericho?

That's it, I'm not sure.

If it's Nablus, then it's absurd.

Why?

Because a person doesn't have a permit, and to get a permit he has to go through the checkpoint.

No, if it's Jericho it's absurd, yes. They have to get to Jericho from the checkpoint. The work permit is only for people from the Territories who work in the Jordan Valley.

And if someone in the valley needs to work in the Territories?

They're free to travel in that direction, everyone can pass freely. If you come from the direction of the valley and live in Ramallah, then you can cross. If you live in Ramallah and you want to get to the valley, then you can't cross unless you have a work permit.

Do they sometimes send orders down to the checkpoint like, "Today we let people with this or that kind of permit cross"?

No. In Gush Etzion it's like that. Every shift would have entirely different orders. Here, not at all. Always the same orders.

74. A truck entering Ramallah? You need a permit

Unit: Nahal (Reserves)
Location: Ramallah district
Year: 2005

A year ago I did reserve duty once at Qalandiya. I ended up staying there two weeks, half a term.

What happened there?

What happened there? It was terrible.

Why was it terrible?

First, I should say that I was happy to see that the whole checkpoint process had improved, because at least they now have set procedures. Qalandiya was much better organized than what I remember . . . Now there are soldiers who are supposed to be there . . . soldiers from the military police who have the training to work at the checkpoints, with procedures and things. I got there, it was the first time they'd called me for reserve duty in three years. But it was still very frustrating, because now there are these procedures, but since I'm a civilian, I think about the procedures and I don't like them, and I try to do something about it. There's an order that trucks without a goods permit are forbidden to enter Ramallah. A guy comes with an empty truck, and he wants to go in.

But he doesn't have a permit.

He doesn't have a permit, and he doesn't have any goods either, he has an empty truck. I say, "What do you want?" He says, "I want to go home to my wife and children." "You can't." "What do you mean, I can't?" I go, "You can't enter with the truck. If you want, go park the truck somewhere, and take a cab." He says, "Listen, it's my truck, it costs a million and a half shekels, I'm not letting it out of my sight." No, no way, you're not letting him in. All kinds of situations like that, very frustrating. I'd thought when I came to reserve duty that maybe, you know, I could do something. There's the thing, it can't be that the only people in the field are the ones who want to be there. If left-wingers don't do reserve duty, who'll be left? It'll be the ones who do all the terrible things. I said, no, I have to go to reserve duty. There really isn't anything you can do unless you're there.

75. How many permits does a person need?

Unit: Civil Administration
Location: Jordan Valley
Year: 2006

Were you in charge of issuing permits?
Yes, permits, magnetic cards, things like that.

What kind of permits did you give out?
Entry to Israel and for movement within the Territories.

Is there a special permit for Palestinians who come from Nablus to work in the Jordan Valley, in Jericho for example?

There used to be, now I think it's open. Don't take my word for it, because I haven't been there in seven months. The last time I was there, in Beit el Kabr, I think they opened traffic from Nablus to the valley, but the council used to give us lists.

Which council?

The Jordan Valley council. For Palestinians who work in the settlements, if that's what you mean.

And for Palestinians who don't have work?

They need a crown permit, a red permit. Like everyone else.

What does that mean?

A red permit.

What if you want to go from Jenin to Jericho?

You don't need a permit. In the past, you only needed one in Nablus if you were going through the valley. You had to have a crown permit. Now you don't need one anymore, I think. If I'm not mistaken. I think you don't need one anymore. But they'd issue it in Nablus, not where we were. Residents of Jericho could pretty much move freely. The restriction was only on residents of Nablus.

And not on Jenin?

Jenin, maybe . . . I don't remember.

Because you need to come down from there to get to Jericho.

Yes, but from Tubas, for example, you could enter Jericho, no problem, you didn't need a permit. I think it was just for the Nablus sector.

Tubas is Nablus.

Tubas is considered the Jenin sector. The District Coordination and Liaison considers it part of the Jenin DCL, and so I think it's just for residents of Nablus, because then there was a wave of terrorists from the Nablus sector. And the thinking then . . . I think it was just for Nablus residents. That's what I remember. Also there were Palestinians working in agriculture in the settlements. So they'd submit a list and they'd get . . .

Permits.

No, they didn't need them. The lists were in some binder and they'd bring in the list and we'd know. Now they also need a business permit, a green permit. There are special permits for businesses.

So how many permits does a person have to have?

There are a few things. If you need to get into Israel, there's a blue permit. For travel from Nablus . . . I think, all that's left from the crown permits, the red permits, are the ones for taxis and public transportation. Don't take my word for it, I'm not sure. I'm not up-to-date. And there's the business permit if you work, that gives you more hours. You've got more time to travel, from five to twelve or from five to ten.

A permit works according to hours?

Yeah, there are hours.

The crown permit, that's just for taxis? Regular people don't use them anymore?

No, they don't need them anymore, I think. It's no longer necessary, I think.

Were they canceled during your time?

They were in the process of being canceled. No need. I don't know if . . . I think they still issue them. But I'm not sure it's needed. Don't take my word for it. I'm not sure.

Which ones did you issue?

All of them.

76. Two villages, two different DCLs

UNIT: CIVIL ADMINISTRATION
LOCATION: NABLUS
YEAR: 2005–2008

Say there's a bride who lives in Marda village near Nablus, and a groom who lives in Dir Istiya. They want to drive from her village to the neighboring village to get to the beauty parlor. In the morning the commander at the checkpoint lets them cross, but when they come back, a different commander won't let them return. He asks them, "How did you leave?" She had to get back to her village in Marda, go back and get ready, and leave with her family for Hawwara, where the wedding's supposed to be in the evening. The groom's family is supposed to be taking care of transportation. These are two villages with two different DCLs: one is Qalqilya, and the other Nablus. In the end, everything was okay, and they went above and beyond, and let an extra eight vehicles go through for the wedding. I remember dealing with it for half a day, half of my last day.

You had to coordinate between the DCLs?

No, just one DCL dealt with it, it's between two regional brigades. There are two different sectors of two different DCLs, it's a very complicated area. Marda is Qalqilya, which is basically Shomron, and Dir Istiya is Qalqilya and Efraim, and Hawwara is Shomron and Nablus. You know why the boundaries don't line up? Because they're according to the Civil Administration, which is what used to be the military government, which was based on Jordanian oversight. When the army occupied the Territories in 1967, it didn't take the old map, it made its own map.

77. It's called "segregation"

Unit: Civil Administration
Location: Nablus
Year: 2006

In 2006, we received a complaint from students from a-Najah University in Nablus, because they weren't allowed to use the Bet Iba checkpoint, which had been open, I think it was open up until a few months before this, and then was just closed. I don't remember why. I think it has something to do with the settlements there, because the checkpoint leads to them, among other things. The checkpoint was closed for almost every possible reason. The army, the brigade, they call it "segregation." Segregation means that you only allow residents of certain ages to go through. Men above a certain age, say around thirty-five, forty. And women from a younger age. They didn't allow the students to enter. They live in the villages near Nablus. It's as if you were a resident of Ness Tziona, and you want to go to Rehovot, and they won't let you. I remember this case specifically because it was the first complaint I received. A nice English-speaking student called, I was glad I could communicate with him, and it's very disappointing to give him this answer, tell him there's segregation, do a makeup.

Did they give you the reason for the segregation?

I did. I explained to him what it was, and that he couldn't enter because of his age. I don't remember the exact age, but if he'd been a different age, he could have entered. Another time, four women, some of them sick and some of them accompanying the sick ones, were detained at the Bet Iba checkpoint. They were sick and needed medical attention. This was two months after the thing with the students.

Was it still the same segregation?

I can't say for sure, but there was still segregation.

You don't know the ages?

Now I don't know, back then I certainly did. We applied tremendous pressure, both myself and ——, who was a coordinator in Civil Administration. We made it so that at least the sick women could cross the checkpoint. The others had to take a long detour to the checkpoint in Ein Bidan, and then they apparently met up.

Who gave the segregation order, and when was it repealed so people could cross again?

There are segregations which can last for months. I remember a segregation that stretched from all of Samaria to Jericho, the whole eastern side. A Palestinian from Ramallah who wants to get to Jericho only has one route available, via Jenin. A resident of Jerusalem who wants to get to the Dead Sea? Go via Afula.

Which checkpoints can you pass through?

I don't remember the names. I think via Beqaot, Tiasir.

Did you know exactly which checkpoints people could use?

Yes, the Palestinians also knew.

What was the reason?

Terrorist attack warnings. It was explained to me that it's in order to prevent terrorist attacks.

How long did it last?

I don't remember. There are certain segregations on certain days and at certain hours, and sometimes it lasts for weeks.

Who ends the segregations?

Someone on the major general level if it's more than a few days, and the decision can go up to the brigade commander.

Are there segregations which don't have a set time limit?

I think there's a set limit. There is a military orders group—there's no reason to get into that—but when there's segregation, they say for how long it'll be, and they extend it for a certain amount of time.

And you know when it ends?

Yes, and I tell the Palestinians. The Palestinians know because there are rumors, and the village leaders and the Palestinian police also announce it.

So you're not so involved in the announcement?

I don't announce it at all. I have no connection to the village heads. But if a Palestinian calls me and asks if he can transfer goods via Efraim, which is a "back-to-back" checkpoint in the area of Tul Karem, even though today is Memorial Day for the fallen IDF soldiers, then I tell him yes, he can do it until twelve noon. We're also like a kind of information service, which leads to a few undocumented conversations during the day.

That's a whole other story, moving from checkpoint to checkpoint . . .

The real story is that this lousy checkpoint is only there to protect the settlements.

Bet Iba?

Yes. Another interesting story is about a taxi driver who took a sick person to the hospital in Nablus, and he wanted to return to his house in Bet Furik, so he had to cross the checkpoint there. The checkpoint closes at eight. Israelis move to daylight saving time in April, the Palestinians change the clock two weeks later. He and the sick person are waiting at the checkpoint, but the checkpoint is closed. The soldiers that were there didn't open it for them, and they only let them cross in the morning. They stayed the night in Nablus.

No one did anything?

No. Here's another example: a sixty-year-old Palestinian with cancer. He got permission to receive treatment at the Asuta hospital. A volunteer waited for him at the Reihan checkpoint, who would then take him to his appointment at the hospital at ten in the morning. The soldiers wouldn't let him cross. It was seven in the morning, and it takes three hours [to get there], and he doesn't want to miss his appointment. It seems that this man had a permit for the Gilboa checkpoint, and not for Reihan, so they made clear to him that he had to go to the Gilboa checkpoint, which is an hour's ride for Palestinians, and from there he could cross the checkpoint to [enter] Israel. I have only one thing to say: Why? He's a sixty-year-old guy with cancer, what difference does it make if he accidentally went to a different checkpoint—which I'm not sure even helps in terms of transportation time. If he'd been traveling from the beginning with the permit that he had, then maybe he would have arrived faster, disregarding the fact that they didn't let him cross. But what's with you? All of a sudden you'll start following procedure. It goes without saying that he missed his appointment, and I think he just went back. Another example: a twenty-day-old baby sick with jaundice. This happened. They didn't let the ambulance with the baby cross the a-Zaim checkpoint, a Jerusalem checkpoint. They let it pass only after forty-five minutes. A twenty-day-old baby doesn't carry out terrorist attacks, as far as I know. Another incident was in Jenin at the Reihan checkpoint—today it's a more established checkpoint, but back then there were four border policemen who just sat there and said, "Come on, go ahead." They didn't allow humanitarian equipment, for example, to be transferred to Barta'a and Reihan. A truck driver who was transporting fruits or vegetables called me and said: "I'm coming from Jenin, I want to enter the village because the people there don't have anything to eat." Only at the end of the day, after he'd spoken with us at nine in the morning, only at a quarter to five did they allow him to cross.

A truck or a van?

He sat there for eight hours and waited, and afterward they let him cross. There were a few trucks there.

Did they inspect it?

They checked it, but that's not their function. They just didn't let him cross, because it was on someone else's orders, and that guy was stuck somewhere else. There were very basic complaints that the agricultural gates weren't opened. I didn't see it as intentional that soldiers were one, two, three hours late. Meaning that a Palestinian would wait for three hours to get to or leave his land and get back home, and it happened more than a few times. It happens because of the soldiers' negligence, or the operations room, or an operation which presumably prevents soldiers from opening it. Because who opens the agricultural gates? Soldiers.

78. There's nothing to be done, anyone who's late can't cross

UNIT: KFIR INFANTRY BATTALION
LOCATION: TUL KAREM
YEAR: 2008–2009

Patrol is about being an active force in the field that can be called up whenever needed, you just go around, and if something happens at a checkpoint, they immediately send you in because you're the closest. Sometimes you go to open gates.

What does that mean?

There are places that have fences that Arabs have to pass through in order to get to their lands, so you open the gates in the morning when you need to—each gate has a fixed opening time, you make a list of who passes through and who doesn't, who passes through and doesn't return, all kinds of things like that.

Is this about access to their agricultural lands that are on the other side of the Separation Barrier?

Yes, something like that.

Does it happen like it's supposed to?

It happens like it's supposed to unless there's a problem. Sometimes the operations are hurried up, so there are people who are just a bit late and there's nothing to be done, they can't pass through because they were late. It's not our problem. Sometimes we push the time limit a bit, and wait a few extra minutes for people. But if they don't come on time, there's nothing to be done.

79. We blocked access to his livelihood

UNIT: NAHAL BRIGADE
LOCATION: JENIN DISTRICT
YEAR: 2005

It's known that in the Territories you get exposed to a ton of paradoxes, dilemmas, all kinds of things that . . . For example, we were once in some pillbox tower in Mevo Dotan, where it was forbidden for them to go to the hilltop above it, because this was seen as controlling the pill-

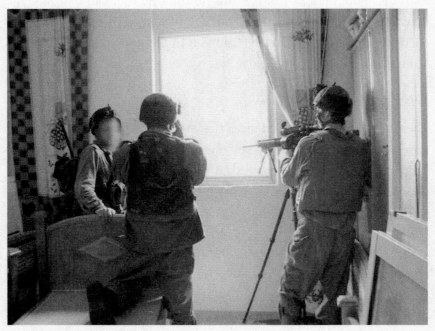

Straw widow, Nablus, 2008.

box a bit. But the hilltop happened to be someone's orchard, and he was forbidden to go there. And every time he went up, we told him to leave, and we tried to help, and he said to us: "But the land is mine." We told him we'll get him a permit, then the next company commander really did try to get him a permit, and he just ran into, you know, the bureaucracy and its inflexibility. This was just a guy who, like, just because we put up a pillbox there, we blocked off his access to his livelihood. It sounds trivial, it sounds whatever, but you know, hey, it was as if someone had told his parents that suddenly this guy couldn't make a living anymore. It destroys his home, there's nothing more to say, it just destroys his life.

80. The farmers burst into tears

UNIT: ARTILLERY
LOCATION: QALQILYA DISTRICT
YEAR: 2002

The operation was routine: the operation was to go out on vehicles and patrol the nearby Arab villages. There were a lot of excavations going on there. And it's really a heartbreaking place, the whole area of the separation fence. We were exactly at the point where they dug the fence, [these were] residents whose fig or olive groves you were uprooting, and it was really difficult for me to see.

Are you a farmer?

No, but you know . . . Someone comes and says to you: "Okay, your home is now mine. Your land is now mine. Everything you invested in for forty years." You know, older people, farmers. People for whom this tree is food. And you say to them: "Forget about it, get out of here, it's no longer yours."

Did you oversee the work?

No, but I guarded there. There weren't violent incidents. Again, because of how close it was to Israel. And if there were—then there were other units, who were more experienced in combat than we were, and they actually went into the city.

Do you remember meeting with these people whose trees they uprooted? Did they go there?

Yeah, you meet them. You get to . . . It's hard, because a person comes to you in tears.

Do you remember a specific incident?

I remember one incident in particular. It gives me goosebumps just thinking about it. Someone whose olive grove they'd uprooted came to me in tears—I'm sorry, his fig grove—and he said to me, "I planted this grove for ten years, I waited ten years for it to bear fruit, I enjoyed it for one year, and now they're uprooting it." The guy had already worked thirty years, and he says to me, "I worked for thirty years to buy the land, I planted for another ten, and I just waited for the trees to bear fruit." He'd only had a year to enjoy his trees, and then the IDF bull-dozer comes and says: "Forget about it." Best-case scenario—you meet a bulldozer operator who's prepared to plant his trees somewhere else.

There was no replanting procedure?

No, definitely not. The bulldozer operators were Arabs, and anyone who still felt some kind of relationship . . . whose heart still broke, then he'd take the hoe, dig, and replant the tree on their [Palestinian] side of the fence. It was rare that someone with that job would . . . It costs a lot, and his boss would say to him, "Why are you playing, stop playing." So the uprooting happens on that same day and that's it, afterward they're already digging [to construct the Separation Barrier].

When you got there, was this kind of work just starting, or had it already been going on for a while?

It was just beginning—it was really just starting the very first time we went into the field.

With the surveyors?

Yes, our main duty was to protect the surveyors. The job of the surveyor is to take his radio and start walking the area.

The surveyors don't see what's going on? Even before the bulldozer arrives, they don't see that there's someone's tree right there?

Yes, but the landowner doesn't realize that the guy walking on his land is the surveyor, he only sees the bulldozer. And even if he understood—what difference would it make?

They didn't speak with them beforehand?

I don't think so. I don't know. I imagine . . . They don't have mail or cell phones for the most part. Someone with authority comes and takes your . . . It's as if I were to come and take your cell phone—who would care? "Get out of here . . . if you want, sue me." Even if you're a citizen with a blue [Israeli] ID and all of its privileges, you try to get money from the National Insurance Agency and they tell you, "Yeah, good luck with that" . . . Like, so who is he [the Palestinian farmer]? You know what's going to happen. You know that even if he sues and everything—he'll just get lice.

The people there didn't argue, or stand in front of the bulldozers? Trees, you know, you can't give them back. There's no compensation for something like that.

They promised them they would give them money or something, or different land. There is a law that if the state takes more than 40 percent [of your land] you are entitled to full compensation. They can take up to 40 percent, and you can't do anything. If they take 41 percent, you get full compensation. Which is a general rule in the state, it doesn't interest them if it harms them or what's on the land. I was unsure if they would take it. There is nothing to do. What do I mean, there is nothing to do? It sucks to see it, because they promised him they'd compensate him—your sense is that he won't get anything.

How long did the work last there?

When I left it was still [going on] . . .

So it took time.

Building a fence is a big deal. Because you are talking about moun-
tains . . . you dig the land, you measure it.

So the farmers didn't resist at all?

At first, when the bulldozer came to uproot the trees, the farmers burst
into tears, trying to stop the bulldozer, standing on the side, crying.

There was no physical resistance, protest, not even a sign?

There was—I saw them standing on the side with a sign, but we're talking
about farmers, not political activists. We're talking about one man, who
has really bad luck. You can't say you're harming an entire population. A
single person controls a quarter, so you don't even run into another person until you get to the next forty. Each time it's just one person's land.
It's not like you come to a university and there are tons of people. You're
not harming a single place full of people, each time you're just seeing a
single person. And then he has no power—he can only stand at the side
and cry. There's no farmers' union. That in itself was heartbreaking, it's
not fair. You know, the idiocy of this country, they took this guy's land,
and tomorrow they'll say they're stopping construction of the fence.
Which happened more than a few times. They decide the fence should be
here—on the guy's land, his courtyard, his private house—but tomorrow
they decide, after they've already destroyed the roads, that the fence
doesn't work there, "Let's get it out of here. Get it out, it's no good there."

Did they move the fence in your sector?

A change in route.

No, in your sector—where you were.

A change in route. They started digging, then all of a sudden they
decided the location wasn't right.

What's this whole thing with the surveyors?

A surveyor gets an order. The surveyor is the cheap part, you know
what the hours are like for the excavator?

But the surveyor checks the land beforehand.

Fine—in Israel we do things on a different schedule. First we do the excavating, and then only afterward we check to see why the location isn't right.

Where did they move the fence to?

Sometimes ten meters, sometimes they decided to cancel it or go around . . . because what's the fence for? It surrounds the settlements. One settlement is included in the Green Line, one isn't. They decide whether the fence should go around the settlement or not, and what the fence's distance from the settlement should be—in other words, they deal with crap.

81. He said: "I live in a prison"

Unit: Border Police
Location: Allenby Bridge
Year: 2002

In the place that's called the border, I tried to stay human, to somehow cross the line. When I say cross the line, I don't know, I'm talking about Mussa, for example. Mussa was . . . we worked on the bridge with people who came from Jericho, Palestinian civilians who came from Jericho every day to the bridge to work. It's janitorial work and stuff like that.

At the checkpoint?

At the terminal. Let's call it a terminal, it's not a checkpoint. I wasn't at a checkpoint, okay? Let's call it a terminal because the Airport Authority finances the whole thing.

That's important to know.

No, really, it wasn't an IDF checkpoint. The documents there are from the IDF, meaning the IDF was indirectly involved. You didn't see soldiers there, it was more a civilian place, civilian and police, not the army, okay? Mussa was one of the young guys who came to work there: a twenty-two-year-old husband and father of two. Twenty-two, twenty-three, yeah, you know, they get married young because there isn't anything to do except . . . when you're under siege there's nothing to do besides be with your wife in the bedroom, keep having children . . . In one of my chats with him, what do I mean, one of my chats? Much as I wanted to sit and talk with him, I couldn't. There was no way. So at most, he'd be working, I'd come by, say good morning, *salaam aleikum*, and like that, and that's it, nothing else. So one time I ran into him in passing, I asked how are you, what's up, and somehow we got to—he said things that have stayed with me till today. Meaning, you're with someone who lives an hour and a half from the sea, and he's never been there.

An hour and a half from the Mediterranean?

An hour and a half from the Mediterranean, fifteen minutes from the Dead Sea. I think they went to the Dead Sea before the Intifada, but there are things which they, I don't know, he said, he used the term "prison." He said that as quiet as they are in Jericho, in military terms and in terms of the refugee camps near Jericho, and the people themselves—meaning, it's a religious, agricultural population, they weren't involved in a lot of the problems there—despite that, you see the anger in their eyes. I felt he was accusing me when he said that. He looked me in the eye and he said, "I live in a prison, I can't go to the sea, I want to go to Tel Aviv, to buy things for my wife." And it eats you up inside. Talk like that and situations like that, slowly you start changing your views. Meaning, I went in, I enlisted in the army very—I don't know if you can say right-wing, but very into it—wanting to do everything for . . . And your service creates doubt, meaning that based on what I experienced, I started doubting things.

When did you begin to get it?

It happened slowly. I don't know if there was a single moment when I finally got it.

The Fabric of Life: Administering Palestinian Civilian Life

An Overview

The testimonies in Part Three depict the influence that the Israeli security forces and authorities have on the lives of Palestinians in the Territories. The state's spokespeople argue that Israel does not withhold basic necessities from Palestinians or take actions that prompt humanitarian crises. Instead, despite its security needs, Israel ensures the Palestinian "fabric of life." These claims and others like them—that the West Bank has a prosperous economy, for example—are intended to suggest that life under Occupation can be tolerable, and that there is nothing to prevent Palestinians from living reasonably well.

On the basis of such claims, Israel portrays the Occupation as a justifiable defensive measure. Any harm sustained by people living under the Occupation is considered reasonable or proportionate. The Israeli authorities claim, for example, that by granting passage and permits in "humanitarian" cases, Israel allows people to conduct normal lives. But it is precisely the dependency of millions on a complex and convoluted bureaucracy, one in which they play no part and which does not represent their interests, that exemplifies the degree of control exercised by Israel over Palestinian life. The soldiers' testimonies reveal that in order to run their lives at the most elementary level, the Palestinians are reliant on Israel's good graces. Palestinians in need of special permits, for example, to reach a doctor, or their workplace, or their family, depend on the benevolence of the soldier at the checkpoint or the mercy of the officer of the Civil Administration—the government body that oversees civilian life in the Territories. Palestinians have to constantly plead with various representatives of Israel to be recognized as mercy cases and have their needs considered "humanitarian."

The Civil Administration is subordinate to the Ministry of Defense. Soldiers in the regular and standing army and civilians working for the Ministry of Defense serve in the Civil Administration, which administers and allocates infrastructure and resources in the Territories, determines the status of land, issues building and planning permits for Area C, provides work and transit permits at checkpoints, controls trade, registers the population, and governs many other services. Palestinians also have to turn to the Civil Administration for various humanitarian requests and to submit complaints and claims regarding damage to property and personal injury resulting from the IDF's operations. Testimonies from soldiers and officers who have worked in the Civil Administration, included here, provide a rare glimpse into the bureaucratic world on the other side of the Green Line.

Since the outbreak of the Second Intifada, Israel has tightened its grip on the Palestinian population. In addition to offensive military operations, which received widespread public attention, Israel has set up physical barriers and complex bureaucratic systems, increasingly inhibiting Palestinian movement. Thus, for example, a resident of Nablus who wants to reach Jericho for business purposes or a family visit needs a permit from the Civil Administration. And the Separation Barrier, the building of which began in 2002, has created a new and even more complex division of the West Bank, adding the need for even more permits and certificates. The "permit regime" that exists in the Territories today affects virtually every aspect of Palestinian daily life.

The testimonies here also show the inability of Palestinian government bodies to provide a normal life for their people. The Palestinian Authority does not control daily life in the Territories: the Israeli authorities control the movement of people and goods through the Separation Barrier and within the Territories, whether businesses open and close, how children are transported to school, university students to their campuses, and people in need of medical attention to hospitals and clinics. Israel also holds the property of hundreds of thousands of Palestinians, sometimes confiscating it for ostensible security reasons or to expropriate land; in a notable number of cases, confiscation of property is completely arbitrary. Houses, agricultural land, vehicles, electronic goods, and farm animals may all be taken at the discretion of a regional commander or a soldier in the field. Soldiers can also "confiscate" people for a training exercise: troops burst into a house in the dead of night and arrest one of the residents only to release him later—all to practice arrest procedures. Overall, Palestinian life is made conditional and transient, dependent on the caprice of checkpoint guards, area commanders, and settlement security coordinators.

The Israeli forces make use of terms like "fabric of life" and "proportionality" to describe and characterize a range of their activities: checkpoint operations, demolitions of houses and infrastructure, forced entry into Palestinian houses, even targeted assassinations. The soldiers' testimonies in Part Three give a more accurate account of the Palestinian fabric of life under Israeli occupation: arbitrary, transient, and devoid of dignity.

The Occupied Territories after Operation Cast Lead, 2009

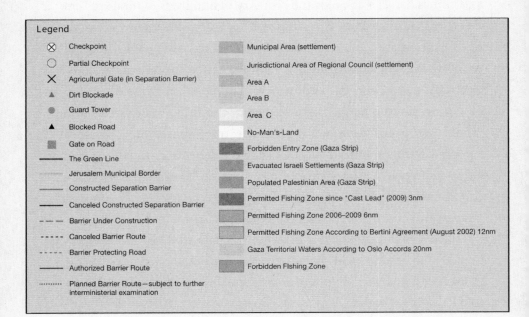

Legend

⊗	Checkpoint		Municipal Area (settlement)
○	Partial Checkpoint		Jurisdictional Area of Regional Council (settlement)
✕	Agricultural Gate (in Separation Barrier)		Area A
▲	Dirt Blockade		Area B
●	Guard Tower		Area C
▲	Blocked Road		No-Man's-Land
■	Gate on Road		Forbidden Entry Zone (Gaza Strip)
—	The Green Line		Evacuated Israeli Settlements (Gaza Strip)
	Jerusalem Municipal Border		Populated Palestinian Area (Gaza Strip)
	Constructed Separation Barrier		Permitted Fishing Zone since "Cast Lead" (2009) 3nm
	Canceled Constructed Separation Barrier		Permitted Fishing Zone 2006–2009 6nm
---	Barrier Under Construction		Permitted Fishing Zone According to Bertini Agreement (August 2002) 12nm
-----	Canceled Barrier Route		Gaza Territorial Waters According to Oslo Accords 20nm
-----	Barrier Protecting Road		Forbidden Fishing Zone
—	Authorized Barrier Route		
....	Planned Barrier Route—subject to further interministerial examination		

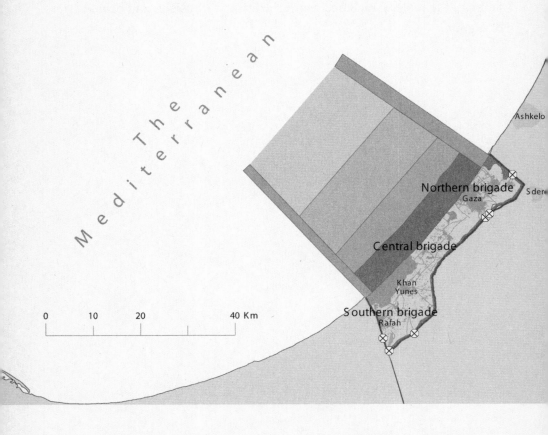

Hadera

Umm
al Fahm

Beit Shean

Jenin

Menashe
regional brigade

Mahola

Makiyot

Netanya

Tul Karem

Taibe

Efraim
regional brigade

Tira

Kedumim

Nablus

Ro'i

Bek'ot

Qalqiliya

Herzliya

Kfar
Saba

Karne
Shomeron

Shomron
regional brigade

Argaman

Massu'a

Kfar
Qasem

Ariel

Aviv

Petach
Tikva

Ma'ale
Efraim

Jordan Valley
regional brigade

m

on
on

Lod

Ramla

Binyamin
regional brigade

Netiv
Hagedud

Modi'in
Illit

Ramallah

Giv'at
Ze'ev

Jericho

Ma'ale
Adumim

Jerusalem

Jerusalem
envelope

Beit Shemesh

Betar
Illit

Bethlehem

Ezion
regional brigade

Efrat

Halhul

Yehuda
regional brigade

Mizpe
Shalem

Hebron

Bani Na'im

at

Yatta

a-Dhahiriyah

r
a

The Dead Sea

Map by Shai Efrati

82. Tipping out crates to set an example

UNIT: MILITARY POLICE
LOCATION: QALQILYA DISTRICT
YEAR: 2006–2008

After your service, if you were to look at your company, would you say things were run properly? Was there a gulf between what you'd been taught and what was expected of you and how the checkpoint was actually run?

People from my company did things in a very strict way, especially in Reihan. In Qalqilya, it was less strict in terms of what they did at the checkpoint. They were strict in Reihan, but at the same time, there weren't too many deviations.

How were they strict? In what way?

The DCL has it in for certain Palestinians who transport goods. For example, there was this guy who had a Mercedes mini-truck and was transferring agricultural goods in crates, all kinds of vegetables. In general, we had to pass a magnetometer over the crate, above it and below it. You put the crate on its side and continue on to the next one. You can also make someone spill out the contents of the crate. It's not a large crate, it's a crate made of old plastic. Of course, you don't help the guy empty out the contents of the crate. You tell him to do it, and afterward he picks everything back up. As far as our procedures went, this was legitimate. They told us to empty out a few crates as an example. That same guy, I remember, had a ton of goods with him. After the checkpoint closed we spent another hour checking him. I remember there were a few times they told me to empty out this guy's crates.

Why him specifically?

There was a girl who came to him at the —— facility at the pedestrian crossing and he told her he'd give her father forty sheep if she married him, but I heard from her that he'd been annoying her. But that's nonsense, you don't get tough because of that—you do it because it's your job. Sometimes people took things personally—because someone annoyed you, you dump out his crates. But we were also supposed to do it to set an example. You don't dump out everyone's stuff.

How many crates did this guy have?

In the small truck there aren't crates, it's a tub. There's Mercedes trucks, there's the Isuzu, which is small and you can put crates in there, but this was a bigger truck, like medium size, and you have maybe two hundred crates.

And he had to dump out two hundred crates?

The case with the girl? Yes.

Is that a common punishment?

It's a kind of punishment, but it would only happen rarely. In his case, it happened because he annoyed her.

83. I didn't understand the point of these mappings

UNIT: PARATROOPERS
LOCATION: SOUTH HEBRON HILLS
YEAR: 2003

What I remember from there that really made me angry was mapping the houses.

Why?

Because the arrests I could understand. They'd tell us, "Okay, now we're going out to arrest a man with blood on his hands, he carried out an attack, he took part in planning an attack." I could understand that, okay. When we'd go out to do mappings it really bothered me because I couldn't see the point of it, the reason. It felt like something that crossed the line a bit.

You're a platoon commander now?

Yes, I'm a platoon commander. Why cross the line? I get that there's some operational need for mapping, and it helps our operations somehow with intelligence, and maybe helps us deal with terrorists later on. But it was very hard for me to come in the middle of the night, with eight or ten other soldiers wearing flak jackets, helmets, weapons, magazines loaded, going into someone's house, waking them up, start searching their house, start asking them embarrassing questions.

Like what?

"Who are you, and what are you, and what's she doing here, and how many people live here?" I don't know, the questions depended on the situation.

There wasn't some kind of form?

There was, but it doesn't always work like it says on the form. Sometimes it also . . . Basically, what bothered me really was going into people's homes in the middle of the night in this threatening way. I remember being really angry seeing how it affected the little kids. It really upset me. You see a small child, three, four, five years old, a young girl, you go into their house in the middle of the night, you come in, you take . . . she sees her father shaking—her father, the man, the authority figure, is shaking—they come, take him aside, interrogate him, ask him questions. Sometimes soldiers who do the questioning more aggressively, maybe it's their voice, maybe they add a shove here and there if they think someone's not cooperating. And this was really hard for me. The mappings were really hard for me. Because the mapping is for some kind of intelligence purpose, it's not like I'm there to arrest a suspect who we know shot at a passing car last week and killed some innocent civilians. So it was really tough for me. And listen, I wasn't, I didn't have the kind of influence where I could say,

"Okay, we're not going out to do mapping." There's no such thing as not going out to do mapping. So when I'd do the mapping, I'd try to do it in the best possible way from a humanitarian perspective. I wouldn't bother the families too much, I wouldn't throw stones at the door in the middle of the night to wake them up with a start, because that's what they do, it's one of the steps in the procedure.

But isn't that the procedure for an arrest?

Yes, but it was also the kind of procedure for this, too, because you knock on the door and no one answers you, so you throw a rock. And people get confused between an arrest and a mapping, so they throw a rock.

Straightaway?

Yes. Sometimes they also break windows, they throw the rock at a window.

Were these mappings in a rural area?

A rural area, also rural-urban. The Yatta area, Dura area. The whole area of the South Hebron Hills. Mapping in that area.

Is there in fact an official form? Have you seen it?

Yes.

What's on it?

I don't remember exact details, but ID numbers, names.

Of all of the people in the house?

Of all of the people in the house.

Kids, too?

The kids don't have IDs, but we note how many kids there are.

How would you map the house that we're sitting in right now?

I write down the ID numbers and names of everyone who lives here, everyone who's inside the house.

In Hebrew, of course.

Yes. I write down how the house is built.

Do you draw a plan?

I don't draw a blueprint, but I do write down how many rooms there are.

That's according to the form?

Yes, according to the form. How many rooms there are, how it's built, if there's a storage area, if there's some structure, if there's some kind of attic. Really mapping it.

If you were to see a form like that, would you be able to understand how the house is built?

Not always, but I'm not sure that what we did was really serious. Maybe yes, maybe no. That I don't know. I also don't know who gets this information and what they do with it. It must have some kind of use, but not that significant, and not always—I don't think it always has a function. I'm sure that in many cases they just did the mapping, and they don't really have any use for the information. There's also mapping of houses that have already been mapped.

How do you know that?

Maybe they'd say, "They were here already, you already did this last week, you were already here, there already."

And you did it anyway?

Yes, as part of the mapping. The form might be some kind of cover, but going there again is a way to show our presence, going into their houses again. The army's interest in this, what they'd say to us was, you have to be active, you have to go out and act so they won't come to you. So you have to be active in their territory.

What else did you have to check?

Who owns the home, who actually lives there, who's there now. Just because—if you have someone there who doesn't live in the house, then it's worth checking why he's there. That's it, mostly. Maybe their occupations, too.

What else did you ask that wasn't on the form? You said there were embarrassing questions.

Embarrassing questions depend on the situation. It really depends on the situation. Of course embarrassing questions were thrown out there, I remember that embarrassing questions were asked. I can't tell you exactly what.

Were there questions that went into private matters?

Of course there were. Maybe not all the time, but there were questions like that.

Were there mapping operations?

Yes, sometimes there are mapping operations.

How many houses did you map?

In one operation?

No, in total. Did you cover all of Yatta? It's a huge place.

We didn't cover all of Yatta, but the mission was to cover all of Yatta. So our company comes in, we map a certain amount, and then another company comes, and they map more houses. The objective is to map all of Yatta. I'm sure that they've mapped Yatta a few times already.

Could you actually go into Yatta, into the village?*

Yes.

You moved around there freely?

With vehicles, two armored vehicles.

*Yatta, a sizable town, is within Area A, under the control of the Palestinian Authority.

84. The mission: to disrupt and harass

UNIT: NAHAL BRIGADE
LOCATION: HEBRON
YEAR: 2005

When we made the rounds in Hebron it was shitty, but I can't say it was anything unusual. It was during Ramadan, and we kept chasing kids who threw firecrackers.

Arab kids?

Arabs, yes, it was during Ramadan. The point is, I had been in Arab villages in Israel the previous Ramadan, just traveling around, and it was just the same there. It had nothing to do with Hebron in particular, nothing to do with the fact that they hate you there, everyone just throws firecrackers at everyone else. It's more fun to throw them at soldiers. But our platoon commander didn't think so, he thought they were all potential terrorists, so we chased them. Two whole weeks. Not a single kid caught. It was really pathetic.

For two whole weeks you were chasing children in Hebron?

Yeah, and we didn't catch a single one.

So, say I'm driving around in Hebron, trying to catch a kid . . .

Driving, sure, but we were on foot patrol.

So what did you do for two whole weeks?

Well, like I said, we never caught any children. We'd chase them. It reminds me of the stories about Romans going into caves with all their gear on and getting stuck inside. You're there with your heavy ceramic bulletproof vest and all that bullshit, and they hold the firecracker and run. The fact is, we never caught them. I don't remember catching anyone. Maybe we did, maybe just one time. Truth is, I once heard that our platoon commander caught a child who had nothing to do with anything. He caught him, yelled at him, and let him go. What else could he do? That was our mission in action. I remember being told quite clearly, "Our mission is to disrupt"—these were the exact words—"to disrupt and harass people's lives." That was our job description, because the terrorists are local residents, and we want to disrupt terrorist activity, and the operational way to do that is to disrupt people's lives. I'm sure of this, and I think it's written that way to this day, if the order hasn't been changed. Disrupt their lives, disrupt the lives of the people who live there, because this disrupts terrorist activity. That's the whole point.

How does it work?

You mean, what do we actually do? You wander around the city . . . Guys there say they have nothing to do? It's like this, You go around the city, go into abandoned houses—abandoned at least by the time we get there—sometimes we'd go into houses that weren't abandoned, and we'd carry out totally random searches. Sometimes, say we saw a kid throw a firecracker, then we'd run over there. But maybe it's a lie, we'd also just pick out any house. It's not like we had any intelligence in advance. We'd carry out random searches in houses, and the people there were totally used to it. They weren't surprised, not even stressed.

Checkpoint, Jericho, the District Coordination and Liaison, 2003, Armored Corps.

They'd get irritated, depressed, they have no tolerance for this bullshit, but they're used to it because it's been going on for so many years now. Soldiers come in, turn the house inside out, make a huge mess, and leave. That's what we do. Sometimes we do all kinds of lookout shifts. There's a cemetery there, so we'd sit in the cemetery and watch all kinds of couples there, or I don't know, anyone else walking by. That's what we did for quite a while. Sometimes we'd put up checkposts for vehicles— stand at some junction, and check cars in the neighborhood, that's what we'd do.

What would you look for inside the cars?

It sounds funny, but it wasn't at all clear. I think it's like searching for weapons, but no one really believes you'll find anything.

Not even your commander?

I don't think so. It depends which commander. If he was a highly moti- vated officer, then yes.

But does everyone do this?

Yes, that's the designated mission. The company commander says to the officer, who says to the squad commander in charge of the patrol: Your mission is to be there or there for an hour and a half, and do this and that.

Didn't you feel completely stupid doing this?

Totally stupid. That's what I'm saying. It's one of the reasons I didn't want to be squad commander. I could feel how much these command- ers have no say, they're just little cogs in the system, almost like pri- vates. And so I thought, why should I bring that on myself?

You carry out these searches, and the population suffers.

Exactly, they're totally fucked. That's exactly the point. That's what's so shitty about it. As long as we were up north, no one suffered because of our actions, it's just trees up there. But in the Territories, it's the popu- lation that suffers.

85. Every incident resulted in "limiting civilian movement"

UNIT: CIVIL ADMINISTRATION
LOCATION: GENERAL
YEAR: 2001–2004

After large operations, terror attacks, or when someone was killed, were there times when the administration would suddenly crack down on the general Palestinian population?

That's natural, isn't it?

Yes, but do you remember specific things that happened?

I don't remember a specific incident, that period was full of them, but yes, every kind of incident like that results in civilian punishment, there's nothing to be done. It's not civilian punishment, it's limiting civilian movement.

Like what?

Like giving fewer permits to go into Israel, for example, which is a step the administration takes when there's nothing else to do. Cutting down the opening hours at checkpoints where you can transfer goods, above all you take economic steps: you stop transferring money through banks . . . it might sound inconsequential to you, but it's not.

How is this related to the administration?

The administration approves the transfer of money between banks, from Palestinian banks to other Palestinian ones, between a foreign bank and a Palestinian one, between an Israeli bank and a Palestinian bank.

Is there a division of the DCL responsible for that?

Yes, back then it was economic that approved all the transfers. I think there was a reorganization of the economic branch there, but I think it's still there, I don't know for sure.

What decisions do they make?

It's government policy, there's nothing to do about it, it's just policy.

How was it defined? Didn't you say they didn't call it punishment?

It wasn't punishment.

Then what is it, how did they define it?

They didn't define it. It's not a punishment. Not transferring money is certainly not a humanitarian act, but it's not a punishment. Punishment means not allowing the transfer of bread, flour, oil, and eggs. That's punishment, and that never happened. They don't do things like that. Money isn't a necessity, that's just how it is. Again, I'm talking about not transferring money for a week. It's not like you don't transfer money for months—that would be a humanitarian problem. But money isn't something that's . . . believe me, it never happened that the bank didn't have the money for withdrawals. That never happened, I never heard of it. And if it had happened, I promise you they'd transfer the money.

What other kinds of responsive steps were taken? Could you affect movement on the roads?

Yes, there was that famous plan to separate the roads . . . which wasn't implemented, as far as I know.

What was the plan?

The plan was to separate Palestinian and Jewish roads. It went to the Supreme Court, I don't remember what the ruling was.

What was the plan a result of?

This was in 2002, the end of 2002, there were terrorist attacks on the roads, shooting attacks, a period of shooting attacks, and they decided to just separate the roads. They didn't do it in the end, there was a plan to do so, we worked on it for a really long time, and in the end it didn't happen, I don't think they ever implemented it, because they had to build all this infrastructure.

What was the plan?

A Palestinian and a Jewish road, based on the idea that this would allow free Palestinian movement in the West Bank, meaning there wouldn't be any separation between blocs, there'd be humanitarian movement without allowing them to go on roads with Israeli vehicles, and carry out a shooting attack . . . it's easier to secure a road that only Israelis drive on. But it won't help.

Who formulated this plan?

I think it was the Central Command's instructions, but who formulated it? Some division, but it was mostly the Civil Administration, what's called the infrastructure branch. They separate roads and build roads. Tunnels, bridges, and maybe part of it was implemented—I don't really know.

86. Do you know what a naval blockade means?

Unit: Navy
Location: Gaza Strip
Year: 2005

It's mostly about punishment. I hate that the most, "They did it to us, so we'll do it to them." Do you know what a naval blockade means for them? There's no food for a few days. For example, it could be there was an attack in Netanya, so they impose a naval blockade for four days on the entire strip. No seagoing vessel can leave, a Dabur patrol boat is stationed at the entrance to the port, if they try to go out, within a second they shoot at the bow, and they'll even deploy attack helicopters to scare them. We had a lot of operations with attack helicopters—they don't shoot too much because they prefer to let us deal with it, but they're there to scare people, they circle over their heads. All of a sudden a Cobra is right over your head, it passes low, it stirs up the wind and throws everything around. There were a lot of incidents like that. The attack helicopters worked with us a lot.

And how common was the blockade?

Very common. More common than a special isolation, which was relatively rare. I wouldn't say more than once a month, but it could be that it'd happen three times in one month, and then three months of nothing. It depends.

The blockade is for a day, two days, three days, four, or more than that?

I can't remember anything longer than four days. If it was longer than that, they'd die there, and I believe the IDF understands that. Seventy percent live on fishing—they have no choice. For them it means not eating. There are whole families who don't eat for a few days because of the blockade. They eat bread and water. Like in the Holocaust.

87. How can you impose so many curfews and expect people to live?

UNIT: CIVIL ADMINISTRATION
LOCATION: HEBRON
YEAR: 2002–2003

Earlier you said a few words about how you could understand some of the complaints.

I did.

Like what?

Not things that happened to me specifically, but things I heard about in the media, things that happened, about delays, that they didn't want to let a pregnant woman cross—situations which apparently happened. They put up checkpoints all the time, and one of the biggest responsibilities I had there was to understand where all the checkpoints were located. The checkpoints were put up at random, and apparently this was pretty unpleasant, and the complaints were about how they couldn't get to work. I remember something that bothered me personally—I didn't understand the whole thing with the curfews. In Hebron there were tons of curfews, I don't remember the number of days, but I do remember just being in shock at how we set curfews so often and expected people to live like that. I really didn't understand how they expected people to exist. If you make people's lives so difficult, how do you think you'll solve any problems? You're only creating more people who are going to hate you deep in their hearts for the rest of their lives. I'm sure that if they put me under curfew for 360 days, what would I do? The way I saw it, it just wasn't realistic, and I remember talking about it and no one understood what I was talking about. They said, "security risk." Great, security risk, but these are people, and they need to live. Where do they get their food? How do you make money to eat when you're under curfew?

You talked to officers and friends?

I'd talk to officers and friends. I did 8/6* and I had a lot of time to forget that I was in the army. The six days when you're in Israel, you easily forget what you're doing. The eight days on the base go by quickly because you sleep there.

88. Three thousand Palestinians at five posts

Unit: Military Police
Location: Qalqilya and Tul Karem districts
Year: 2005

How does Reihan[†] work? There's you and the combat soldiers?

The combat soldiers were with us at the checkpoint, then there were artillerymen, and there was a certain period when one of the units from Kfir was there. Anyone who came to the checkpoint was inspected completely, and we worked according to intelligence, because there were strong and precise intelligence warnings. They said that a blue pickup would arrive with weapons, and there really were weapons there.

*Eight days on the base, six at home.
[†]A checkpoint

The intelligence was precise, we did quality inspections that were more sensitive. Now, in the Eyal area, it's like at the mall—you check the trunk and they drive on . . . That's why there was resentment . . .

Some of the soldiers were stationed in the vehicular terminal and some in the pedestrian?

Yes.

Let's talk about the pedestrian terminal with the glass boxes, because that's the newest part of the way checkpoints work today. A guy walks up—what kind of process does he go through?

He walks up to the crossing, and he stands there and is inspected—there's a large magnetometer, which beeps if it identifies weapons or bomb belts, so we make sure there there's no threat at the crossing itself. Afterward he goes to the X-ray, and there he removes all of his things, down to his pocket change, and then crosses again there. All of his things are examined by the X-ray, he gets dressed again, he goes on to the ID check, and then he goes through. There was a lot of pressure in Reihan, once in a while Palestinians would cross three at a time, and they didn't wait a long time. Eyal in the morning was a completely different story, because it was peak crossing time, and there were three thousand Palestinians for only five ID posts. Out of boredom, we came up with a contest to see who could let more Palestinians into Israel so that the shift would go by more quickly. There it was really five hours without rest, maybe some rest the last half hour, but you worked and pushed people through. You got up at two-thirty, at four or five you're at the crossing with puffy eyes, pushing the Palestinians through.

At what time do they start coming to the checkpoint?

Before four, the checkpoint opens at four.

What time does the congestion start to ease up?

After four or four and a half hours.

Is it like that every day?

Yes. Five days a week, and on Friday there's less congestion because the majority of people don't work. Sunday is the busiest day, by far. On Sunday you wouldn't even get a break sometimes until the last minute. I would get a break only after five hours. The shifts there were divided up—you could either do ten hours straight or a five-hour shift, five-hour break, and another five-hour shift. It was crazy because you were stuck in this small box, alone, the orders were no music, nothing. After the peak hours you felt like just killing yourself. The soldiers would slack off and bring MP3s, and I even brought a portable DVD player to pass the time. I was completely burned out, I felt things that I'd never felt before in my life. I blessed the day I was released and ran away from there, because I hated being at the crossing in every way . . .

Going back to the pedestrian terminal in Reihan, when they go through the X-ray screening, is there any contact?

None. Only through the microphone. You talk to them, and it's crazy because sometimes they play stupid, sometimes they know what they're doing and they just want to annoy you, and you go crazy because you can't show them, you have to direct them via the box, and you don't always know enough Arabic to explain it to them, you just improvise sentences.

Are men and women together at the checkpoint?

Yes, but the moment they needed to do a more thorough investigation, something involving removing clothing, men and women went to separate cells, where a male or female soldier would check them, depending on their sex.

If you already have an X-ray machine and a magnetometer, when is there ever a need for a more thorough investigation?

When the magnetometer doesn't stop beeping, or when the people being checked don't do what you tell them to, then you take them aside.

You said that you check for a permit—does everyone need a permit?

Yes, otherwise they don't have permission to cross.

At what age do you need a permit? Kids certainly don't need them.

I don't remember the procedures there, but a child has to cross with an adult accompanying him, or he has to have a copy of his father's ID to show what city he's from, and that his father's allowed to cross.

In terms of luggage, are they allowed to bring a suitcase?

They can transfer anything except for electronics, because you can't check that. At the X-ray machine there were people who knew how to check, but they couldn't check that.

What about someone who comes with a car?

If he has a permit for it, he can cross in the car.

Does having a vehicle permit allow you to transfer goods?

We had a list of who was allowed to transfer goods.

What's the definition of "goods"? If a person has a vehicle permit but not a merchandise permit, and he comes in a car carrying half a liter of oil, can he cross?

Yes. The restrictions are more about sheep, candy, vegetables, things like that.

Is it about the kind of thing or the amount?

The amount. I remember twenty-four baking pans, for example.

Everything was defined?

Yes.

89. Restricted hours for crossing the checkpoint

Unit: Military Police
Location: Qalqilya district
Year: 2006–2008

Were there also crossings for pedestrians at the Zufim checkpoint, or just for vehicles?

Pedestrians could definitely cross there. In the morning, there were people who were from Zufim or were permanent residents.

Did they have freedom of movement?

They had to be checked, but yes.

Were the agricultural crossings always open?

Of course. The Zufim checkpoint was open twenty-four hours for the residents there. For the most part, the agricultural gate is open only at certain hours. Aside from that, there's a facility in every area where they check pedestrians.

Permanent residents couldn't cross there?

They could. It's a bit vague.

Can a Palestinian cross at two in the morning?

No. There are defined hours at the checkpoints, even if you're a permanent resident.

But if someone Jewish comes at that time, can he cross?

Yes. Even though we carried out our work in Reihan as strictly as possible, there were always people who could cross as long as we were at the checkpoint. Only if they came from the Israeli side, for example, could they cross late at night, because there was no reason to keep them on the Israeli side. The authority to check someone was ours alone, and no one else's.

You said there were blockades set up between the Palestinian villages, Azun-Atma and Beit Amin.

It's like in Hawwara—you play bingo. You have a short version of the ID number, the last four numbers, and you've got the program on the computer. You check the number—for the most part, there's not much reason to keep inspecting. The thing is that there's no fence to prevent people who live in Azun-Atma from crossing into the Israeli side because they're there. If they leave the village—but they can't leave the village because there's a prohibition because they're Palestinians—but if they were to travel west, they'd be considered illegal aliens. The reason for the crossing is to prevent Palestinians who don't have a permit from going to visit Azun-Atma, or to catch a wanted person who wants to go there.

So if someone's not a resident of Azun-Atma, can he go there?

No.

90. The line wasn't straight, so the officer shot in the air

UNIT: ARMORED CORPS
LOCATION: SOUTH HEBRON HILLS
YEAR: 2001

There's a checkpoint at the Dahariya intersection. South Dahariya. Palestinians cross there to go work in Beersheba. Dozens of Palestinians have to cross there every day, some on foot. One of the officers with us wanted to maintain order, he wanted them all to stand straight in a line, even. He ran beside them and told them to straighten up. They didn't do it too well. So right near the first person he saw at the front, a fifty-something-year-old guy, and next to him an eight-year-old boy or something like that, a small boy . . . the officer shot in the air, and the line became orderly.

He shot in the air to straighten the line?

To straighten the line. And another time he just beat a guy up . . . He hit him in the face with the butt of his Galil, kicked him in the balls, spat on him, cursed him . . . he just shat on him. Right next to this guy's little boy. He just humiliated him completely. That was rare . . . it would happen . . .

Was he an officer from your company? From the Armored Corps?

Yes, and we also had another soldier there who made special preparations. He invested two weeks in them, so he could beat up Arabs. And just anyone who wasn't, who didn't do exactly what he said, whoever wasn't immediately obedient, he'd give it to him in the knee, leg, stomach, head, and anyone who wouldn't answer his questions directly, "Where's your ID," "Where are you from," like those thugs who beat you up, anything that didn't seem right to him, you'd get a beating. There are people who need this kind of power, they get power-crazy and turn violent. I'm not talking about Arabs who were running away and soldiers would shoot at them, or people who bypassed the checkpoint . . . but this whole thing with the beating, it was really idiotic.

And when you're a witness to it, you . . .

At that moment you're silent . . . and you . . . you can't stop it. I'm talking about if you're in regular service. It wouldn't happen on reserve duty. If I were to see something like that now, I wouldn't let it continue. We fought with border policemen, we tried to keep them out of there, we really fought with them. It was difficult. Look, we're . . . the majority of people are good, it's not that most people are a problem, there's just a problematic minority. The problem is that this kind of behavior was legitimate. So beating up an Arab, cursing him, humiliating him, pointing your weapon in his face and then shooting in the air a second later—these things were legitimate. It was down to the individual, it wasn't like, let's have four, five soldiers beat this guy up and . . . but there were people who knew they were going to beat someone up every day. They talk about it openly, they take photos . . . they photographed a Palestinian they bound like a contortionist—shocking things.

91. They told us, "Dry them out"

UNIT: NAHAL BRIGADE
LOCATION: TUL KAREM DISTRICT
YEAR: 2001

It was just after the terrorist attack at the Dolphinarium Club.* They wanted to establish a brigade on the seam line. So they sent us to the Taibe area. We were in Avnei Hefets, and our duty was to go on patrol and prevent the passage of illegal aliens. There's an open field there to the north of Taibe, and we were stationed there. There was nothing to be done with the people there. The majority of those who cross are, of course, people going to work. We never caught—with the exception of some drug addict who lived in a cave, which was maybe the most interesting thing we came across, most of the people, all of the people we detained there, were people who tried to get into Israel to go to work. And there was nothing to be done with them, there weren't any facilities to jail them. It's impossible. So the procedure was just to take their ID, keep them there for a few hours, have them sit there, and then send them back home . . .

And would you give them back their IDs?

Yes, after a few hours. You catch someone, run his ID number, yes, Shabak, it never happened that they detained one of those people, you keep him on a rock for a few hours and continue with what you're doing. There were some guys, some Russians, the crazy ones, I remember, they just grabbed someone . . . I once saw them, they were generally at a different post, they sat among themselves, the Russians went together to the post. And I was young, so I'd go wherever they assigned me, so one time they caught someone, and for no reason they decided they'd give him the treatment, meaning they'd take his ID. In principle they were at a lookout post, which they generally were—we were down

---

*A Tel Aviv night club that was bombed in June 2001. Twenty-one Israelis were killed and more than one hundred injured.

below, they were on the lookout, and they'd say to us, "There's someone crossing there." So we'd go out, try to catch him. Sometimes we had some pickup truck, or we were on foot, you go, grab him, take his ID, make him spend a few hours in the sun or shade, depending on how you felt at the moment, and then you send him home.

Yeah, it could be anywhere between two hours, between two and six to eight hours, it depends when you caught him. The procedures weren't very clear, because they didn't know what to do with these people. They said, "Dry them out." "Drying them out" is pretty vague, it leaves room for the imagination . . . So these Russians, who were in principle at a lookout post, which was more of a screwing around and no exercise post, meaning they didn't have to run from place to place. So by chance someone walked right by their post, and they grabbed him. They grabbed him, and tied him up straightaway. When we'd catch them, we'd sit them down, give them water . . .

Do you sit everyone down together, or just wherever someone's caught?

It depends. Sometimes we'd catch a few people together, so we'd sit them down together, or we'd decide that we didn't want them sitting together, "You sit here, you sit there." So when the Russians caught him, they tied his hands behind his back, blindfolded him, took his picture in all kinds of poses, one with a weapon in the air and things like that, like they caught some serious terrorist or something. And it was just some guy on his way to work.

Were there violent incidents?

Not really, aside from that incident, I don't know exactly what happened there, because I only arrived at the end. When we came to collect them, we saw that they were . . . they said, "Yeah, one second, we have to release this guy, cut his ties . . ."

At the end of the shift at Abir, do you have to go back to the post?

Yes, so we had to go get the Russian soldiers. And we saw that they'd caught this guy and done this stuff to him. I don't remember incidents of violence there. Yes, there's the issue of them knowing that we're in control, right? But real violence?

A-Sahla Road (the "Tnuva Road"), Hebron. In the forefront, the road is open only to the Palestinians who live above the stores, which are permanently closed. Beyond the point where the soldier is standing, the road is "sterile," off-limits to Palestinians.

Which includes what?

It includes that they don't talk to you. You talk to them. You tell them what to do. Whoever talks, you say, "Shut up! I don't want to know." Because they're always telling you about their family and whatever, saying, "I need to work and I need to . . ." You don't care—"Shut up, sit!" and so they lose . . . I take their ID, and it's gone. "Sit here, you won't want to not be here when I get back." They're always there when you get back. No one goes anywhere without his ID.

92. You take a man and take control of his life

UNIT: LAVI BATTALION
LOCATION: SOUTH HEBRON HILLS
YEAR: 2003

There was one incident which I think is the most . . . it's the thing I regret the most. It's the worst thing I did during all of my service in the Territories. There was this guy who came out from Yatta and went past a barrier. He was on his way from Yatta to Hebron, to the milk production plant. He had a truck full of containers of milk. I think there was a curfew in Hebron at the time. In short, he was not allowed to cross. I caught him right as he was crossing the barrier, and it was the third time that week that I'd caught the same guy—under different circumstances, but the same guy, at more or less the same place. My fuses blew a bit, because I took him out—I asked him to get out of the car, and so on, but he started arguing and yelling, so right away I did two things, got out the cuffs and blindfolds. I went into the jeep, and brought him to the gate. It was, I don't know, ten in the morning, something like that . . . and somewhere between eleven and one in the morning I released him. Meaning, this was summer, meaning, all day. He had like two thousand liters of milk with him, and all of the milk spoiled. It was all day, he just sat at the gate with a blindfold on and his hands tied. When I look at it now, I'm ashamed because of two things. First, because of how I treated another human being. Just taking a man and taking control of his life like that? I physically took him away, bound him, brought him to that post and said, "Okay, sit here." I took him as a bound prisoner. And no one else was responsible for that. It wasn't as if I got an order, right? No, it was what I decided to do. And this was acceptable. From the perspective of everyone in charge of me, there was no problem. Okay, you detained someone, there's the way you treated another human being, and the fact that there was property involved, meaning the milk. Something of monetary value was lost. Meaning I made the man lose who knows how many shekels, but let's say the milk was worth at least five hundred shekels. In Yatta that's a lot of money. Really. Fine, so I didn't take the money from his pocket, but my actions caused him to lose it. And to me that's still less important than the way I treated him as a human. It's not okay. Because really, what's the big deal? He's not a terrorist, he wasn't wanted, he's not someone who came up to me or threatened me with a weapon. He's a regular guy. What was the point of what I did? Nothing. Did it contribute to the security of the state? No. I just did harm to someone. And that's not okay.

93. I made him crap his pants

UNIT: BORDER POLICE
LOCATION: WADI ARA
YEAR: 2003

Working with the population—that was our entertainment. At least in Katzir. I don't know what was going on at that time in Jenin, but it was fun. Working with the people was . . .

"Working with the people" is a nice turn of phrase.

Yes. Working with the people. That's what there was to do. Then all of a sudden, they built the fence and there were no more people around. There was the Israeli population you had to be careful with, there's Barta'a, where you could still do a little . . .

So the operations moved to Barta'a?

There was a slight shift, yeah. But again, they tended to keep Barta'a for the IDF, it was more their domain. So the work we did was mostly along the fence.

What happened when they caught someone?

Then we went in. If you capture someone, then you can go in. Really, the majority of the time when I saw violence was in the period before they built the fence, when it was just routine. Pouring out the kids' bags and playing with their toys. You know, you'd grab a toy and play "monkey in the middle" with it.

Did the kids cry?

All the time. They cried and were scared. Meaning, you couldn't miss it.

The adults cried, too?

Of course they did, they were humiliated. The goal was always, "I got him to cry in front of his kids, I got him to crap his pants."

There were times when people went to the bathroom in their pants?

Yes.

Why?

From being beaten, for the most part. Being beaten and threatened and screamed at—you're just terrified. Especially if it's in front of their kids—they yell at them and threaten and scare them, so you're also scaring their kids. One time, there was some man we stopped with his kid—the kid was small, like four or something. They didn't beat up the kid, but the policeman was annoyed that the guy brought his kids so they'd feel bad for him. He says, "You bring your kid so they'll feel bad for you—I'll show you what feeling bad is." He goes and beats him up, screams at him, saying, "I'll kill you in front of your boy, maybe you'll feel more . . ." It's terrifying. There's a lot of stories about pride.

Did the guy piss his pants out of fear?

Yes.

In front of the boy.

Yes. Lots of stories about pride, like, "Check me out, I got him to crap his pants, I got him to whatever." They talked about it all the time, it's not some kind of . . .

Where did they talk about it? In the cafeteria, in front of the officers? Did people talk about it openly?

Yes. I think that an officer who says he doesn't know about it, he's totally lying. At least the officers, the high-ranking officers knew. The platoon commanders had less to do with it, but the company commander, the assistant company commander, the operations officers— they even encouraged it to a degree. Again, not directly, they didn't come and say, "Come on, beat them up," but there was a kind of legitimization, otherwise it wouldn't have happened. Again, it's a fact that it happened less in Jenin, and in my opinion not just because there was less work with the population.

94. We had a kind of temporary prison camp

UNIT: PARATROOPERS
LOCATION: NABLUS DISTRICT
YEAR: 2003

I was a squad commander by this point. It was also one of those crazy periods, the same story I told about Hebron, only this time inside Nablus. No static posts. I remember I'd say to the soldiers who were interested, that they should be thankful they weren't in Hebron. One checkpoint is called Havah 7, Bet Porik, one checkpoint is called Meteg 3, which is at the northern, northeastern exit between Nablus and Ein Bidan, and one that's called "the valley of the runaways," which brings back a lot of memories that I hadn't remembered until now. The valley of the runaways . . . most of the checkpoints there, nothing really happened, because there was a squad commander. Unusual things started happening when there were fewer available squad commanders, and so soldiers started being squad commanders . . . the central checkpoints in Nablus, Hava 5, Hava 7, Hava 6—normally nothing unusual happens there, because they're open to the media. Those people are always there—Machsom Watch, B'Tselem, you know. But sometimes it's not clear where the checkpoint is—it's a moving checkpoint, what's called a checkpost, or an unestablished checkpoint, which you set up with an APC so you can close off a wide area and prevent Palestinians from exiting there. You always patrol or set up the checkpoint in a different post each time, and no one sees you there, no one knows where you are, it's abandoned land. When I was there, not too much happened, either. But things could happen there because there's no real supervision.

Are there things that are part of the procedure, like detaining people, drying them out, confiscating their keys? Are those things you're familiar with?

Okay, yes. Look, at the checkpoint, detaining someone is the right thing to do. I can tell you that today, for all the reasons, detaining someone is preferred, it's the least terrible thing. A soldier is in a life-threatening situation at a checkpoint. If there's no order there, then the soldier could die. It's an issue of life and death, because all of the checkpoints there are very dangerous, you're very vulnerable when you're at a checkpoint. You're a soldier, you're standing there, and it's easy to attack you. The moment a checkpoint commander loses control of his checkpoint— people aren't standing in a straight line, people get too close and wander around the checkpoint freely, then there's a good chance that some- one will come and blow himself up, or shoot the commander and take advantage of the chaos. A checkpoint that's routinely chaotic, or if the commander of the checkpoint is always disorganized, it's only a matter of time until a terrorist, especially in a dangerous area like Nablus, will figure this out and attack it. And so the question is, what can the com- mander do to maintain order at the checkpoint? So he can use physical violence, which works, it certainly works. Cruelty works. If you take a person who's going crazy and smash him in the head with the butt of your weapon, it works, it's effective. It's unethical, and commanders don't normally do it. And because of that, commanders detain people. It's a less effective method, it frightens them less, but there it is, it works.

What does it involve?

A person who gave you some trouble, who disturbed the peace at the checkpoint, who spoke to you in a certain way . . . you have to keep your authority, you have to keep it so they respect you at the checkpoint. What can you do? It sounds terrible, and it is. That's the reality of the checkpoint. Everything to say about the checkpoint has already been written and said, whoever's seen the movie *Checkpoint* understands it, I think. In the end, you have to have people respect you, and you have to keep order at the checkpoint. So you take that guy who got out of line, those few people who were making trouble for you, and you tie their hands behind their backs and sit them down for ten hours, five hours.

Who decides? The checkpoint commander?

The checkpoint commander who's there. And again, I have to say, that as long as checkpoints exist—and this is an entirely different discussion, if there should or shouldn't be checkpoints . . . apparently there have to be, because there isn't much of a choice in certain places, and there are also places where the checkpoints could go. That's clear to me. And when they'll be able to evacuate the settlements in general, it'll be possible to get rid of many checkpoints. But there's a certain number of checkpoints that'll still exist. And as long as checkpoints exist, detainment is the most humane way, among all the other ways which are less humane, to keep order at the checkpoint. And what can you do? You also have to protect the lives of the soldiers.

As a checkpoint commander, who tells you that you're allowed or not allowed to detain someone?

That's during the company commander's briefing. They told us that it was acceptable to detain people. No one legitimized physical violence.

What other means of punishment or authority are used?

In the more extreme cases, they take people to the company. There was, like, a temporary prison camp in the company that we set up, where people could stay for two days. It's for cases where people really made a lot of trouble. You take them to the jeep, put them in the improvised prison camp we set up, with a tin roof, and mattresses.

Are they prisoners?

Yes. Their hands are tied behind their backs, and they sit in the temporary prison camp for a day or so. We give them water, food, but they're bound there for a day in the company prison camp, and there's someone who guards them. It's a kind of tin roof, with a mattress underneath, and surrounded by barbed wire.

What were the criteria to merit a day or two in the temporary prison camp?

I don't remember. It was for people who really caused trouble. Someone you detained, but he kept making trouble, started acting crazy, acting violently, or it was for someone you caught regularly.

95. He mumbled a bit, I hit him in the face

Unit: Engineering Corps
Location: Ramallah district
Year: 2005

When I got there, they immediately briefed me on the Qalandiya checkpoint—this was the old Qalandiya checkpoint, before it became a terminal. Because of things that happened to us there, the checkpoint was turned into a terminal. At the checkpoint there were twenty-four soldiers on a shift: twelve at the vehicular checkpoint and twelve at the pedestrian one, who were mostly on alert and acted as an intervention team. The pedestrian checkpoint was already sterile—not like in the past. When I got there, the pedestrian checkpoint was sterile, with only glass passageways and the military police crossing unit there. There was an alert force at the pedestrian checkpoint, and the other force took over the vehicular checkpoint. I was at that checkpoint, and the first time I was there I actively opposed what we were doing. Because of my opposition, my platoon commander took me in for a conversation and told me that he was forced to dismiss me from all my duties and remove me from the company within a week, and that they would find me a new company, headquarters apparently, because I expressed political opinions that were against military procedure. My "political opinions" were that while I was there, no one was going to lift their hands. This is a checkpoint where the women of Machsom Watch are there in twenty-four-hour shifts, or back then they were, and I said that no one turns to them, talks to them, or bothers them in any way, and that what they do is legitimate, and it's their right. You can speak to them through the IDF spokesman, but we don't have authority to talk to them otherwise. Those are the orders of the military, and I represented them faithfully. The soldiers didn't listen to me, and they aimed their weapons even at the Machsom Watch women, they cursed at them, broke some bones.

There was a lot of abuse at the checkpoint... It was around December or January, and it was a rough winter, not like this year. It's cold in Ramallah, and Qalandiya's exhausting—you stand there for twelve hours on your feet, a bullet in the chamber, it's considered dangerous . . . you have a helmet on your head, and a flak jacket, and all your equipment is on, you're always on your feet, twelve hours or 8/8, but it's the same thing, and you're always working. You're freezing cold standing there, and you see the Palestinians driving up in their warm cars. We came up with a game: most of the Palestinian cars were old, and the trunks don't open from inside the car, so we'd tell them to get out and open the trunk, so they'd have to go out into the cold and rain. It angered me, seeing them in their warm cars, to the point that I forgot they don't want to see me there, either.

One time, a guy by the name of Amjad Jamal Nazer—I remember him well—I asked him to get out and open the trunk, and he asked why, he said he could open it from the inside. It was hailing, and I was feeling a bit sick, and I told him to get out and open the trunk. He refused. I followed procedure: he said he wasn't getting out, so I took his car, took his car keys, and told him to stand on the side. He mumbled a bit, I hit him in the face with the butt of my gun—and just like that I was part of the cycle of violence. My soldiers couldn't believe it, they were so excited. I was a deputy commander at the vehicular checkpoint, and this was a step up for us, this incident. The checkpoint became very violent, because of the weather and the subpar conditions. Our food was always late, and for that, too, we blamed the Palestinians. The soldiers would send Arabs to bring them food from inside Ramallah when I wasn't paying attention. Of course they wouldn't pay them. They would collect prayer beads, take them for themselves. At that time, I didn't know it was considered a war crime, to take prayer beads or even watermelons. I was extremely against it. I didn't take part in it, but it happened all the time. A lot of squad commanders and sergeants took part in it. I have to say, the officers were opposed to it, and they tried anyone who was involved in these things. They were strongly against it.

So those were the kind of things they took?

Prayer beads, mostly food. They didn't take money. There were other things—I don't remember what exactly.

Cigarettes?

Cigarettes. It happened a lot that they'd stop a truck with cartons of cigarettes, and it was like a bribe, like you see at the Mexican border, they took two cartons and let them cross.

And what if the driver doesn't want to hand them over?

Then he doesn't cross, even if he's right at the entrance to his house. But he gives it to them. I almost never came across situations like that. We were always there with a finger on the trigger, literally and figuratively. They told us that it's a very dangerous place, and so anything goes. It's like that today, too. It wasn't like the brainwashing they gave us in Yakir, where it's pastoral and beautiful. It was dangerous at Qalandiya, and we felt it. After a month at that front, a day before I was supposed to go home, a friend of mine at the sharpshooting security post was shot with four bullets and badly wounded. Another soldier at that post was also shot and killed. It totally changed the rules of the game. They closed the whole checkpoint, the checkpoint was hermetically sealed for twenty-four hours, and no one came in or out of Ramallah. We went into Ramallah with no reason, security-wise. We turned Ramallah upside down, real hatred, we arrested eighty people that night. We went crazy.

What do you mean?

We broke the lightbulbs of every house we went into with the butts of our weapons—as an operational pretext, we claimed that the light bothered us. We used the butts of our weapons, the barrel—physical violence on an indescribable level. The level of . . . it went up dramatically, the checkpoint became extraordinarily violent. From our point of view, they'd killed our friend. He was a good, personal friend of mine, and I took it personally. I removed any restraint from my soldiers at the checkpoint. The violence became a daily reality. We took people out of their cars by hitting them with the barrel of a gun. The sharpshooter standing above us had orders not to move his sight from the car being inspected, keep a bullet in the chamber, always keep an eye on the person. Any disruption—you could shoot. We started shooting at the legs of Palestinians who didn't follow our instructions. There was an incident or two where we shot at their legs. They didn't listen to our orders to stop fifty meters before the checkpoint and to lift up their shirts and turn around. That became the procedure. One time we didn't hit this guy, he ran away and we caught him. One time we hit this guy's leg, and we injured him. Needless to say, he was an innocent, unarmed civilian. With that, we finished up our time in Ramallah, which was, by the way, the calmer Ramallah. That was our company norm for many years, our violence was the pride of the company. We were dark, crazy, not like the 4th Infantry, who are nice Ashkenazis who behave with the Palestinians.

The battalion commanders, brigade commander, did they know what was going on in Qalandiya, did they know about the violence?

No. The battalion commander of 605 was very opposed to it. I think he knew about it some of the time, and when he found out about things he punished people and was against covering it up. But he didn't know about the majority of the violent incidents. It stayed at the level of sergeants, platoon commanders. At most, deputy company commanders, company commanders.

96. You want the keys? Clean the checkpoint

Unit: Civil Administration
Location: Bethlehem district
Year: 2002

A Palestinian came to the DCL and said, "They took my car keys at the checkpoint." I said, "Why did they take them?" "Because . . ." he started talking. I said to him, "Listen, I want to see this for myself." It was the al-Hader checkpoint. He got into my jeep, we drove together to the checkpoint. I said, "Show me which officer." He pointed out the officer, a first lieutenant in the paratroopers. I went up to him, and asked, "Did you take his keys?" He said, "Yes." So I said, "Why?" He said, "Because he stopped here and dropped people off, and it's forbidden for them to drop people off." I said, "So what did you decide to do?" He said, "To punish him, to teach him a lesson." I said, "What was the lesson?" He said, "To clean the checkpoint, keep everyone in line, and after all that, I'll give him back his keys. Until then, he won't get his keys back." It was incredible. The guy was such an idiot. So of course I told him to give the keys back now, I took down his details and passed it on to the brigade headquarters and everything. I don't know if he was tried. They did some kind of briefing as a result. That's it, about the first lieutenant. He just admitted what he'd done. He said, "I took the keys so he'd learn a lesson, because otherwise they never learn. It's the only way they understand." He said to the Palestinian, "Make some kind of order here, organize a line, make sure everything's in order, clean the checkpoint, and then I'll give you back the keys."

97. The roads open for four hours every two days

Unit: Civil Administration
Location: General
Year: 2002

At the beginning of the Intifada, there was trouble with the curfews, for example, they'd just set a curfew and that was it. Forget when you're supposed to open, when whatever. The Civil Administration established regulations for these kinds of things, established that every two days it has to be open for four hours, and they made sure it was open for four hours, but they didn't inform the population, and they didn't announce it on the radio or . . . they just closed a ton of roads. They'd make sure that no village was completely blocked, that an ambulance could get in, and that every village has an exit, and all kinds of things like that.

And how would you know whether a village is blocked?

Earlier I told you that we make connections with individual Palestinians. You just have a man who isn't . . . he's the contact person, you call him, ask him what's going on in the village, what about this, that, what's happening. He tells you. And if he tells you that something's not okay, he's always got your phone number, right? He calls you. And if he tells you something's not okay, then it's your duty to deal with it.

How did the curfews work in the beginning?

In the beginning, this was also in Hebron, there are charts . . . you can request them from the Ministry of Defense, they'll even give them to you, we did it at the time and it's in the bureau of the minister of defense, it was moved to there. But at the beginning, there was an extended period without opening any . . . I think about once a week. I was still in Bet El, but at first there were these very extended curfews, and after that they really did open things: every forty-eight hours for four hours, and on Fridays, because of prayers. Also on Saturdays things were generally open, because there's not a big IDF presence in the area. Slowly, things worked out.

Who decided on the curfew?

The brigade commander.

So there's no kind of system or that you're required to consult with the administration?

No. First of all, he always consults with the administration. But the reason for establishing a curfew is security, so there's nothing the administration can do. That's why the brigade commander makes the decision and he has to inform the division commander, but he doesn't . . . and he has organized guidelines. There are rules.

And where is the administration on this issue? If, say, an administration officer says . . .

If, for example, after forty hours . . . first of all this law has . . . it's a regulation put out by the legal adviser in the West Bank, by the army's legal adviser in the West Bank. This is the regulation he set, but it has exceptions. Meaning, if something happened, you could bring it up to the General Commanding Officer, and he could approve a curfew of longer than forty-eight hours. But those incidents were unusual—

there had to be a really big terror attack. And the administration is meant to remind the brigade commander every forty-eight hours, or to say, "You have to open for four hours, between hours X and Y." And that's it. These are the kinds of things the administration announces ahead of time, so that the population knows about them and is prepared to go out.

How do you update them?

You call the radio, you tell the broadcasters. Even the Fatah radio broadcasters. Back then, there were no Hamas stations. I think today there are.

And they announce it?

Yes.

98. Villages with no water

Unit: Nahal Brigade
Location: Nablus district
Year: 2001

Bet Furik and Bet Dajan are villages that have no water. They bring water in trucks from Nablus.

What do you mean they don't have water?

They're not connected to the water system. You didn't know there were places like that? So that's it, they have these trucks, and every day they transport these containers back and forth, they travel to Nablus and fill them up with water. According to what the truck drivers told us, people there have water pits in their houses, something like that, and they fill them up.

Were there times when you'd prevent the water trucks from going in?

Generally, there was pretty open travel for the trucks, even when there was curfew for everything else, the water trucks could still cross. But during the time when Gandhi* was killed, they decided that was it, no one goes through, not even the water trucks. I remember I annoyed my company commander at that checkpoint, saying this situation couldn't continue, and actually, that same day, that afternoon or maybe the next day, the villages had no water. I don't remember when exactly, but we got a list of authorized drivers pretty fast, and almost all of the drivers were on the list. There were a few who didn't have authorization, and only drivers with authorization could cross.

99. A kind of humanitarian environment

UNIT: CIVIL ADMINISTRATION
LOCATION: GENERAL
YEAR: 2001

I think the Civil Administration didn't wake up until the middle of 2002—it didn't understand the shift from the Oslo Accords to the Second Intifada. It took about a year, a year or more to understand the shift. That it had to take a more military stance and show less concern for communication issues with the Palestinians. So at first the question was "How do we manage? We cut communications with the Palestinians, and so what do we do from now on?" At first the administration was lost, but slowly it found its feet again, it found itself back in the role of quasi-government.

What does that mean, "the administration was lost"?
The Oslo Accords basically determined that the District Coordination and Liaison would maintain contact with the Palestinians. Of course, once the Intifada broke out, the DCL and people like that, people who dealt with the security connection, things like that, their jobs no longer existed. Who was there to meet with? You're not allowed to meet, the government has ordered that you can't meet. So what are you supposed to do? What's your job? Slowly you create a new job for yourself.

*Tourism minister and Knesset member Rechavam Ze'evi.

So what happened in the field? On the one hand, you had a government order, and on the other hand, you had your work to do.

No, so then the Civil Administration focused more on what's called protecting the "fabric" of Palestinian life: access, roads, all kinds of civilian things which are for the most part for the Palestinian population's benefit, and basically ensure a kind of humanitarian environment, and make sure there's no humanitarian disaster or anything like that. That was basically the objective of the Civil Administration during that period. And also to strengthen ties with Palestinian people, but no longer with the Palestinian government. You no longer see the Palestinian government, you see more of the Palestinian people. You forge ties with unofficial sources, as it were.

How does that play out?

For example, at the beginning of the Intifada, transferring goods was very problematic. We went from a time where really anything could go in, and come out, to this new time suddenly, when you have to consider all the time whether to let something out from a security standpoint. So, for example, we worked on organizing the import and export of goods.

How does that work?

In "back-to-back" zones, such as Tarqumia*—you know what I'm talking about. They set up "back-to-back" zones, for example. The last one they set up was in Bitunya,† after 2002. They allow the transfer of goods and inspect the goods to see that they're really bringing in food, or cement, or fuel.

Did the administration establish the guidelines?

Yes, the administration is a pretty small office, but it has a lot of power. At the beginning of the Intifada it didn't get much respect, but it's an office with a load of power.

---

*A checkpoint in the Hebron area, one of the largest in the West Bank and a main point for the passage of goods.

†A checkpoint in the Ramallah sector also predominantly used for transferring goods.

So, let's say there were no goods transferred at some point, and then . . .

No, they couldn't find a secure way to transfer goods, so the Civil Administration, with government funding, of course, went and built these concrete areas. There was one in Tarqumia, but not in Hawwara, Bitunya, or Jalama. Today I think there's one in Qalqilya, but I'm not sure, I haven't been there in a long time. That's what the administration does, it makes sure goods are transferred.

100. One of the workers was crushed to death

UNIT: EREZ CHECKPOINT
LOCATION: GAZA STRIP
YEAR: 2003

Every time they had to get an ambulance across, an ambulance would come from both sides, a Palestinian ambulance and an Israeli one, and they'd transfer the person from one ambulance to the other.

When do they transfer someone to an Israeli ambulance? Why do they need to cross into Israel?

I imagine they go to hospitals for injuries, or if a woman's in labor, for example. I sit in the operations room, so I don't know the details exactly. I know there's someone sick, I have his name, ID number, and I check with the District Coordination and Liaison to see if he's okay, and then I allow them to transfer him, but I don't know the person's medical history.

No, but you hear that a woman's in labor, or that someone's sick . . .

They tell me about special cases, such as a case involving a pacemaker, because they pass everyone through a metal detector, and there's certain medical equipment which sets off a metal detector. There's a separate inspection for those kinds of cases.

So everyone goes through a metal detector? Even "back-to-back"? What kind of incidents were there?

If a woman's in labor, and has to wait until she gets to the other side, she'll give birth at the checkpoint . . . I imagine that a woman in labor would have to go through the process, and there were all kinds of sick people there, kids who needed medical attention.

When do they open the checkpoint?

In the morning, from eight to ten, and again in the afternoon. There's a crossing into Israel, and there's also a small checkpoint for workers crossing from the strip to areas nearby. They go out, work, and come back.

So where were you?

The battalion was responsible for both of these crossings, we're a crossings battalion, responsible for all of the crossings, and for everything that goes through the crossings. Sometimes there were instructions to change the opening and closing hours, but for the most part it was open two to three hours in the morning, and again for three hours in the afternoon.

How many people would cross?

I don't know exact numbers. I know that a lot of people crossed. They don't tell us about everyone who's crossing. They say, "The crossing is open, the crossing is closed."

You weren't curious to see the things outside the operations room?

When I first got there, I'd been in the battalion for something like three weeks, and then they brought me down to the company. When I was in the battalion, I once went to the checkpoint to see what it was all about, to see who I'm talking to all the time, and I remember that people were waiting to cross, and it was so crowded, and there was a person who was pressed too hard against the gate, and they brought him through the checkpoint to treat him and he died—he was crushed to death at the checkpoint.

He wasn't sick or anything?

As far as I know, he wasn't sick, but the checkpoint is built like this: here there's bars, there's a revolving door like at the university where you can't exit or enter, and then there's a direction to exit. They wait for them to open the crossing, and they push one another from the pressure, and one of them was just crushed by the bars.

Do you remember the approximate width of the crossing?

The place with the revolving door was one-by-one, they stand next to it, there's a pretty wide iron fence, and the whole platform of the crossing is about the size of this room. It's divided into two lanes, there's a door and there's another waiting area. That whole part was full of people.

What happened?

I don't know, I was in the army for a month and a half, and this was the first thing I saw, and it was a shock. He fainted, they tried to treat him, they brought in a medic, and he was unsuccessful.

Where did they keep him? Where was he released from the . . . ?

I don't deal with things like that. I stood on the side, I'd arrived in the middle of the chaos. I imagine that if someone faints, they let him pass.

And then what did they do?

I left after the medic was unable to treat him. I left—it was enough for me. I didn't need to see any more and I left. I assume they removed the body and brought it to the appropriate authorities, certainly through the DCL.

What did they say afterward in the debriefing?

I don't know what happened at the debriefing.

But did they speak about it afterward?

It wasn't something they talked about in the operations room or dealt with there, I imagine that they spoke about it more over at the DCL, because it's relevant to their work. And at the checkpoint, I imagine. Though if a soldier's standing at the checkpoint before it opens and everyone's pushing each other, he can't just say, "Okay, stop pushing . . ." They're like kids waiting to get into a concert who keep pushing each other, even when you tell them to stand nicely. Of course there's a difference, but I think that in this case, the very most that can be done is that the soldier standing there can try and tell them not to overdo it or move. But no more than that. You can't do anything meaningful when you're faced with the fact that many people are trying to cross in a limited time.

Did the story about the man who was killed get any attention?

As far as I know—no. But I didn't look for news about it, and I think there's nothing to do about it. Israelis are more interested in news about a terrorist attack, or a near-terrorist attack, or a thwarted terrorist attack, more than in an Arab who was killed. Mostly, the news tries to show our side, and what happens between us and them, and how they attack us.

101. We shot at fishermen, cut their nets

UNIT: NAVY
LOCATION: GAZA STRIP
YEAR: 2005–2007

There's an area that borders Gaza, an area called Area K, which is under the navy's control. Both before and after the disengagement, nothing changed with regard to the sea sector, everything remained the same. The only thing that changed was that Area K divided Israel and Gaza, Area M was between Egypt and Gaza, and in the middle there was another partition, which prevented boats from crossing from the Rafah harbor to the Gaza harbor. This partition disappeared with the disengagement, and then afterward it was open again. That was the only plus. I remember that near Area K, between Israel and Gaza, there were kids who would get up early in the morning, kids as young as four or six. Seventy percent of the population in Gaza lives on fishing. It's their bread and water and everything. If there's no fish, there's no food. They'd go to the off-limits areas early in the morning, around four or five every morning. They'd go there because the other area is crowded with fishermen. It's a small area, and the fish swim up there because there are no fishermen. The kids always tried to scout it out and cross over, and every morning we'd shoot in their direction to scare them off, it got to the point of shooting at the kids' feet where they'd stand on the beach, or at those heading in that direction on a surfboard. We had Druze police officers on board who'd scream at them in Arabic and curse them. Afterward, you could look at the cameras and see the kids crying, poor kids.

What does that mean, "shoot in their direction"?

It starts with shooting in the air, then it shifts to shooting close by, and in extreme cases it becomes shooting toward their legs. I didn't shoot at anyone's legs, but there were other ships in my company that did.

What distance did you shoot from?

Far, from five hundred or six hundred meters. You shoot with a Rafael heavy machine gun, it's all automatic.

Where do you aim?

It's about perspective. In the camera, there's a measure for height and a measure for width, and you mark with the cursor where you want the bullet to go, and it cancels out the effect of the waves and hits where it's supposed to, it's precise.

You aim a meter away from the surfboard?

More like five or six meters away. There were cases I heard about where they hit the surfboard, but I didn't see it. They said the shrapnel hit them, the ricochet of the bullet hitting the water. There were other things that bothered me, there's this thing with Palestinian fishing nets. Their nets cost around four thousand shekels, which is like a million dollars for us. When they disobeyed us a lot, we'd sink their nets.

They leave their nets in the water, the nets stay in the water for something like six hours. The Dabur* comes along and cuts their nets.

Why?

As a punishment.

For what?

For the fact that they'd disobeyed us too many times. Let's say a boat drifts over to an area that's off-limits, so a Dabur comes, circles, shoots in the air, and goes back. Then an hour later, the boat comes back and so does the Dabur. The third time around, the Dabur starts shooting at the nets, at the boat, and then shooting to sink them. That never happened with me, but I've shot at the boat and nets.

But how do you know whose net it is?

The boat is dragging the net. It's always connected to the boat.

Is the off-limits area the one that's close to Israel?

There's the area that's close to Israel, and the area along the Israeli-Egyptian border. The sea border is three miles out, something like twenty miles wide, about thirty kilometers.

This is when you take into account the twenty miles between Gaza and Egypt and between Israel and Gaza?

Yes.

These twenty miles, are they taken from Israel's area or from Gaza's?

What do you think? Of course Gaza's. Not only that, Israel's sea border is twelve miles out, and Gaza's is only three. They've got just those three miles, which lie in the direction of the Mediterranean, because of one reason, because Israel wants its gas, and there's an offshore drilling rig something like three and a half miles facing the Gaza Strip, which should be Palestinian, except that it's ours. They work there like crazy,

---

*A navy patrol boat.

and Shayelet 13, the Navy Special Forces unit, provides security. A bird comes near the area, they shoot it. There is an insane amount of security for that thing. One time there were Egyptian fishing nets that crossed the three miles, and we dealt with them, it was a total disaster.

Meaning?

They were in international waters, and we don't have jurisdiction there, but we'd go out and shoot at them.

At Egyptian fishing nets?

Yes. And we're at peace with Egypt.

102. Training in the middle of the village, in the middle of the night

UNIT: PARATROOPERS [RESERVES]
LOCATION: TUL KAREM DISTRICT
YEAR: 2007

In principle, the army, since the time of the last war, came to the conclusion that it needs to take advantage of every day of a soldier's reserve duty to get him completely prepared for the next war that's coming. And so regular pre-operation training was converted to expanded pre-operation training. Much more serious, a lot more exercises, on a much bigger scale. Normally you do the firing range and some kind of dismounting from the Hummer to remember how to do it. And that's the preparation for the front. Now it's a much bigger exercise. Now, I started my reserve duty on March 11. It was the second time I did reserve duty in Ariel. We knew that reserve duty would begin with three or four days of training, and then we'd continue to the front. On the Friday before—the eleventh was a Sunday—on the Friday before, I went to my parents', and on the way I'm listening to the news, and they're talking about an exercise carried out by the Central Paratroopers Brigade, pre-operations training in the village of Beit Lid. Now—that's me. Meaning, it's clear to me that if that's what the battalion before me did, then that's what I'm going to do on Sunday.

So I listened carefully, and apparently, it was an exercise done on terrain like Lebanon's, in the Shomron, where we'd simulate movement
toward targets, with lookouts and ambushes and all kinds of things
like that, and it would end with occupying some village. Now, what
they said on the news was that there'd been complaints . . . again, the
local villages are Arab, so their complaints aren't heard as loudly, but
soldiers in the company, in the battalions, had complained. First of all,
they said they hadn't received orders about opening fire. Now, why
wouldn't you get orders for opening fire? Because basically, on the one
hand, you're doing a training exercise, and there are tons of other
forces out there, and tons of soldiers who've been walking all night and
are tired . . . you start putting a bullet in the chamber or loading a
magazine, and you'll end up with some friendly fire. On the other
hand, it's not an Israeli village, it's not like you're doing the training
exercise on a kibbutz or something like that. There's a real threat. And
Intelligence knows there are a lot of hunters there—they hunt a lot of
wild boars in the area. There's a chance you'll see someone armed with
a weapon in the middle of the night. What are you going to do? Nothing. They had no orders. More, the soldiers thought the whole man-
agement of the exercise was pretty strange. That you go into a village
in the middle of the night, where there isn't . . . and by the end, you're
using blanks and stun grenades and explosives. It's a village where the
people living there presented no threat beforehand, no threat afterward—or maybe afterward they will—and you basically disrupt their
whole night. Children pee in their beds, mothers scream, the things
that happen when you go into . . . An attorney spoke on the radio, and
they put my deputy brigade commander on, the deputy brigade commander of that same brigade. And the guy's talking, how important it
is after Lebanon to train and whatever, and everything is okay. And he
concludes with a sentence that stunned me. He said, "I was the last to
leave the village in the morning, and the locals, all smiles and understanding, blessed me to go in peace." Which is, beyond the ignorance
and the arrogance with which he allows himself to speak, you know,
apologize, say that the military attorney general is checking it out, give
a military response maybe, but I just wish an exercise like that would

happen on the kibbutz where the deputy brigade commander lives. That at four in the morning they go in with stun grenades and all that, and I want to see him throwing rice in the morning* when the soldiers leave. Because it's really chutzpah, like nothing else. Now, I imagined, in my naïveté, that it would be different for us. Meaning we'd get there, and since the story had already made it to the media, and there's a military attorney general and other legal authorities involved, that someone would take care of it. Now, I got to reserve duty on Sunday, I signed off because I had to return to the center of the country for a day, and then I came back to reserve duty. When I came back to reserve duty, it was already Tuesday, and then I understood that they were at the height of preparations for this exercise. The location and whatever wasn't exactly talked about . . . In short, they were at the height of preparations for the exercise. Now, the story of everything that I'd heard was still running through my head, and I wanted to see if there'd be some kind of difference. Since I arrived at the second-to-last briefing—not that there were many—but I arrived at the second-to-last briefing by the deputy company commander, a security briefing, and he opened with, "Guys, I don't care. You can go to the media, tell them whatever you want, but what's important to me is that you do this, this, and that . . ." And then I said that if this is the tone, if this is his manner of speaking, then nothing's going to change. And in reality, what happened was exactly what the soldiers of the previous battalion exercise had said—the same thing with us. We walked all night and did ambushes and invasions here and there and everything, what you do during an exercise like that. And in the early hours of the morning we found ourselves in al-Hayad, ready to start the incursion into the village itself. Again, I don't remember receiving unequivocal orders about opening fire. It could be he said something, but since I don't remember it now, and it was just a month ago, apparently it was vague enough that I didn't exactly understand the procedure. And even if he did say it, I don't think that after a night like that I'd be able to differentiate between a soldier and a Palestinian, I don't know what kind of

*A traditional gesture of welcome.

Palestinian or Israeli Arab goes out with his weapon to hunt boars near the village, anything unpleasant could develop in this situation . . . what we did was what they'd outlined. We entered the village and captured houses, but we didn't go into the houses.

But you went into the courtyards.

You go in . . . we went into an area near the wadi. It's an Arab village and it's different . . . the definition of a courtyard, what's yours and what's mine, are different. But we certainly went through houses, inside the courtyards of houses, we didn't just stay on the roads. Now that's just what I saw, I'm not the whole battalion. I don't know what the rest of the battalion did . . . I do know, and maybe this is the only change that took place, that after they said to us that from now on we were supposed to go into the houses and take them using urban combat techniques, then they said we weren't. I don't know if that meant that the forces before us did it during the exercise, and that we weren't going to, or if in principle that's what you do during a war when you go into someone's house, I don't know. And that still has to be checked, if they really went into the houses. Because if they did, then they'd learned something. Okay, so look, we finished the exercise in the middle of the village. We started marching toward the buses that were waiting a few kilometers away. Look, you see the residents there standing, looking around, smiling and whatever. The deputy brigade commander's words came back to me, of course, but it's not smiles and understanding. It's smiles and understanding that this is the fourth or fifth time this exercise has happened in their village without anyone coordinating it with them beforehand. I don't know if they informed them the night before, or if they didn't. That's it, in any case, with that exercise. I was stunned that no one in the reserve unit, that there wasn't, you know, when you're a conscript no one raises his voice at all, but among the reserve unit there was no voice of opposition, asking . . .

No one said anything?

Listen, everyone was there, I don't know of anyone who didn't take part in the exercise. I didn't hear of anyone getting up during the

briefing and say, Listen, this isn't right, this isn't appropriate, this isn't . . .
no. Nothing.

103. They file the complaint and move on

Unit: Civil Administration
Location: General
Year: 2001

Confiscating IDs is forbidden, and it's not supposed to happen. Most
of the checkpoints do it all the time, I think. And just grabbing someone on the road and taking his ID shouldn't happen at all. It's illegal,
according to the legal adviser. It's hard to say, it happened a lot, I
think.

What does it mean for a Palestinian not to have an ID?

It's like you without an ID, but seventy times worse. Because you, what
do you need your ID for? To open a bank account, more or less just that.
They need their ID for everything. To get a permit they need an ID, to
move one meter they need an ID. It's like, taking complete control.
There's not a thing he can do about it. Apart from the financial damage.

So what do they do?

They go back home in a roundabout way, if they can. Meaning, we force
them to make another trek just to go home. Most of them start by calling the Palestinian Authority, and then the PA would turn to us—all of
it goes through the DCL—and then either they'd come and get back
their IDs, or they'd just get a new one. At some point it wasn't through
the PA anymore, they'd know to go to the District Coordination Liaison
to get the ID.

*But how can you get to the DCL—aren't there checkpoints along the
way?*

Correct. That's where the roundabout way comes into play. We force
them to do very strange things.

You force them to bypass the checkpoints, because they're not able to cross at the checkpoints.

Yes, correct. And God forbid someone stops them without an ID, forget about it. He goes straight to the Ofer base detention facility or something. At some point they learned to travel with a spare ID, because they didn't have much choice. But soldiers would confiscate loads of IDs. Loads.

You don't complain to your higher-ups?

You do.

And then what?

In the end, the soldier at the checkpoint is king. He's the king. It doesn't matter how many conversations and briefings there are. We briefed the brigade commander and the battalion commander and the company commander and the platoon commander and the soldier. And he's king. He's there in the heat for eight hours with a helmet and flak jacket—he's king. And if the Border Police is there on the road when there's no one else around—totally. That's how it is.

And what do the higher-ups say?

The higher-ups say, "No, no, no, it's not okay." And that's it. They take active steps, but what can you do at the end of the day, when a soldier is standing there by himself? Either he's a decent human being or he isn't. Either it went to his head or it didn't. I'm pretty sure everyone knew it's illegal and not okay. Where did this thing with confiscating keys come from? I don't know who came up with it. It also doesn't seem legal to me.

Did you get complaints about that as well?

Of course. But again, we get a complaint and that's it. Aside from filing it, what can you do?

You don't have any power or authority?

No. Meaning, even if I did, even if I were to do a debriefing and a briefing for all the forces in the sector, what would it do? You can't educate Border Police. I think they made most of the problems, but it's a strategic decision to have them directly involved with the Palestinians. The government knew what it was doing. Because the Border Police are the best at beating them up. And that's it.

104. Inefficiency and indifference

UNIT: MILITARY POLICE
LOCATION: EYAL CROSSING
YEAR: 2008–2009

The checkpoint was built with lanes—a Jewish lane, a Palestinian lane, and a lane for trucks. The Jews had to put a sticker on their car, and there was a fight about it, "Why should I have to put a sticker on my car? Why should I have to be checked whenever I leave my house?" It was tense with the settlers, with the Palestinians, with everyone.

Palestinians needed a permit as well at this checkpoint?
Yes . . . The orders were contradictory, and they changed them every second. They'd play with you—yes, and then no.

Which orders would change?
The amount of meat they could have, for example. Anything you can't inspect, you don't allow it through. Someone trying to cross with a sofa—you can't inspect it, so you call and then he can cross.

Did you check meat according to weight?
By sight. You look at the approximate number of bags. If someone tried to hide some meat, I'd send him back, even just a kilogram. The checkpoint was plagued by inefficiency and indifference.

This was the trans-Samaria checkpoint, checkpoint 107?
There was checkpoint 709, which was next to Tul Karem. The one we were talking about is checkpoint 109.

With the exception of trans-Samaria, are all of the checkpoints along the fence?

I don't know about 709 because I wasn't there very often, and they took it down for a while, so I can't say. There was the Efraim gate, which is a crossing, which was like 107. The Efraim gate was in Tul Karem, and 107 was in Qalqilya. Both of them are pedestrian terminals, at peak times the number of Palestinians was around three thousand. The one at 107 is a pedestrian terminal, and 109 is for vehicles. Both of them are more or less in the same place. The Efraim gate was near 709, near Tul Karem. The Efraim gate is for vehicles, and 709 is for pedestrians. There was another checkpoint near trans-Samaria for Palestinians, and there was an inspection pillbox there, I don't even remember what it was called. There was a twelve-hour post there, where you were paired with someone else and you'd carry out inspections.

What was the purpose of that checkpoint?

Like all checkpoints, to prevent terrorist activity.

But why are there only two soldiers there?

Yes, just two soldiers. You're there for twelve hours and soldiers are stationed outside the post, inspecting vehicles. And we're there with a metal detector and an X-ray, and we're inspecting pedestrians at the same time. This went on for twelve hours a day.

Is there also a glass wall there?

Yes. You're alone in the room, you speak with them through a loudspeaker, you hear beeping, people, you get crazy headaches. We did a lot of stupid things to get through the boredom. We'd call to other posts and hang up out of boredom. We'd swear at each other over the PA system. I'd swear all day there.

How do you control such a large number of people?

You don't. In the middle there are gates that lock, but sometimes for everyone to cross, there were times when the gates beeped and someone was able to cross even though he hadn't been checked. We saw that the IDF didn't provide enough people to do the mission, and there was a lack of communication between you and your commanders, and in the end people would sleep in the booth, out of indifference they'd leave the gates open and let people cross.

Even during the congestion?

Yes—it's the most congested when you've just woken up, which is when you're the most tired. The hours when it opened were difficult in a really crazy way.

This was when you'd behave differently?

Yes, you'd sometimes curse at the Palestinian[s] trying to cross . . . we held them up outside. If anyone so much as yelled "Soldier!" near the gate, we'd keep them another twenty minutes. Total indifference.

Were there times when checkpoint 107 was closed?

Yes, because you can cross into Israel from there. It was closed on Shabbat and the holidays, and the orders weren't very clear, because sometimes you came across a barrier where someone with such-and-such kind of documentation could cross, and someone with another kind couldn't, and then they change the orders a second later. You don't know what's going to happen tomorrow. You wait for the eleventh hour to see what's going to happen. Sometimes they close it right at the last second, and you don't know what to say to the Palestinians there. The whole Eyal company, the checkpoints overall, the guidelines are equivocal, there's no prior information. You get the feeling that they just throw you in and you figure things out along the way. It annoyed us, because as soldiers we didn't know when to prepare to go to sleep, how to organize a shift, and what to expect.

On the Palestinian side, we didn't know how to answer their questions, whether they can bring their brother or their son. It happened a lot that someone would come, and you say one thing, and in the middle of the conversation another soldier comes over and says something different. The guy gets annoyed because he was stuck in the DCL for nonsense. Or, they don't let someone cross with his son to see a doctor, because he doesn't have a permit, but if he says some bullshit, like he's going to see his mother in Israel, then they do let him cross. There were no clear answers, the DCL always changed its mind, it wasn't organized, they didn't know who could cross and who couldn't. The general orders were very clear, but during the actual process you didn't know what you were supposed to do. You can't say anything to a Palestinian who's yelling at you, you depend on the orders. So you call the commander and he says, "You deal with him, just tell him no." You fight with him for an hour. He goes to the DCL and they tell him he can cross, you call the DCL and you realize there are many situations where a person gives up and goes home.

Were you ever in a situation where there were three thousand people at the entrance and you told everyone to go home?
Yes.

How many times a month does that happen?
It's not times per month. I yelled at them to go home when the checkpoint was closed, I myself did that more than five times during my service. That's not every month, but it happens a few times a year. Afterward they try to get through via another crossing, and another mess starts there. The Qalqilya area is really a mess, unlike the Jenin area, where the orders were clear.

105. Anyone raised his voice, we'd tie him up

Unit: Armored Corps
Location: Nablus
Year: 2003

There was this checkpoint inside Nablus itself, this road that connected Bet Furik with other villages east of Nablus. We'd give them a hell of a time there. We'd detain whoever we felt like at that checkpoint, chase after runaways. That's what we did at that checkpoint.

Detainees, Ramallah. Photographer: Sagi Blumberg

By definition? Someone told you, "This is where you can detain whoever you want"?

It was a checkpoint. You had to check everyone going through to make sure there were no wanted people and so on. I don't think our superiors gave us instructions to detain anyone. The company commander had orders that we had to detain whoever tried to run away, and anyone whose IDs we needed to clear with the police. We'd pass on the details to the police, to our ops room, and our war room would pass them to the battalion war room, and from there to the security services or the police. It would take about twenty or thirty minutes for them to get back to us for every number we passed on. With all the communications glitches and the rain and sun and everything else, people were held up for quite a while. Anyone got rude in the meantime, or raised his voice, or just got on our nerves, we'd tie him up, meaning with handcuffs.

Handcuff and blindfold him?

Handcuff him. Blindfolding was only for when they went really overboard. We'd make them kneel, dry them out.

For how long?

It could be up to eight or nine hours. Until we'd get tired of it. Then when we changed guards we'd instruct the shift replacing us to leave him there for at least another two hours. "This one is really rude." Or, "That guy, let him go soon, he's not guilty." Stuff like that. That's how it worked, essentially.

106. One of the veteran soldiers decided to humiliate him

UNIT: ARTILLERY CORPS
LOCATION: WADI ARA
YEAR: 2001

One of the things we did was catching illegal aliens near the seam between Umm al Fahm and another place there. Seeing these illegal aliens and whatever, I remember one of the veteran soldiers . . . like every time there was this thing of chasing after people running away, and I never understood what the big deal was. They'd catch them, make them sit next to us, and they'd just humiliate them with all this degrading talk. Like saying shut up to adults, to young people, just to people . . . and these are the nicest people in the world, and the soldiers said to them, "Shut your mouth" and whatever, and there were really unbelievable situations. It shifted from trying to humiliate someone and then suddenly being nice to him. Suddenly he brings him popsicles and cigarettes when he comes back, things like that . . .

Who, the soldier brings these things to the Palestinian?

No, the Palestinian brings him the stuff. And then all of a sudden it seems okay, but . . .

The soldiers would take bribes, gifts?

They'd just detain them, for no reason. You check their papers, say "have a good day," whatever. Let's just say they weren't as humane and professional as possible. I bought an Arabic conversation book and learned how to say "You can't walk here," and I asked my parents for help, they speak Arabic.

Wait, so the soldiers detain people even if they have papers and everything? They just hold them?

Yes, for no reason. "Sit here, stay here." And there's no need. If someone can't cross, then just tell him to go back. And if he can, then let him cross. But there was one argument where that veteran soldier just decided to humiliate this guy. It was just when we were about to leave the post, and he told the guy to lie down on the floor, and this was the most like . . . he was a twenty-five-year-old guy, a student, nice, and this soldier just decided to humiliate him. He made him lie down on his stomach . . .

This was a soldier or a commander?

A veteran soldier, he had more say than the commanders. The guy was dressed nicely, button-down shirt, jeans. He just told him to lie on the floor on his stomach. And he put his foot on his neck, here, and cocked his weapon and yelled at him, "Why are you crossing here, don't cross here anymore . . ." And this and that . . . and the soldier started telling him to do all kinds of things, telling him to stand, then telling him to lie on his stomach, he told him things like that. I yelled at him, "Enough, let him go, stop," I was in shock. The situation really threw me. I thought the soldier was an animal, not a human being. I think he's a shitty human being. I couldn't stand him before all this, and afterward I couldn't stand him even more. But no, I didn't pass it on or anything. There was no one who'd listen.

Why didn't you tell anyone?

Because this guy was pals with everyone. I think even the officers knew about it. The commander was also there. The commander didn't see it as anything unprofessional, apparently.

An officer?

A commander, a squad commander. I decided right then and there that I want nothing to do with this crazy place, if this is how they humiliate people who've done nothing wrong. And even if they did commit a crime, you're not allowed to lift your hand against them, it's forbidden. I was shocked. I don't know if the guy was Palestinian or an Israeli citizen. There's a good chance he was an Israeli citizen, because Umm al Fahm is Israeli. There was another situation in the same place, where they stopped someone's car and started yelling at him. It was always the group of veteran soldiers who'd do this kind of thing. And we'd do what we had to do—check his documents. They did it for some action, or just to pass the time, so they'd have something to talk about at home. To kill time, I guess. They started dismantling this guy's car. Yelling at him. The guy said he was a member of B'Tselem and a citizen of Umm al Fahm. They kept abusing him anyway. They don't even know what B'Tselem is. They were idiots. And then it ended. Aside from that, from those two situations, that's how it was.

107. It's the power that you have

Unit: Civil Administration
Location: Jericho district
Year: 2001

I'd go out on patrols in different sectors to see how the soldiers—our soldiers, too—to see how they treated the Palestinians. It disgusts you as a human being. But you're part of the system, and more, if you aren't part of that base, then there isn't much you can do. Disgusting things. Every Civil Administration soldier knows what an open-sided shelter is. There's the open-sided shelter outside the DCL, and the Palestinians wait there. All the Palestinians who come to request a permit wait there. And there's the window. They approach the window—a bullet-proof window, on the other side of the glass, our soldiers are sitting there and printing out permits. They give them the permits. A Palestinian

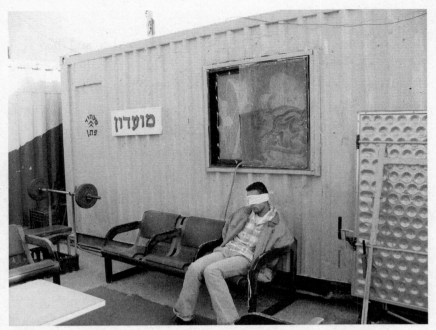

Detainee being held at IDF post, Nablus, 2004. The photographer served in the
Paratroopers Brigade.

can sit and dry out in that open-sided shelter for five hours, and even
longer, for a few days.

Because?

The "because" is very hard for me to explain. It's not that the soldier
lets the Palestinian dry out for no reason. No. He has to go through a
Shin Bet check—I don't remember the exact procedure anymore. But
let's just say that if these were Israelis, it wouldn't be like that. I saw for
myself disgusting things. In the DCL, there was a shade for the window,
so the Palestinians couldn't see you. So you can lower the shade and
they just sit outside, but when the shade goes up you can see soldiers
inside playing soccer, and all kinds of nonsense, and laughing at everyone sitting outside, telling someone to "Come," so he comes over, and
then saying, "No, no, sit." It's just the power that you have. At some
point it fucks you up, if you're a human being.

108. The checkpoint commander called himself "the doctor"

UNIT: GOLANI BRIGADE
LOCATION: JENIN DISTRICT
YEAR: 2002

I remember we had a squad commander in the company who called himself "the doctor." He really liked looking at people who came with X-rays. I also had to open it to see the name on the X-ray and whether it matched the ID. He'd look at the X-ray, peer at it as if he were deciding to do some kind of physical inspection. It was all a joke . . . Someone once said he had a headache, so the commander felt his skull and said, "No, no, you're okay." Something like that. It really cracked the soldiers up. I remember everyone talking about how cool that squad commander was.

109. You're undermining my authority

UNIT: PARATROOPERS
LOCATION: HEBRON DISTRICT
YEAR: 2001

I remember the subtleties of the checkpoint better, not the extreme cases of abuse, rather what caused them. That's where my awareness of the checkpoints came from, I'd think about it a lot. There was one time, afterward I used the phrase even as a commander, where some soldier took a Krembo snack. I grabbed him afterward, even though by then he couldn't give the snack back, there was no one to give it back to, and I said that he shouldn't do it, I don't remember exactly what I said, I said something about it. And his response was, "You're undermining my authority." To me, these words stand for the terrible thing that checkpoints do to a normal person—not to someone who beats up Arabs, and there are plenty of those. This is what checkpoints do to an average kind of guy, someone who does nothing out of the ordinary. This kind of guy has no authority, but he doesn't need any authority toward a forty- or fifty- or twenty-year-old who comes to cross the checkpoint. There's no issue of authority here. Feeling "I'm above them" is irrelevant—you're already above them. You tell them when they can cross and when they can't, if they're unruly you get annoyed, and you have the power to get annoyed because you have a weapon and you can close the checkpoint. So you control them. And when you suddenly say to someone, "Don't do so-and-so," you're undermining his authority. So this phrase, "You're undermining my authority," stayed with me till my last day of service, and to me it says everything, because we're talking about something minor, it's not a soldier beating someone up, it's not punching an Arab or hitting him with the butt of the weapon. It's a basic outlook, everything begins with that. I don't know how many of our soldiers reach that point, but let's say it's infantry, Armored Corps, Artillery, Anti-aircraft, Engineering Corps. It's a lot. And there are plenty of others, it's not just them. It doesn't matter how much they oppose ideologically, it makes its way into you, this sense of supremacy. When I'm at the checkpoint, the hardest thing for me is how annoyed the soldiers get, it's not just that they get annoyed for no reason, it's like when a teacher gets annoyed. "You're not doing what I told you to? I'll show you what's what." Fuck, I'm standing here directing their traffic like a retard, so they better listen to what I'm saying. Of course, the more extreme response is, "I'm standing here with a weapon so do what I tell you. I decide who crosses and who doesn't. I decide when to open the checkpoint and when not to." It's also kind of arbitrary. For those higher up, and I don't know at what level, but I'm convinced—and I have many friends who are angry that I say this—but I'm convinced that the arbitrariness is a strategy. A strategy to undermine their confidence, their stability, so they won't know what's going to happen tomorrow. I'm convinced of it. I don't think it's some kind of stupidity from someone higher up, I think it's a policy, a strategy. I'm convinced.

110. You feel like one more second and you'll spray them with bullets

UNIT: CIVIL ADMINISTRATION
LOCATION: JERICHO AREA
YEAR: 2001

There's a checkpoint right next to the Jericho DCL, checkpoint 327. The battalion at that front would take charge of the checkpoint, and we'd send a soldier or an officer there to reinforce them for a few hours with this whole business of permits and things like that. And when I went there, they'd be standing there for, say, eight hours on average, more or less, with a helmet and flak jacket, in the sweltering heat of the valley, which is hard to describe in words, and they just deal with non-stop shit all the time. And if there was no soldier or an officer of ours, the soldiers were clueless about what kind of permit lets you cross and what permit doesn't. And all of this stress with the Palestinians—until you see it for yourself, you can't understand it, it fucks you up. I really understand the soldiers who went crazy at the checkpoint. It fucks you up. It's hard to explain. Jericho is hard because of the bridge there and the people who want to go to Jordan, there are just so many people going through there. And you don't really understand the orders. So, people can cross? They can't cross? If they have a passport, then they can? I don't know. The soldiers line everyone up and you have to start looking through their vegetables, inside the truck, because the day before they found a rocket in the Jenin district. And you have to check inside every ambulance . . . and the woman with the elderly mother is yelling in your face, and you yell at them all the time, "Get back, get back," and you go crazy. At first you think you're a Nazi soldier, you feel like some kind of Nazi soldier, then at some point you let go of that idea, because how long can you feel like you're a Nazi? So you just go with it. And it fucks you up. Really. Any soldier who didn't go crazy, I think there's something wrong with him. Or he shut himself off entirely.

What do you mean by "At first you think you're a Nazi soldier"?

Because you yell at them in a kind of Arabic-Hebrew, because soldiers don't know Arabic. We know a bit, so we try to help them. Then you yell at them in a kind of Arabic-Hebrew, "Get back." And they don't pay attention. So you start to raise your weapon, as if you're really going to do something with it, and everyone there, women and children start to cry, and they're also yelling, and it's hot, and you feel like one more second and you'll spray them with bullets. You just don't understand what you're doing there. At least I didn't.

111. What's the thing with closing the parking lot?

UNIT: CIVIL ADMINISTRATION
LOCATION: NABLUS AREA
YEAR: 2006

There was a story about soldiers creating dirt barriers in the parking lot between Askar and Ein Bidan in Nablus. It's a parking lot specially set aside for Palestinian public transportation and private vehicles. It's something like three kilometers from Nablus. Based on a report, the soldiers got to the parking lot, and they shot in the air and told the Palestinians to leave the area. After all of the residents left, the soldiers built dirt mounds with a backhoe and blocked access to the parking lot. The army didn't bother to check that there were no cars at the checkpoint. The backhoes came at four or five in the morning, they made dirt blockades. The Palestinian bus drivers came to the lot around seven or eight in the morning, and they had no way to get out. There were a lot of cars there, and whoever had a small car did what every Palestinian did, they bypassed the barrier. But the trucks and the buses, there was something like thirty vehicles there, they just couldn't get out. So twenty private cars and three buses were stuck in the parking lot. By the way, one of the jeeps was still in the area.

Was it an army jeep, or the District Coordination and Liaison jeep?

The army jeep. We even got the license plate number.

How did you get the details?

The Palestinians saw the license plate.

Did you verify it?

I couldn't verify it, I did the primary investigation. Afterward, it became clear that the backhoe created a double barrier and hermetically sealed the area. The army claimed that all of the vehicles were able to get out, and the Palestinians claimed they couldn't. In the end, the locals paid the workers to take down the barriers. But the trucks and three buses still couldn't cross. They took down part of the barrier, and the private cars that were detained until 15:00 crossed at 18:37. The battalion sent word that it would send a team to open the barrier. At 22:39 it still wasn't open, at 22:48 it still wasn't open. At 22:48 they asked for permission to bring a private Palestinian backhoe to open it up.

Who brought it?

The Palestinians brought it, they asked us for permission. The Palestinians lost a day of work. At seven o'clock the next morning they started opening the barriers, and at ten o'clock they crossed. A daylong story, started at eight or nine in the morning.

What was the reason for closing the parking lot?

It had access to the village or something, I don't know.

112. We confiscated keys and vehicles

Unit: Nahal Brigade
Location: Nablus district
Year: 2001

Vehicles were confiscated there, they confiscated people's keys if they pushed in line or came to the wrong place, so they decided to "educate" them.

They took people's keys and then gave them back, or they put them aside and said something like, "Bye, go home"?

Yeah, like that. They confiscated a lot of IDs, of people who weren't allowed to cross, or something like that. They were supposed to return at night and ask for them back before they closed the checkpoint, at eight p.m.

So they'd wait all day?

They could go back to their side, to the Palestinian side, as long as they didn't cross the checkpoint.

Why do you confiscate someone's ID?

As a punishment. People weren't allowed to cross, but they tried anyway.

113. Closing roads? It's political

Unit: Nahal Brigade
Location: Hebron
Year: 2008

Were there curfews while you were in Hebron?

No.

If I'm not mistaken, didn't the Supreme Court rule during your time there that David road had to be opened?

The Supreme Court made its decision before we were there, and Palestinians were permitted to use it. Later the road was closed, I don't know why. It was closed when I was in Hebron. This whole thing about disrupting people's lives, opening and closing roads, it's mainly a question of policy. There's never any unequivocal security reason to do it. There isn't a legal one, either. Opening things up to allow movement and life and development, or shutting them down, it's a debate between government and the administration. I remember that in

Rantis, there was a high-ranking commander who spoke to us once, who said he was unequivocally opposed to revitalizing the fabric of life. He'd prefer to do anything other than blocking the roads, going into villages, preventing people from leaving their homes. What I started to understand, and only after a long time, was that he didn't necessarily represent the army's view or the government's. There are conflicting interests on this. It depends who gets the ruling, and how he thinks. Hebron was complicated because there actually were areas . . . I remember when they explained it to us, Hamas was organizing there. People who were killed in Hebron during our time there were killed by other Palestinians, in clan warfare, so opening the roads was dangerous—again, it depends on which area it is, and it requires familiarity with the issues. It's more a political question and less a military one. They tell you the road is blocked, so it's blocked. This has a lot of impact on people's lives there. There were incidents where people broke through, and we had to detain them. It also has to do with a policy of punishment, but we didn't have the authority to punish people, so we'd detain them for three hours, which was defined.

Were they restrained?

We preferred not to restrain them. We detained them, took down their details, and you have to have authority to detain a person as . . . I don't know if every soldier could, but you could as the mission commander. They'd use detention to make the point that the roads really were blocked. I don't think it worked. I tried to be decent. I told the person that he'd been detained for a security reason—I didn't have to tell him whether he was suspected of anything specific, just that he was detained. I'd keep them for three hours. It sucked, plenty of people complained about it, and I couldn't bear people's bitterness and their hatred. I could have acted differently if I'd taken a different approach with them. There were also observers who checked that we were detaining people for only three hours. After three hours, I released them.

114. You give Muhammad money

UNIT: NAHAL BRIGADE
LOCATION: RAMALLAH DISTRICT
YEAR: 2001–2002

There was some guy, I think his name was Muhammad, who became a friend of ours.

What does that mean?

He understood the game. He understood that the person who makes the decisions isn't . . . he got it that there's no reason to get the right permits and whatever, the way to do things is with the soldiers in the field. So that's how he got friendly with us. He'd ask, "Hey, do you need cigarettes?" He would distribute gas in the area, so he'd always come and go, and if you needed something, then you give money to Muhammad and he'll bring it . . . or he wouldn't take the money.

Food? Something to drink?

Drinks, cigarettes, little things like that, sure. And in exchange, he'd cross more easily than other people.

115. Some of the detainees weren't medically fit

UNIT: NAHAL BRIGADE
LOCATION: JENIN
YEAR: 2005–2007

Salem is for prisoners who'd been caught with security violations, and they served their sentences there. The conditions there were worse than Megiddo, which is a huge prison. In Salem there's no doctor, there's a doctor who comes once or twice a week, and the prisoners at Salem have supposedly been examined by a doctor, who determines that they're fit for detention in a facility without a doctor. Whoever's unfit goes to Megiddo, sort of.

Why "sort of"?

There were all kinds of cases I know of, where people who, if they'd seen a doctor, wouldn't have gone to Salem. For example, someone with heart problems before catheterization, or someone with diabetes.

That kind of thing happened? So they went to Megiddo?

Yes, but they were at Salem, that's the whole point. There are cases I remember, a boy with testicular pain. There'd be screaming from the cells. Oh, and there's a sewage pipe right under Salem, and it really stinks in the summer, it really, really stinks like nothing else. So we yelled for the sergeant on duty to come, after twenty minutes of this screaming, and they took out a fourteen- or fifteen-year-old boy from the prison cell, and there's a translator there, someone who knows Arabic and he translates and communicates between the jailers and the inmates. He realized the boy's balls hurt . . . there was a medical protocol for the inmates. The protocol for a guy whose balls hurt was to get him to a hospital, to go see a doctor. I kept pressing for the battalion doctor to come. He said that he would come in two days, and in the meantime I should give him Tylenol.

What did you say to that?

That Tylenol doesn't help with testicular pain, that he needs to go to the hospital. He said that the boy couldn't go, and that he'd try to come tomorrow. Another incident, there was a really fat guy . . .

What happened to the boy?

He's okay, a doctor came and transferred him.

You told him to sit in his cell, and you gave him Tylenol?

There wasn't much to be done. I brought him Tylenol to help with the pain, and psychologically it calmed him down. I told him that if it continued to hurt, he should call me.

Did it still hurt?

He didn't call me.

Did you see him afterward?

I don't know, I don't remember. I think I did.

He was okay?

Again, I remember he didn't call me that night. I was there on a shift as a medic. I knew he was supposed to have a hernia operation before his arrest, I knew because there'd been papers signed that a doctor saw him before he went into detention, but maybe the examination wasn't comprehensive, because this boy shouldn't have been in prison. Afterward, I realized that a doctor doesn't always do an examination.

How did you realize this?

When they asked me to see if he was medically fit, they told me that a medic can also do the examination.

Are you officially the prison medic?

There were a few medics in the prison. I was the medic until a certain point, until I couldn't be there anymore. I had a lot of confrontations with the staff and with my company medic, and with the battalion doctor over this issue, so they told me not to go there again. There was another older man who had a heart attack in the prison. Again, someone with heart problems who's supposed to be catheterized, he shouldn't be in a prison without a doctor. It took the army's medical ambulance forty minutes to arrive. We needed the battalion ambulance. This was after I'd threatened to go get a civilian, I said I don't care what the repercussions are. He was okay in the end. A week later, I saw his son at the prison gate, and he told me that his father had a heart attack but he's okay. He was also diabetic, and the veins in his legs were swollen.

How many days did it take for him to get treatment?

I don't remember, this was three years ago. When I arrived, there wasn't even a medicine cabinet.

Where was the medicine?

With the company medic.

In a travel case?

Generally, there was no medicine there or at the checkpoint. I had my company medic's things if I needed them.

You took the case with you?

I took what I had to, usually.

Of your own accord?

I think so, I don't remember exactly. Things for blood pressure, thermometer, Tylenol, Stop-It, stuff like that. But it's clumsy and limited. People in Salem live in bad and unhealthy conditions.

Does a diabetic have his own medicine?

Listen, they speak Arabic, and I don't understand Arabic. The translator had to explain things to me, but there were words he didn't know how to say in Hebrew. What's really terrible there, what was hard for other soldiers to see, were the conditions, the living conditions, because there were definitely life-threatening cases there, the one guy with the heart attack was the last case I was there for, and afterward I couldn't go back. I think someone else thought it was an attempt to get attention, there are also people who don't care . . . the guy wasn't someone who threw stones, rather he was someone categorized as "security-lite."

It doesn't sound security-related, detaining someone with diabetes.

They're security-lite if they haven't carried out terrorist attacks. Brothers of terrorists, relatives, people who threw stones, members of organizations in possession of material that was . . .

How do you know all these things?

I looked in their files. Anyone who comes to the detention center, you have to look up his medical history, which is in his file.

How is the file organized?

Name, details.

Two pages? Criminal records and medical records?

There's a picture, official details, description of the crime, how long—
and his entry papers to the prison.

Who fills it out?

In principle, the doctor or the medic.

You filled them out?

Yes, I filled out forms: pulse, blood pressure, questions about health,
medicine, family history.

Who signs it?

I sign it.

What does it say at the bottom? Signed by . . .

The doctor I think, I'm not sure. They said that a medic can sign it.

Who said that?

The doctor, I think.

The doctor gave you permission?

Yes, they requested a medic to examine incoming detainees.

Who requested this?

I don't know.

They gave you an order?

Someone told me, go examine these people.

PART FOUR

Law Enforcement:
A Dual Regime

An Overview

The testimonies in Part Four address the enforcement of law and order in the Territories. Palestinians are subject to military rule: that is, control by the use of threats backed by punitive actions and assaults that demonstrate the ruling army's power. Thousands of orders, regulations, and ordinances are given by different bodies—the Ministry of Defense, the Civil Administration, the Head of Central Command—as well as by commanders and soldiers. Instructions change frequently and often are contradictory. New regulations appear constantly, while others expire without warning. A soldier at a checkpoint has the authority to "exercise discretion as a commander on the ground": detain, arrest, or use force against anyone whom he perceives, for whatever reason, as a threat. Thus the Palestinian population, which is perceived by security forces as a threat, is itself subject to an endless succession of threats based on the complete military authority of the State of Israel.

Alongside the millions of Palestinians who live under military rule, hundreds of thousands of Israeli citizens live in the Territories, primarily under the jurisdiction of Israeli law. The settlers—who in 1967 began to establish Israeli settlements with the assistance of the government—are tried in Israeli courts, and the laws enforced on them are those of their own state. The settlers, however, are not merely Israeli citizens entitled to protection by the army and rule of law: in practice, they are also partners in the military rule of Palestinians.

There is a close connection between the IDF and settlers: many military units are positioned adjacent to settlements, or even inside them; settlers often treat the soldiers to food and coffee, give soldiers historical, geographical, and political overviews of the region, and even host them for Shabbat and holiday meals. More important, testimonies in this part bring to light the fact that settlers participate in significant military activity: they command soldiers and guide them, and even participate in the operational decision-making process. Additional testimonies in this part demonstrate how in many instances soldiers in the Territories receive and carry out the instructions of settlers and security coordinators of settlements, especially with regard to the expulsion of Palestinians from agricultural land adjacent to their settlements. Such is the method through which settlers succeed in dispossessing Palestinians of their land and expanding the territory of their settlement.

The testimonies in this part demonstrate the dual status of settlers in the Territories, and show what happens when settler activity deviates from the law or from policy written by heads of the security forces, generally as part of efforts to drive Palestinians from their land. Activities that under normal circumstances would constitute undeniable violations of the law transform, in the context of the Territories, into differences of opinion between settlers and law enforcement authorities, and ultimately conclude in compromise, which usually comes at the expense of Palestinians and their rights. These moments of crisis and compromise reveal the depth of the partnership between the two parties. The failure to enforce Israeli law on settlers does not reflect incompetence on the part of law enforcement authorities; rather, it is evidence of the double status given to settlers: Israeli security forces consider the settlers as allies with whom they share a common enemy, and view them as full partners in the military control of the Palestinians, yet they also give the settlers the same right to protection as Israeli citizens. In this way, settlers are able to act in the Territories as representatives of Israel—as if they were a branch of the security forces.

The Occupation is based on this dual regime: the civil rights of the settlers are protected and anchored in Israeli law, while the Palestinians are controlled by the use of threats and military force. Soldiers' testimonies describe how the IDF serves, trains, and advances the political ambitions of settlers in the Territories at the expense of the Palestinian population. The testimonies also describe the way in which the settlers aid Israeli security forces in exerting control over the Palestinians. The double standard to which settlers in the Territories are privy constitutes a systematic phenomenon: settlers play an essential role in a system that controls the lives of Palestinians and ensures Israel's hold on the Territories.

116. The mission: providing security for the settlers' rampages

UNIT: ARMORED CORPS
LOCATION: NABLUS DISTRICT
YEAR: 2000

One operation in Hawwara has been etched into my memory. It's an Arab village, not exactly quiet, but it's no Jenin.

What happened there?

Basically, what happened was, the Jews decided to go on a rampage in the Tapuach area. There are settlements there and all kinds of outposts.

You weren't in the village . . .

We weren't in the village but Hawwara was in our sector. They sent us to get the mess in Hawwara under control. That's at the beginning. We didn't know what the mess was. We got there. The settlers had decided to attack the residents of the village, and we—we're supposed to protect them and make sure nothing happens to them.

The settlers were in Hawwara?

They came to protest, and they started throwing stones at the village, at Hawwara, on the main road and creating disturbances. There was a group of people from outside Israel who were demonstrating in support of the Jewish settlement, and they were goading on the settlers. I remember I was on the verge of hitting one of them . . . they were a group of fanatical French Jews who'd come and were taking pictures of what was going on there . . .

What were the Arabs doing?

Nothing. They were scared.

Did the settlers have weapons?

They had weapons and threw stones. Children were hurling stones at adults.

Were there women there?

Women were there as well, but not many. But there were settler women there. So we're standing there, and the French group was bothering us, the IDF.

What did you try to do? Stop the stone throwing, or just protect the settlers?

Protect the settlers and make sure that nothing happened to them while they're throwing stones, while they're going on a rampage . . .

Was that the official order?

What can you do? Security is the most important thing. Security. Protecting the settlers. You get there, they're united, they're throwing stones. You back them up, you provide cover. Now, on the one hand people from the village are gathering on rooftops, and you're scared to death because you're exposed to Palestinians, and on the other hand, you don't know what to do, because you're protecting the settlers who decided to start this whole thing. It got to the point where we just wanted to stop it. We didn't want to let the settlers into the village.

Wasn't that the first thing you wanted to do?

No, we waited for the police.

Meaning, you didn't move the settlers in the meantime?

No, but at some point I think one of the officers tried to stop them from throwing stones so they'd leave and get out of there. It got to the point where he was afraid. We tried to stop them from bothering the Palestinians, but we also had to protect them and protect ourselves . . . it was crazy, absurd. And they, the settlers, didn't care. They didn't care about the soldiers, and certainly not about the Palestinians.

And when you come and try to stop them . . .

You hit them.

You hit the settlers?

Yes. And then the guys from outside Israel come, the French people, and they start taking photographs, and then you start hitting people. They're lying under your jeep, and you want to hit them, too. They come with their video cameras, and you grab an eighteen-year-old boy and shove him into the car, and some idiot woman with a video camera comes and videotapes you. And in the meantime the settlers continue their rampage. You want to slap them and throw them out, the settlers, too— one by one, they're throwing stones! They're throwing stones and maybe . . . they start shooting, they shoot! Throwing stones at houses and people . . .

Did anyone get hurt?

Not too bad. Not that we didn't go and treat them, it was three hours . . .

Who was injured? The settlers or the Arabs?

No, no, no . . . the Arabs.

Did anyone get hit in the head?

Are you kidding me? I think more than ten people got hit in the head.

Were they bleeding?

They start bleeding and they run away. Someone was standing in the window of his house . . . By the way, those same settlers, there was one day when they shot at the water tanks. They just shot the water tanks in Hawwara.

How did this end?

It ended with us throwing them out.

You threw them out?

Yes.

You took them out physically?

No, in a car. They came in their cars, got out, and started throwing stones. Because of the potential danger to soldiers, it was hard to stop them. For the first hour or so you protect them, you let them throw stones . . .

You let them throw rocks for an hour and no one says anything?

You don't understand what happened. We were on a vehicular patrol when we got there. We didn't know what was happening. Afterward, we realized we needed to prevent disturbances like that from happening.

And the settlers still kept throwing stones?

Yes. And there were a lot of them, and they were doing whatever they wanted. They have eight or nine vehicles backing them up, something like that, and they stopped the traffic. And you're fighting with them, and then the French group came . . .

They don't try to injure the soldiers? The local population?

No way! They poke their heads out the window, they get hit with a stone, and they go back inside. Think about it, they're in shock. People live there. They stick their heads out their windows, they get hit with a stone. They walk down the street, they get hit with stones. At that moment, their lives and routines were in danger.

So who got up and said, "Let's stop the settlers . . ."?

Our battalion commander decided it was enough. That it was too dangerous if they resisted and a terrorist group suddenly arrived. And things changed pretty fast. We put the settlers in our vehicles and we got rid of those Frenchmen and we started putting out the fire. We didn't do it out of humanitarian concern. We didn't stop the settlers because the IDF became humane all of a sudden, it was just so that there wouldn't be a huge mess, so that some terrorist group wouldn't come along or something—we were thinking of the soldiers, not the people.

117. We shot in the air to chase the farmers away

UNIT: NAHAL BRIGADE
LOCATION: SOUTH HEBRON HILLS
YEAR: 2004

All the residents are obliged to go out on the night patrol with the commander of the settlement security detail there. And there was one guy who people paid to do the patrol for them. So normally it was one or two, three people who did it. And there it was the same story. The settlement security coordinator would come and define the precise borders of the settlement. There was a place at the edge of the settlement, and he'd say to me, "Here, you see this place, this line, this is the settlement's territory, and that area over there"—there were also these open farming areas, and there was no fence around the settlement—"they're prohibited." It's an open area, there's a field, but the settlers said, "They can't go there, they can't enter the area. They sometimes come with their tractors to work the land, but they're not allowed to, it's not their land." Okay, I get it. One day he comes to me and says, "Get over here, they're coming to work on the land." Now, I'm just a young squad commander, and I get there, and he goes, "Here, come and shoot a few shots in the air to scare them." The settlement security coordinator has a weapon, but he doesn't use it because I'm the soldier, and he's forbidden to use it. Okay, so I shoot a few shots in the air. The farmers looked up, but it didn't stop them, they were right at the entrance to the settlement's land. And there also happened to be a group of reservists on patrol, going by at the same time. When the reservists arrived—they're already used to things, they're not scared—they said, "Those guys will give you trouble." Okay, so he comes, takes his weapon, and shoots next to them.

Who?

The reservist aimed at the farmers, moved a few meters to the side and fired, to show them we're serious. He shot, and then he said, "Come here." And then they started going down to them, the reservists went down to them, the Palestinians. The reservists got there and grabbed the Palestinians, brought them to where the settlement security coordinator and I were standing. I go, "You can't be here, you can't . . ." The reservist also took a guy and slapped him, kicked him. I was in shock, I didn't know what to do, what to say. I had a feeling that something, you know, that it wasn't right. The reservist goes, "This is the only way they learn, this is the only way they won't trespass next time." And you say to yourself, maybe this is the only way they'll learn. That's it. Then he released him, saying, "Don't come back here." They went back, got on their tractor and drove away. That's what happened in Bet Haggai.

You didn't think to yourself, maybe it is their land?

Honestly, I didn't think about that. I didn't doubt it when the settlement security coordinator told me it was his land.

Where was the reservist from?

I don't know, he was from a reservist company that was there.

In Bet Haggai?

No, they were just in the sector, they were on a patrol. They came in a jeep.

Did the settlement security coordinator call them?

I don't know why the reservists came, that I don't know. It could be that they were just by chance passing through, or maybe the settlement security coordinator called them. The reservists came, the settlement security coordinator told them the story, and then the reservists took charge and did what they did.

An officer?

No.

What were the commands for opening fire in Bet Haggai?

Normal. You say "Stop, stop" if someone gets too close and whatever.

Did the Palestinians come close?

Those two in the tractor? No.

But you did open fire.

I shot in the air.

But that wasn't the order.

What can I do? Listen, I went back to the company afterward and told everyone, "Listen, something crazy happened there." It seemed logical then, it's the army.

It does affect you, sure.

I know that I wouldn't have beaten up anyone.

The settlement security coordinator didn't shoot?

No.

He briefed you at the post?

He did the briefing once, when we arrived. He briefed the soldiers and me. First me, and then the soldiers.

And the platoon commander?

He wasn't there at all, he was in a different settlement.

Was the settlement security coordinator the authority for the platoon commander?

No, I was the commander in the area.

But who commanded you?

No one, I was the commander in the area. When you go out on a patrol, for example, there's a commander in the field. Who was my commander? —— was responsible for me, but he wasn't with me at the settlement.

But he's responsible for all the settlements.

Yes, he's responsible for all the settlements.

He never came to check up on you?

No, he was at another settlement. Or maybe he did, I don't know.

So who gave you orders, the settlement security coordinator?

The settlement security coordinator doesn't get too involved in the guard duty and whatever. He doesn't come up to me every day and say, "Today you'll be doing this and that, go clean your weapon." He's only there if there's an emergency or something like that. It's not like he's supervising me. If he says something to me and I don't do it, it's not like I'm refusing an order.

But you do things.

I do things, because he's there and he knows the place. I'm just a squad commander, I go there for a week on settlement security detail, I don't know what's going on around me, or what's what. So he's an authority, and I listen to him.

It makes a lot of sense that he'd come up with that division of labor.

Yeah, maybe. It could be that he made it up, I have no way of checking.

Did the Palestinians present a threat?

No, they didn't present a threat. I didn't feel like they presented a threat. You know, that's the settlement's area, so they shouldn't go there. In the Territories, every Palestinian is a potential terrorist. There's some kind of boundary that begins at the settlement—I don't know if it's legal or not, or how it's defined—but there's some kind of boundary. If they're allowed to walk around freely near the settlement, then it's much more difficult to protect, so they have to keep a certain distance.

118. The settlement security coordinator told us what is allowed and what isn't

UNIT: NAHAL BRIGADE
LOCATION: SOUTH HEBRON HILLS
YEAR: 2002

I did settlement security detail during basic training at Avigail Farm. Bottom line, it's really nice. All of a sudden you don't have commanders beating you over the head, you live with six other guys, it's really like a farm there, a commune. There's a really pretty view. I got into arguments with the settlers, I'd always talk with them.

About what?

About the settlements and everything, and with what right they . . . I said to them, "Bottom line, you guys are criminals, you're breaking the law, it's illegal for you to be here." They said, "We stretch the law, the law will bend according to what we do. We stretch it."

Who said that?

One of the guys there at Avigail Farm. The settlement security coordinator there.

What does that mean, "We stretch the law"?

How did he explain it to me? There's the role of the regional council. They're a group of idealists. Settlers come to the head of the council—I don't remember what the council's called, Mount Hebron I think, or South Hebron Hills—and they say, "We want to establish a settlement, give us a place to do it." They came and looked for a place with the Ministry of Defense. Wait a minute—the settlers said there's a place, but they hadn't received building permits from the Ministry of Defense yet. But they already started building, the permits will come at some later point. That's it, they start building, and there they are. Maybe now they have permission to be there, but back then the settlement location wasn't approved by the Ministry of Defense. That settler called it stretching the law, "We establish the facts on the ground, and they'll accept what we do." Of course, there's a lot of tacit agreement, a lot of corruption, you could call it the Ministry of Settlements and Defense.

When you were at Avigail Farm, what kind of structures were there?

There was a water tower, two caravans, some house they'd built, and an abandoned bus, where a girl lived.

A girl?

Yes, a woman and five boys or so. And aside from that, they were a really nice group of people, you know, really great. They didn't seem like the type of people who uproot olive trees and beat up Palestinians or chase after them. They just wanted to establish a settlement, they didn't care what might happen along the way as a result. They're not directly aggressive. I just remember the settlement security coordinator coming and saying to me, "Here, this is our territory, and here they can work." When he briefed the soldiers, it was like, "We have trees here, and sometimes on Fridays all kinds of organizations come, all kinds of organizations that work with Palestinians, and they come to harvest the olives, to show that it's theirs. But it's not theirs, so you have to get them out of there." If I'm not mistaken, that Friday people came, and we chased them out, saying "Leave, leave."

Did you know who the olive trees belonged to?

I didn't know, I relied on the security coordinator.

Was there an officer with you?

Yes, there was an officer there.

What did he say?

When I got there, I got my briefing from the settlement security coordinators. I was the commander in the area, and the settlement security coordinator was the authority on what was allowed or not.

He gave you orders?

He—you know, it's not exactly giving orders. He defined things. He said, "This is our territory." Bottom line, I never saw where any of this was written down or what was written down. To me, whatever he said was how it went.

And as the commander, how did you brief your soldiers?

The briefing, "We are here in case the settlement is infiltrated. We guard in case of invasion. We're like the defense."

Were there any orders about the olive harvest?

No, just in general to drive them out.

How did they react?

After we expelled them? I don't remember exactly, but there wasn't too much friction. Really, none.

How many people came?

Not too many. You could count them on your hand. Ten, maybe less. Not many.

You just told them, "You can't be here, get out"?

Yes. I don't remember any argument.

How far was the field from the settlement?

Not far. A hundred meters, really not far. It wasn't a big field, it was small. Bottom line, we were there to prevent infiltration. We also did all kinds of other things: we walked around the hills to demonstrate a presence, we put up all kinds of targets in the forest, just the kind of stuff privates do.

119. He's basically a civilian, and he's telling the army what the law is

UNIT: MAGLAN SPECIAL FORCES
LOCATION: SOUTH HEBRON HILLS
YEAR: 2002

I did settlement security detail with soldiers in Eshkolot and in another settlement nearby, I don't remember what the name was. But when we were there, there was the settlement and some village a kilometer or two away. They work their land in the area there, five hundred meters away in the valley below. The settlement sits on the hilltop, and the Palestinians work the land in the valley below. What I remember—it's a little hazy—is that one time they were out there working. All of a sudden the settlers go out—this is past the settlement border, although it was exactly where the settlement expansion was . . . so we ran to where the expansion was, where it was under construction. The settlers just yelled at them . . . they didn't shoot or anything, but they drove them out of there. I don't know if they left.

Who expelled them?

The settlement security coordinator came, called us over, deployed us, some other soldier and me. He said, "They're crossing the boundary, they're scouting us out, they're . . ." Like what do I know? In short, he yells at them, I don't know if they left. But I remember he came and started yelling at them, "Get out of here, get out of here!" Later I go on patrol with him in the vehicle, and he sees a little girl playing near the entrance to the settlement. She was on the access road into the settlement, but still outside the settlement fence—it was totally not part of the settlement. He sees this girl, and I hear him yell something at her in Arabic, from the megaphone, something like *"Rasak."* I didn't understand. I go to him, "What did you yell at the girl?" So he goes, "If you come around here again I'll break your head." Something like that. The situation there is that your commander is actually the settlement security coordinator. He's the one who tells you what's allowed and what's not, where they can be, where they can't be—he gives you authorization to shoot in the air, although in principle I'm the senior army commander—as senior as that is, right?—in the field. He can tell soldiers to shoot, with discretion. But in principle, he fixes policy. It's not some military authority, some company commander, or an officer in the area, it's the settlement security coordinator who decides what's allowed and what isn't. It's pretty ludicrous, when you think about it, where a civilian tells the army what its limitations are and what the laws are.

120. A settler transportation service

Unit: Lavi Battalion
Location: Negohot
Year: 2003–2004

You said something about the Adorayyim–Negohot road, about it being "infamous" or something.

Yes, I at least had . . . it's infamous security-wise. What happened there, it's the only road that connects the western part of Shekef and Negohot toward Otniel with Hebron and the more eastern side. Every day we used two vehicles to escort settlers from Negohot, we escorted people who went out to work . . . there was an arrangement with the army that the army would escort them while traveling on that road. Every trip had to be approved from above. And this business of proper approval from above felt terrible. On the one hand, you're providing security, but again, you don't know if it's done under the framework of providing security, or the framework of . . . I mean, the settlers there determined what the army would do, more or less. The only times when they'd close the road was when there really was an incident or a suspicion that something would happen. The result was that a large part of our time in that area, at least twice a day, we acted as a kind of transport service for the settlers there. Now, we also brought the kids to school in the morning, so it wasn't for no reason, but there were times where you just brought someone back from work, and you felt like a kind of transport service.

121. The settlers are touring the casbah, so get the Palestinians out of the way

UNIT: NAHAL BRIGADE
LOCATION: HEBRON
YEAR: 2008

You said that you talked among yourselves—what did you talk about?

Because of our background, we weren't the kind of guys who cover up things. Ethically and politically it was hard for a lot of us to be there. It was hard for us to be with the settlers. We were in the center, the center of the casbah, and the center of the settlement, and a lot of the troubles we had were with the settlers. Most of the violence didn't come from the Palestinians, because they didn't have a chance— there's not much they can do with soldiers in front of them. Rather it was the settlers who were violent. I had a notebook in my pocket during my service, and each time the settlers cursed or acted violently, I'd write it down, and I also interviewed other soldiers and wrote that down.

How many of those notebooks did you fill?

A lot, twenty-three. It was important for me to document what I saw, or what close friends told me about. I didn't want things that I didn't . . . it was important to me to document all kinds of violence, from someone cursing a real attack.

What's a real attack?

One of the objectives in Hebron is to prevent friction, so they divided roads between Jews and Arabs. And our "favorite" thing was the Friday afternoon tour of the casbah. Settlers spitting in people's faces . . .

The settlers would go to the casbah on Fridays?

Yes, there was a regular outing with one of the leaders of the settlement, and they'd go on an outing, and we had to guard them. Besides the fact that they needed double the people to guard them, it was the most humiliating thing. Not so much for us, it was more what they did . . . they'd start cursing, and we tried to prevent encounters. We had to move an entire street so that this group could pass through.

What is the procedure regarding the Palestinian population when there's a tour of the casbah?

There was one force on the roofs guarding up there, and another force below with the company commander or the deputy company commander, to surround the settlers and remove all the residents from the street.

You didn't impose a curfew?

No, we just moved them aside. We tried to make it clean, sterile, to disturb them as little as possible, although it was impossible not to disturb them. I don't know how long this had been going on.

Did you encounter real violence by the settlers, beyond cursing?

No. I think that if I even saw them slap someone, that would be a violent act, because they'd be the ones doing it. That's how I see the world. What difference does it make if it's a settler pushing, cursing, or slapping someone—it's their attitude that's the problem.

Did you show the notebook to one of the officers?

No. At a certain point we had a decisive conversation with the battalion commander. He was straight and honest, and he said that we had to come forward if we saw things or he did something—he wanted to investigate it and uncover things. He said he looked into the things he knew about. We told him about having to deal with the settlers. You always had the feeling that it wasn't clear what the army wanted from you, or where the line was. You're not the blue police, you don't have the same rights as the police, and the settlers don't see you as an authority. The settlers are behind you when it's convenient for them, and when it's not . . . So our battalion commander says, "Even if the settlers spit at you or attack you, try to ignore it." He was aware that it was a problem, but he was pretty limited, because it's political.

What did they say about your authority over the settlers?

They said we had the ability to arrest them if something develops, but in practice that's very difficult. The general feeling was that it's not clear what we could do. The police have very limited resources, and I want to believe that they wanted to do more, but I know that it was difficult for them because of the amount of incidents that took place.

So in general, the only thing you can do when you see something like that is to oppose it?

No, we'd get involved, but we were limited in what we could do. It's difficult for a nineteen- or twenty-year-old to oppose something like that. I also don't know how much power we had to do so.

So what did you do?

We'd separate them, the physical friction points between people were relatively few. When things happened we'd try to separate them, and we'd call the police. There were kids who'd go up on the roofs in Avraham Avinu and throw stuff or curse, and soldiers would have to drive them away. I got the sense that the law is pretty terse, where it's unclear what they want from me.

122. Three or four soldiers guarding a shack

Unit: Paratroopers
Location: Elon Moreh
Year: 2002–2003

In Nablus, there's settlers from Elon Moreh and all the issues of the Territories. It's really different there because you aren't inside the city, you surround it. It's harder to control, even though you've got Mount Gerizim and Mount Eval. We had a lot of trouble controlling the area in Nablus because of the settlers' isolated farms, and the state's decided that the IDF will protect them: three or four soldiers guarding a shack or a hilltop that's totally exposed.

Is it dangerous? Normally soldiers on settlement security detail are responsible for that kind of thing.

It's more random than that. As soon as there's an order from the regional brigade or above, it goes down to the brigade, to the battalion, to the company, and finally to you.

Do you know if the hilltop settlements were legal? Because there's the whole issue of illegal outposts.

You assume that if the regional brigade gave the order then it's okay. When you're out in the field, you don't know about where things stand with the Supreme Court. There were a lot of problems with this, because sometimes they didn't want us to go up and guard [the outposts], because the moment you start guarding them, you give them legitimacy. The settlers want to fix borders, grab land, and establish a settlement. They don't care much about someone guarding them. Anyway, all the settlers have weapons. That's another problem, because in the dark you might identify a man with a weapon, and you have to be very careful. There were problems with harassing Palestinians as well.

123. Things that don't make it to the media

Unit: Paratroopers
Location: Hebron
Year: 2002

The worst thing I saw in Hebron happened a day after Elazar Leibowitz's funeral.* I was guarding the Gross post, which is on the roof of a building and is the lookout for Hebron's central square. I was on guard there, and in the middle of my shift, sometime in the afternoon, I see an old man with a cane walking down, an Arab from Abu Sneina. The old man looked sixty-plus, had a cane, he gets to the Abu Sneina intersection, to Gross Square, and all of a sudden three sixteen- or seventeen-

---

*A Hebron settler who was killed in a Palestinian attack whole on his way home from military service.

year-old kids jump him, they push him down to the ground in a second. They grab a stone and they open up his head. They start kicking him down on the ground, bashing his head. Here's a sixty-year-old man with a stream of blood gushing from his head, blood pouring from his head. It all happened in a few seconds, really, just a few seconds. In one second he's on the ground, then they have a rock and they've cut his scalp and there's a stream of blood gushing from his head. They kick him and before the soldiers standing below me at the post were able to get to them, they'd already run away. An officer on patrol showed up, he didn't know what they'd done, so he didn't catch them. They just ran away. The company medic came immediately and started bandaging up the old Palestinian man, and we took him to an ambulance.

Do you know what happened to him?

No. I believe he was okay, because they stopped the stream of blood from his head and they sent him to the hospital. It was just so shocking. I was shocked. Afterward I went to the officer in tears. I'd been a soldier for seven months, I didn't understand what was going on here. I said that it can't be like this, us protecting the settlers, I didn't understand how come it was like this. The incident really shocked me, for me, it destroyed everything. Here's the thing, the first thing I compared it to, what I immediately thought about was the lynching in Ramallah.* The images are still in my mind, even today. It's hard when I think about them, and it really reminds me of the lynching in Ramallah, how they behaved.

And then you went to Carmela?†

I took the story to Carmela Menashe. I didn't tell any of the soldiers in my company, because it didn't seem appropriate, but I quietly went to Carmela Menashe. I had a contact for her.

Were there other soldiers like you?

In each company I think there was one soldier who had a problem with things. The majority didn't have the emotional intelligence or the

---

*In 2000, two Israeli reservists were killed by a mob in Ramallah.
†Carmela Menashe, Israel Radio's well-known military correspondent.

The Sharabati house, vandalized multiple times by settlers, Hebron.

openness to talk about it. And we didn't talk about it with each other, because soldiers don't talk to each other about things like that, there's no serious discussion in a company of combat soldiers. The whole macho atmosphere, everything's a joke, they don't take anything seriously, and at the end of the day everyone's just trying to get through the shit together. Because again, like I said, on the spectrum of miserable people in Hebron, it's pretty bad being a soldier. You're sacrificed.

What happened when you went to Carmela Menashe?

I told her the story over the phone. It didn't get broadcast. I didn't hear it anywhere. And that was another shock, because I understood that basically anything that goes on there, that innocent kids, fourteen years old, eight years old, die there for no reason,* that settlers go into their houses and shoot at them, and settlers go crazy in the streets and break store windows and beat up soldiers and throw eggs at soldiers and lynch the elderly—all these things don't make it to the media.

---

*The soldier is referring to a settler rampage in which a Palestinian girl was shot dead and a Palestinian boy was stabbed in the back.

Hebron is a small, isolated world, and the Avraham Avinu neighborhood is isolated inside Hebron, and more soldiers guard it than people living there. The people living in the neighborhood do whatever they want, the soldiers are forced to protect them. The settlers are the biggest Jewish Nazis I've ever met. And it's here in the State of Israel, and no one knows about it, and no one wants to know, and no one reports on it. People prefer not to know, not to understand that something terrible is happening not far from us. Really, no one cares. And the soldiers there are unlucky, and the Palestinians there are super-unlucky. And no one helps them.

124. An elderly woman . . . the guys beat her up

UNIT: NAHAL BRIGADE
LOCATION: HEBRON
YEAR: 2002

What were your meetings like with the settlers in Hebron?

When I was in the assisting company there were more of them. We were in Jabal Juar at that time. It used to be an Arab school, and for at least a few years now it's been an IDF post. There was an incident there where some settlers jumped some woman, an elderly woman. She was ill in some way. They injured her stomach, a serious stomach injury. It was only later that we understood that she'd been ill. But apart from that, she was very old, and a few settlers jumped her in the Erez alley.

Were they kids? Adults?

Guys. Youths. They beat her up a bit and injured her, seriously in the stomach.

What did they beat her up with?

We heard they beat her with stones. But I don't know what with exactly. We got there afterward, and she was lying there. We arrived before the ambulance—we'd sent for the ambulance. I think the young men ran to Kiryat Arba. Some ran to Avraham Avinu, some to Kiryat Arba. We found her lying there. Both Israelis and Palestinians are allowed to go in the Erez alley. It was like routine there—this woman was lying on the ground and settlers were walking past, and we asked them what had happened, they said they don't know, kept on walking. It was a nasty situation, we didn't know what to do. We called an ambulance.

What were the orders when settlers injured Palestinians?
There were . . . there weren't really any orders, but there was . . .

But what did you feel your duty was when settlers attacked Palestinians?
What did I feel my duty was? To separate them.

125. The cute boy took a brick and smashed the girl's head

Unit: Nahal Brigade
Location: Hebron
Year: 2003

My main problem in Hebron was with the settlers, the Jewish community. I got the feeling we were protecting the Arabs from the Jews. And neither side liked us, but it felt like the Jews did whatever they wanted and no one cared. We were stuck in the middle. Here's an example of something that happened right near me: I was on guard duty, and one of the soldiers at another post called a medic over the radio. Someone replaced me at the post and I ran down to see what had happened, and I see a six-year-old Palestinian girl, her whole head a gaping wound.

At post 44?
Yeah. This very cute kid who'd regularly visit our post decided that he didn't like Palestinians walking beneath his house, so he took a brick and threw it at this girl's head. Kids there do whatever they want. No one does anything about it. No one cares. Afterward, his parents just praised him. The parents there encourage their children to behave like

that. There were many cases like that. Eleven-, twelve-year-old Jewish kids beat up Palestinians and their parents come along to help them, set their dogs on them—there's a thousand and one stories.

126. Settlers' homes are inside the army base

UNIT: KFIR BRIGADE
LOCATION: HEBRON
YEAR: 2006

I remember the blow that I felt when I found I had settlers' homes inside the base. There's the house, the caravan, another caravan that they've parked inside the base. You know what I'm talking about?

Bet Romano?

No, Bet Romano is the yeshiva, with the stairs that go from the yeshiva to the base.

Metal stairs?

Yeah. So when you reach the top of the stairs there are two houses in front of you, two families live there. They call it the caravan neighborhood, or it has some other name now, I don't know.

They walk around the base?

Yes, they walk around the base freely, and they also leave using the entrance gate. On Shabbat we're forbidden to close the gate, because they have to use it to get out. It's unbelievable, you can't close the gate because it's, you know, it's Shabbat, and you can't open and close the gate. Even though there's a soldier right above, he has to leave the gate open so they can go out.

Did it bother you as soldiers?

It drove me crazy. It really drove me crazy. I also remember that once one of our commanders had some argument with a soldier, and this commander started screaming at him. The soldier was known for being difficult, and the commander was yelling at him. All of a sudden, one of the windows opens, and some redhead settler, you know who I'm talking about, he was well-known, sticks his head out and shouts at the commander, "Who do you think you are, yelling at him like that?" This guy's screaming. You know . . . "Come here, tell me, aren't you ashamed? What's it your business? You're this, he's that . . ." Like he wanted to protect the soldier. And everyone, you know, everyone starts arguing with him and whatever, and then one of the sergeants comes and yells at the settler, "Shut up, go home, who do you think you are?" Exactly the right response. Who's this settler to open his mouth? He could have just said, "Stop yelling, you're making too much noise." That I could accept, but what's he getting involved for? So then one of the officers went in to talk to him. You know how it is. In the end nothing happened.

Did you eat Friday night dinner with the settlers?

I wouldn't agree to go. They invited me tons of times, but I wouldn't go. But they'd always invite me . . . Sometimes they'd invite you, "Come, sit with us, come for a Shabbat meal." I never went.

What was your interaction with them like? The last time I was there, there was a gate.

They walk through. If they go to Bet Hadassah, they walk from there.

Where do they park their cars?

I don't know, I think they park them below in Bet Romano, at post 38. I don't know where they park. You have some contact, you see them go by.

And their kids?

They run around the post with bikes, totally freely. I also remember, this was the most unbelievable thing, I remember that we would do our training at the post, and I see ten to fifteen religious men there, I don't know, they came to Hebron to see the Cave of the Patriarchs, and they're standing there and watching. Inside a base, an IDF military base, standing and watching us. You know, we're training in case someone attacks you from the side, and they're all, whatever, they're just standing there and watching. Suddenly, you know, you say to yourself, "Come on, this is ridiculous, totally unbelievable. What are they doing here?" You know, and it doesn't seem strange to anyone. There were always Chabad guys walking around the post, "Did you put on tefillin? Did you put on tefillin?" I remember one night I woke up because I heard some girls—you wake up for girls right away—and some religious American girl was walking around the post, asking things. She pointed to my Aleph pin and said: "I want this pin." This is my battalion pin, Aleph Battalion, she wanted it. Just walking around freely, you know.

Did the people from Bet Romano also walk around like that?

Everyone does. It's no—you get it? The settlers just walk around wherever. No one had trouble coming in the base.

Didn't the company commander say anything about it?

He said we're not allowed to close the gate on Shabbat. You can't close it. And you have to open it daily for the settlers.

Were there skirmishes at the gate sometimes?

With settlers? Maybe, I don't remember. I think so. But it's unbelievable, it's totally crazy, the way they're there under your feet. I really didn't like them. And they were there a lot. I remember an episode with the Coke machine. Like hey, it was after I'd finished guard duty, and the one thing that kept me going was this can of Coke I was going to drink afterward. You finish guard duty on Friday, Saturday afternoon, it's hot, it stinks, you've been up there since six a.m., you come back at noon and you're exhausted, you get to the machine and it's turned off and there's a sign, "This machine does not operate on Shabbat." Sonofa . . .

Did you experience problems evacuating settler outposts, or were there other disturbances by the settlers?

So that's just it. Look, during my time there, for example, the wholesale market had to be evacuated.* We didn't evacuate it, the Border Police did, but after the evacuation there was a lot of unrest. Listen, the settlers there are incredible. They don't respect you, they don't value you—the opposite, in fact, they curse at you in the street. You know, after the disengagement,† it's unbelievable. I remember all the arguments.

127. You hate everyone

Unit: Nahal Brigade
Location: Hebron
Year: 2004–2006

I remember seeing those kids in Hebron and feeling proud that they're afraid. These are kids I'm talking about, like, really. And who were they afraid of? The Jewish kids. They don't do anything, but the Jewish kids throw rocks at them when they pass by. The Jewish parents don't say a word. The parents stand around, and you see a little Jewish kid throwing stones and yelling something at the Arab kids, and it was just routine. You come to Tel Rumeida and you see it every day, and it's okay, it's acceptable. And the parents, I don't know if they're the parents, but adults walk around and they don't say a word to the kids.

It doesn't seem strange to you that a kid throws a stone at another kid?

Because one's a Jew and the other's a Palestinian, it's as if it's okay.

Did you also see the opposite, a Palestinian throwing a stone at a Jew?

I remember that I'd say that it was kind of okay, but to myself I'd think, come on, what is he, retarded? That guy didn't do anything to him. I'd

---

*Hebron's historic wholesale market was twice occupied by settlers in an effort to expand their presence in the city. They were evacuated for the second time in 2007.
†The evacuation of Israeli settlements from the Gaza Strip in 2005.

think, this is what causes the whole mess, these little fights, these things that the Jews start. I know their parents teach them to hate them, and so they legitimize throwing rocks and cursing at them. It's the kind of thing you see on TV. So it's clear there'll be a mess afterward. And you don't understand which side you're on. In Hebron it's the strangest thing, you don't know which side you're on. I'm a Jewish Israeli soldier, and I'm supposed to be against the Arabs because they're my enemy, but I'm here, next to a settler's house in the base, and I start thinking that I'm not on their side, that the Jews aren't right. So wait, so no, I have to flip a switch in my brain so I can keep hating Arabs and justifying what the Jews do. But no, wait, I still can't agree with the Jews, because they started it, it's because of them that we're here, and it's because of them that all this is happening, because they disturb them and they're afraid. It's terrible, all of this . . .

So why flip the switch?

Because you have to be loyal to your side.

How old are the kids you're talking about?

Young, like five or six. The ones who run around outside.

Were the adults ever violent?

I remember one incident. We were on a bus, it was during the disengagement, and I don't remember what the story was, but there was some settler woman on the bus who they said was crazy. Her husband or boyfriend had been killed by a terrorist, or something like that, so she was screaming at one of the soldiers who wouldn't give her a place to sit. I remember he was concentrating on controlling himself, restraining himself, and she was hitting him, I think. He held back and held back, and then at a certain point he yelled at her, "Shut up, it's because of you that I have to be here." They hated being there.

The soldiers?

Yes. I think they were mad at the settlers and at the residents of Hebron. They were angry.

This settler child was a favorite of the soldiers. Hebron, Nahal Brigade, Battalion 50.

Don't the settlers bring you pizza at the post and all kinds of stuff like that?

They do, but every so often I'd hear the soldiers say, "It's because of these shits that we're here, they should get out of here, they should leave." On the one hand there's that—again, you're mad at your country that the settlers are here, that the Jews are here. On the other hand, you also hate the Arabs, because they kill your friends and make trouble for you.

So you hate everyone?

Yes. And so I think that you don't think—you say whatever comes into your head at the moment: now I hate this, so I'll curse at him, and then I hate that, so I'll curse at him, and now I hate him, so I'll spit on him.

You spat on Jews?

No, why? They didn't do anything to me.

What about the Arabs?

But they're like, Arabs . . . I don't know, it's true, the guy I spat on didn't do anything to me. I think he didn't do anything at all. But again, it was cool, and it was the one thing I could do to, you know, I can't go and arrest people and be proud that I caught a terrorist, and I can't kill a terrorist, and I can't go on some operation and find some weapons under some tile in their house. But I can spit on them and humiliate them and ridicule them.

128. We confiscated cars, and the settlers vandalized them

UNIT: PARATROOPERS
LOCATION: NABLUS AREA
YEAR: 2003

What was the issue with confiscating cars?

There were a lot of roads, but that's nothing compared to all of the dirt paths there. There was an order at some point that if you found someone trying to bypass the road, or trying to go around you, and you manage to catch him, then you confiscate his car.

What did you do with the car?

You bring it to a lot next to the post. They created a lot.

Who did?

I don't know, I think it was there before we got there, and we used it as a lot. The problem was that there was no one to guard the cars, so settlers from Elon Moreh would come and destroy the cars you'd just confiscated and intended to return to their owners the next day. You confiscate cars, it's a way for the state to threaten you, so that you don't do it again.

Did you also look inside the cars?

Yes. First you take the person for a short interrogation, and then he goes into detention.

Where do you take him for interrogation?

You bring him to the checkpoint, that's where they interrogate him.

Do soldiers from the company interrogate him?

Either soldiers from the company, or if necessary, you bring him to the interrogators at the central brigade. We don't do that. Usually we'd release him after half an hour, and he'd go on his way, and they'd tell him to come back to get his car after a day or two. Our problem was the settlers who'd walk down from Elon Moreh and destroy the cars. We guarded them so that they wouldn't smash the windows, wreck them. The taxis are one of their main sources of income. The guy comes back the next morning with his ticket; you walk over with the guy, you want to give him back his car.

So there really was an organized system.

Yes, he had a ticket and we had a ticket, he signs and you sign, and then he comes back the next day to get his car.

What was written on the form?

His license plate number. After the interrogation, he'd get a note with his number. The idea was only to take his car for a day. He'd drive it out to the car lot, and we'd escort him there.

So you were playing cat and mouse with the settlers . . .

Right. You stand there helpless in front of the guy the next day, you go to show him the car, and you see that it's broken: tires slashed, windows smashed. You catch a thirteen- or fourteen-year-old settler and you've got a problem. You go to the Elon Moreh settlement, and they say they don't know anything, and so then you've got a situation where the company has to allocate another post just to guard the cars. It was a real pain. We were always fighting with those fucked-up settlers—we tried to protect them, and they just stuck a spoke in our wheels. You catch a car and carry out an interrogation so that terrorists won't hurt the settlers, you just have to deal with the settlers all the time. And there are all these young, brash settler kids whose parents never taught them anything when they were younger.

But you know the routine—you see the settlers coming . . .

The absurd thing was that we'd set up ambushes just to catch the kids coming to destroy the cars. You catch them, but you can't arrest them because they're minors—the police can't do anything to them.

They're all minors?

Yeah, the settlers aren't idiots—they send their kids, they don't put themselves in danger. If you catch one of them, you have to open a file. And then the higher-ups speak with the heads of the settlement, and we were helpless. Who's going to fix their cars? Sometimes the cars were in such a state that they weren't worth fixing. It's a shitty feeling you have protecting them and they . . .

129. The settlers went into the casbah, killed a little girl

UNIT: PARATROOPERS
LOCATION: HEBRON
YEAR: 2002

The Jews are by far the most difficult element in Hebron, unbelievable. That's what you find out, after all their craziness, that you live there in this insane way just to protect them. You're standing there in their neighborhood, on their street, and you're wearing a flak jacket and a helmet while they go about as normal. And then suddenly something happens, like the murder of Elazar Leibowitz, who was killed in the Carmel area, not far from Hebron. He'd lived in the Jewish area in Hebron, and then all hell broke loose, craziness in the streets. At his funeral, Jews went into the casbah and started shooting in the air. They killed some girl, an eight-year-old boy got a knife in the back, appalling things.

What was your part in this story?

I was trying to stop them.

What were your orders?

Try to stop them with physical force of any kind. Physical force. But they didn't give us authorization, there's no way, you can't give authorization for that. The problem is that even if the soldier doesn't want to, he finds himself protecting settlers while they do terrible things to the Palestinians. Because if a Palestinian comes and throws a stone, you can immediately start shooting in the air and throwing stun grenades at him, doing a thousand and one other things and no one will say a word. But you can't do anything to a Jew. You can only try to catch a settler and remove him with force. And normally, the Jews who live there know the soldiers' tactics. And when they go to destroy a house inside the casbah, they just go in, destroy a wall. They destroyed the Sharabati house, and there's a mess there, even today. You're one miserable soldier among hundreds of children, and it feels like a game of cops and robbers. A soldier stands at the entrance to the casbah and stretches out his arms, and the seven-year-old kids run right underneath in every direction. He might grab one kid, but four more come. There's nothing to do, they just come and run into the casbah. You try to stop them to protect them, because it's the casbah after all, but they run straight into the casbah anyway, they go into homes, break all the windows, break whatever they can break, destroy everything, and then they declare the house theirs, they say that they've taken another house in Hebron. Their behavior is astonishing. All of a sudden the police arrive, the settlers throw eggs at them, and you find yourself—I found myself in a situation where I was walking right next to a settler woman, trying to protect the baby she's holding while she's walking through the crowd. We're inside an Arab house, in the casbah. There are no Arabs there, of course, but there are around a hundred Jewish kids who've smashed everything in the house. They smashed the wall, they broke through the wall to create a path from the house to their neighborhood, because there was only a wall separating that house from their neighborhood. And I'm in this crazy situation, where the police are trying to get the settler kids outside, and I'm standing between the police and some woman holding a baby. I'm trying to protect her and her baby, and the settlers hit me with an egg, while they were trying to hit the police. And the police are taking all these blows, and the special female patrol is getting hit by the girls, and at the [Leibowitz] funeral we're fighting with all of the settlers—and the next day they bring food to the post.

What happened at the funeral?

The funeral was completely insane. I was inside the post, and at a certain point the settlers just shot at the post. Not Palestinians—Jews. By accident, because they just ran into the casbah and started spraying gunfire in the air. Shooting on autopilot, with no judgment. And because of it a little girl was killed and another boy got a knife in the back. Just mindless destruction.

Where were the police?

The police couldn't control the settlers because it's impossible. They're everywhere—the police can't control a hundred kids running around the casbah. Two soldiers are standing and trying to block the entrance, but it's like they're playing a game with seven-year-old kids. You can't control seven-year-old kids.

What if there were a hundred Palestinian children?

Oh, there'd be a huge difference, that's exactly what I was saying. First of all, Palestinian kids would never do it. If a hundred Palestinians showed up, then in principle they'd also be able to do whatever they wanted. But they'd never do that, because the moment Palestinian kids would try to infiltrate the Jewish neighborhood, there'd most likely be shooting in the air, and then there'd be rubber bullets, and there's a good chance that some kid would die, and then all the others would take off. But a Jewish kid—no one would ever shoot at him.

So you don't have permission to use any kind of force against the settlers?
Just physical contact.

You can't arrest them?
We could. We've arrested them occasionally, but it's rare. Very rare. Our treatment of them is too forgiving. We didn't usually arrest them.

What did they do with all the people who went beserk during the protest? Were there any proceedings against them? Did you know who they were?
Not always. Normally there are all kinds of hilltop kids who come from Itamar and Elon Moreh, and in Hebron no one knows who they are. And so a bunch of sixteen- and seventeen-year-old kids came, created havoc, and left. No one knew how to catch them, and or how to locate them, and most of the soldiers didn't have the motivation to do so. You don't want to be a policeman, it's not your job, it's not your concern, you're there to try and protect the . . . I mean, maybe if you saw kids coming and throwing stones at a Palestinian shop, then you'd try to stop them, because that seems completely unreasonable, but usually you don't put too much effort into chasing after them and arresting them. It's just not like that. There was a lot of hostility. During the whole funeral proceedings there was chaos in the streets, and officers of all ranks actually got into physical fights with the settlers. The settlers came and spat on the battalion commander—just about the worst thing they could do. Again, as I said before, and it's important to say it—the soldiers in Hebron are the greatest victims. No, the Palestinians are the greatest victims, but the soldiers are next. They're in this place where they have to go against their will and support the settlers, who can do whatever they want, abuse Palestinians as much as they want. Soldiers try to stop the settlers, but they don't have the power to do it.

130. The settlers put a hole in his wall

UNIT: NAHAL BRIGADE
LOCATION: HEBRON
YEAR: 2006

Another terrible thing that happened, I was on patrol 30, and a Palestinian approaches post 38, which is the passageway between the casbah and the Jewish settlement. He came up and said, "They're bombarding my house with stones, they're shelling my house." I go, "What?" And he tells us he lives on Zahav road. Zahav road goes by Bet Hadassah, and then there is Big Shalala road and Little Shalala road. Zahav road is totally closed off, except at the very end, where there's a building right next to Bet Hadassah. All of the windows are welded shut, of course. The army welded the windows so that he and his family can't see what's going on in Bet Hadassah, but Bet Hadassah can see their wall. The guy asks for permission to go into their territory from Sirena road. He goes with us, and he sees the state of his house, two rooms and a bedroom, and his whole family is outside shaking. In one corner of the metal post of the house, you see the hole the settlers made from the other side with a five-kilo hammer.

When was this?

Just three months ago. And every stone thrown against that metal sounds like a real boom. And it's right against their bedroom. That incident made me really angry. I called my company commander in a rage, I was really angry. I wasn't able to get him on the radio, so I spoke to him on the phone. He says, "Just remember one thing, when you speak to the settlement security coordinator, remember that he's on our side." The company commander understood my rage. He was also very upset, because you could see the hole they made with the five-kilo hammer.

I want to make sure I understand, they made a hole in the wall?

They made a hole in the wall and stoned their windows. It made me really angry.

Do you remember the name of the family?

No, but I think they were the last family to stay in the house. The only family who'd put up with it.

Do you know what the situation there is like today?

No. I'm afraid to find out whether they even live there anymore.

Was there an investigation afterward?

I really doubt it.

What did you do in that situation, did you call the police?

I called Yoni,* they also called Yoni. We get there, and I go to the house in Bet Hadassah to meet with the Hadassah patrol in the area and tell them what happened. In the meantime, I see a group of young kids standing on the side, saying, "Yeah, we blasted their house." All of them so happy and pleased. At that moment I wanted to do I don't know what to those kids, because they were so happy they blasted the house, like it was the best thing they ever did. That was one of the things that bothered me the most. A family that's so . . .

Why did you call Yoni, was that the procedure?

That was the procedure, you call the settlement security coordinator. And, of course, you call the police, but it takes about a decade for the police to come, for obvious reasons.

So the settlement security coordinator was the first to arrive?

He was the first to arrive.

What did he say when he got there?

He looked at the house and goes, "Okay, I see." That was it.

Did he talk to the kids?

Maybe. I don't know.

*One of the civilian settlement security coordinators.

What authority does the settlement security coordinator have?

I have no idea. He's a good man, he's nice, supports the army and everything, but on the other hand, he's a member of that settlement.

Where does he live? In Bet Hadassah?

Yeah, one of those places. And he just—I have no idea why they called him to come, it's a complete joke, because he's not going to do anything against people from his settlement.

But he has the authority to do so, the responsibility?

He's subject to the Ministry of Defense. That's his authority.

But he's the first person you turn to if something happens?

No, it depends what the incident is.

What about in a case like this?

You go to him and to the police. You turn to him because he's from the settlement, so he can talk to the kids and whatever. Because at the end of the day, try doing something to a kid younger than fourteen. You're not allowed to do anything. So maybe there were fifteen- and sixteen-year-olds there.

So what happens if someone's older than fourteen?

So what?

So you're saying you don't do anything to them either. How does that make you feel?

What can I do to them? I'm not, I'm sorry . . . my company commander was really worked up because that same day they told him he had to stay to protect the Sharabati house. He was very worked up about it. He'd had conversations with the battalion commander, the deputy battalion commander, the deputy brigade commander, about how this is not why he's here. He said he's not here to protect their house. He's here to protect the Jewish settlement, not to protect Palestinians from the

Jewish settlement. He said again how irritated he was. And because they understood there's no way out, they put in a special patrol unit there for when the Palestinian workers were there.

131. Stopping the settlers? The army can't do anything

Unit: Lavi Battalion
Location: South Hebron Hills
Year: 2003

What about the Palestinian farmers?
What do you mean?

I know that there are fights over land in the South Hebron Hills.
First, it wasn't in our sector, so I was less involved with the whole thing about settlers poisoning sheep. I'm talking about the settlers from Maon. They just say, "This is my land!" and they throw out anyone who's not Jewish, okay? The army doesn't do anything about it.

The army doesn't do anything public?
I guess. I don't have any proof, I just assume that the whole senior command staff in the sector knows that there's a problem. But are you supposed to deal with it? Is there is a plan to deal with the problem? No, I don't think there is. It's like when I was in Hebron, the settlers are like the settlers in Hebron. They throw stones and shut down the casbah, and ruin the lives of the Palestinians living there, right? And does the army do anything?

No.
Right. It's the same thing here, the army doesn't want confrontation . . . They took control of a house, a private home where the Muasi family lived. A Palestinian home, and Israelis just took control of it. It hadn't been abandoned, right? They just threw the family out of the house. And what did the army do? Nothing . . . What about the Palestinian

family? Why didn't the army just throw them out? It's not like we don't have units that can go in there . . . How would the army deal with Palestinians who were holed up in a house with weapons? They'd take down the house on top of them with a bulldozer. It's the same thing with all the settlers in the area. A settler does something wrong, and there's no way to enforce the law. And the settlers know it, "So what, you're a soldier, you can't do anything. Go get the police."

They say that to you?

Yeah. They say, "Go get the police." And you know, you already know the police there. So you call the police, and if you report someone who's Jewish, the police won't come. It's the same even with Israeli Arabs, I got an answer from the police once, "We won't come, release them."

132. The brigade commander didn't want to get involved

Unit: Civil Administration
Location: Hebron
Year: 2001–2004

I was one of the people who went in and saw the settler kids there, hanging out inside the Sharabati family house.* We'd received the same complaint from multiple places, from the city of Hebron, from the Palestinian liaison, from the Waqf. I think it was evening, and they sent me in there at night. I got the complaint, and so I went to see what was up. I caught those kids there, eleven- to thirteen-year-olds, playing inside the Sharabati house upstairs. I don't remember exactly what it was, but I remember some of them were smoking. It was a hash hangout. I'd always suspected they were doing drugs there, but that's not important, even though it's true. And I did report it, but there wasn't much else for me to do.

---

*The house, which borders the Avraham Avinu neighborhood, has been repeatedly ransacked by settlers and made uninhabitable for the Sharabati family. The army first welded the house shut in 2002.

You reported it to the army, or the police?

The army, police, everyone.

And what happened afterward?

The Sharabati house is complicated. The report went to the brigade commander. The brigade commander turned it into a very drawn-out process. You know, he didn't freeze it, but he didn't deal with it for a long time. He didn't want to get into a confrontation with the Jewish settlement; it was a sensitive time, after everything else.

Who was the brigade commander then?

The brigade commander was ——. He delayed it. You don't want to get into a confrontation with the Jewish settlement. They're the people who are closest to you, they're like your operations branch officer, that's how it works. At first he delayed things and didn't really deal with it, but there was pressure to act. There was pressure from above the legal adviser, the legal adviser went to clarify things, and then the report didn't go to the captain legal adviser, rather to ——, who was a colonel, and —— wanted results. So things really started to move. The army blocked off the house, put up a fence, and today there are concrete blocks there. I don't remember anymore, but I think they fenced off the, whatever, and there was a period where they had soldiers guarding it. People broke in all the time, it was broken into once a month.

Were there other "Sharabati houses"?

No, but I remember one time settlers burned down a Palestinian house on a Saturday. A house right across from the cemetery. I remember that kids, twelve years old at most, totally burned down the house. I don't know what it's like today. I took photos of the inside. I went to Harat a-Sheikh to escort the fire truck, a Palestinian fire truck which put out the fire, because Kiryat Arba wouldn't agree to send their fire truck. It was Shabbat, and they said that they don't drive the fire truck on Shabbat unless it's an emergency.

And the fire was burning during this whole time?

Yes. The fire was burning down a house across from the Muslim cemetery.

Was the house empty?

No, it wasn't empty. When they burned it down, no one was there, and afterward I coordinated with the Palestinians so they could come and take whatever remained. I escorted them and helped them with moving.

Who took things?

The Palestinians who lived there. It was their house.

You're saying there was food in the fridge.

A woman was living there. She wasn't home when the kids broke in and burned it. She was with her family in Abu Sneina, maybe with her son or someone from her family.

She'd been living there on a regular basis?

No. She lived there, but not on a daily basis. The house was orderly, clean even, but could I say for sure that she was there all week, or every two days? I don't know. After the house burned down, she wasn't there anymore.

Were you involved with the wholesale market during that time?

The wholesale market, I did legal work … In general, after the fire, which was sometime in 2003, I started doing a lot of work with the Jewish settlement, not with them, with the legal adviser on how to advance the issue of the Jewish settlement and how to prevent violence by working in cooperation with the Israeli police. I was a committee member, a military committee, with the Civil Administration, the police, the legal adviser. We wanted to figure out how to curb the violence, which increased dramatically sometime in 2003—there was suddenly a huge jump in violence.

What caused the sudden jump?

I'm not sure what caused it—after that house burned down, there was a weekend of intense violence, I don't know why. Maybe there was a terrorist attack, I don't know, there was definitely something. So I got angry and I called —— and I spoke with him, and I also spoke with the brigade commander that Saturday, and I spoke with the operations coordinator of the government in the Territories, and they decided they'd figure out a system to deal with it, but their system didn't work because it had no teeth.

Did the police in Hebron have any power?

No, any decision to regulate the violence within the Jewish population has to come from above, there's nothing the police can do. You just need to decide, the police commissioner needs to say "Stop." And no one will . . .

But a representative from the police is on the committee? Didn't the police complain about their lack of manpower? Say that they're incapable of working under these conditions? That they need reinforcements? Didn't the representative say things like that at the committee?

No, he didn't say anything like that. The police always complain about a lack of manpower, always, but . . . What were the committee's complaints? That there was a lack of manpower, so they talked about what days to have additional people or no additional people, how to reinforce the station, how not to reinforce the station—all these things are administrative. I was powerless, I really didn't have any say.

133. They close Palestinian places even without an injunction

UNIT: CIVIL ADMINISTRATION

LOCATION: HEBRON

YEAR: 2001–2004

The Civil Administration has a very bad relationship with the settlers.

Why?

We're treated as a Palestinian authority.

And the army?

I told you, the settlement security coordinator is like the operations branch officer. He goes into the brigade commander's office whenever he wants, however he wants. They talk all the time. That's just how it is. They sit in at all of the situation assessments, and they sit in on all the discussions, and they know about a lot of things ahead of time.

How much power and influence do the settlement security coordinators have over decisions that are made during situation assessment meetings?

They're a security force, they're treated as one. They're an alert squad that's treated as a security force. They bring up a lot of requests at the situation assessment meetings, a ton of requests.

Did you get to sit in on these meetings?

Many times.

Do you remember specific requests made by people?

I wasn't with ——, just with ——. But specific requests? I think that after Worshippers' Road* there were discussions about weapons or no weapons or how many weapons and how to use the weapons—those things were discussed.

---

*On November 15, 2002, a terrorist attack occurred on what is called "Worshippers' Road," in which twelve Israelis—soldiers and settlers—were killed. The road is a shortcut connecting Kiryat Arba and the Cave of the Patriarchs.

Patrol duty, Hebron, Nahal Brigade, Battalion 50. The settler was returning from Friday afternoon prayers at the Cave of the Patriarchs. The photo was taken from the elevated patrol on the rooftops.

Discussions about weapons they'd receive?

Training of the alert forces there. Technical military things.

Were there requests concerning closing Palestinian stores or roads?

No, first of all, these are internal letters circulated by the settlement. They personally give the letters to the brigade commander, and at the situation assessment they bring up their complaints. The letter goes directly to the brigade commander, you don't see it, but you know it exists. And yes, the settlers got angry more than once about the opening of Palestinian stores in the Shalala roads area, and there was a period where we tried to open the Shalala roads and it wasn't pleasant at all, the settlers were very unpleasant during that time. At one meeting they requested a mapping of the casbah. The settlers said that the army needed to map the casbah to see which families live there. And they actually did it.

So their requests are granted?

Yes, yes.

They did a mapping . . .

It started from there. Yes.

When was this?

It started in 2003. I don't remember what was going on at the time, but there was some justification. No one said what the justification was, but it was around the time when the committee for improving the old city and the Palestinian Authority decided to gentrify the area there. It was around the end of 2002, and they'd just received money from the Swedish government, so they decided to gentrify the area. If you look back, at the end of 2002, beginning of 2003, you can see all kinds of families from the refugee camps, al-Fuar, or whatever, who appear to live there. There was just a lot of money there.

What was the relationship like between the settlers and the police?

In the city itself it's not all that friendly, but the higher up you go you'll see there is a friendly relationship. Go to the station commander in Etzion, and you'll see there's a relationship. Friendly relations just don't exist on the lower end, at least not from what I saw. They weren't friends with the Druze [police] there. But higher up, yes.

How is it expressed?

I don't know, I never sat in Etzion or spoke with the station commander there on the phone, but I knew and saw letters from the settlements to him, meaning he knew, he was in contact with the settlers. But I don't know how it was expressed.

How was restricting movement in Hebron managed? Who made the decision? How were you involved?

That was before my time. When I came, Shuhada street was already dead, the only thing that changed in the Shuhada area while I was there was that the tiles from Fedesco fell. That was it. With the exception of that, nothing changed during my time there.

A danger to public security . . .

Yes, it's not clear who threw them down, but we picked them up.

Meaning, by the time you got there, Shuhada street was closed to Palestinian pedestrians. It's still—

Yes, that's still the current situation.

When you first got there, who explained it to you?

It's not something that was explained to me—you see it for yourself. No one said anything or showed it to you. After Moshe "Boogie" Yaalon* came to the brigade they went and reorganized some stores that had been closed with or without an injunction. When he came in 2003 and appointed ——, only then did you see where there was an injunction and where there wasn't. Before that it was pretty naïve to think there actually was an injunction.

What do you mean?

Boogie came in 2003, I don't remember, there was some political change, something that happened, I don't remember, what happened in 2003? It could be that it was the *hudna,*† and a political change took place, and he visited the brigades, and I did the presentation for the Civil Administration.

A presentation on what?

I don't remember, on a lot of things, the function of the Civil Administration and so on. Everything, basically. Some of the things he asked about were how to ease things in Hebron, and I brought up the closures. And after he came to . . .

What kind of closures?

Closing stores and streets with injunctions, to make things official. Only then was there an awareness of this issue.

---

*Then IDF chief of staff.
†A negotiated truce between Israel and Hamas reached in 2003.

An awareness that stores and streets had been closed without injunctions?

Yes.

And what did you discover during the investigation? Which places had injunctions?

Nothing.

Nothing, including stores and streets?

Yes.

So they took out injunctions?

It depends, in some cases yes, others no. So you pass the case on to the legal adviser, and he says where it's possible to close stores and where it isn't, where there's an immediate security need and where there's just a regular security need . . . he ranked the security needs, like rings around the Jewish settlement. And in the end that's how they issued injunctions.

What did they take out injunctions for?

I don't remember, it was selective. They took out injunctions for all of the areas that were close to the settlements, I really don't remember anymore.

Do you remember if they took out an injunction for Shuhada street?

I don't remember an injunction for Shuhada street.

So it continues to be closed with no injunction.

Is there an injunction today? I don't know. During my time I was unaware of an injunction.

Here's the question: You carry out an investigation whose purpose is to . . .

The primary objective of the investigation was to ease things for the Palestinian population in Hebron in light of the *hudna* or the other political event that took place, don't take my word for whatever it was. I was responsible for it, I did a mapping of H2,* where there are injunctions, where there aren't. I brought my report to a meeting, and at that meeting the chief of staff said that my findings couldn't possibly be the case, so Boogie Yaalon told the brigade commander to check, and he also found that there were no injunctions. He had two weeks to check, and then it got to the situation assessment meeting in front of the general of the Central Command, I don't know what happened there, I'm an insider. And then they slowly started issuing injunctions. Whatever the brigade commander could issue automatically, he issued for ninety days, which was in very limited areas. Afterward they started administrative work which took a very long time and I don't know if it's finished even today. In the end, things mostly stayed the same, even for places that don't have injunctions. The exception is the Shalala roads.

The Shalala roads were the one thing that changed.

The Shalalas—I personally thought it was a great achievement that they were opened. I'll never forget the day, a Friday, when we got permission to open the Shalalas starting on Sunday.

Permission from whom?

The general of the Central Command. He informed everyone on the radio that they should inform the merchants to go to the left of the square, next to the police square. There are some six thousand, eight thousand people, and I'm yelling at them from the jeep megaphone, all by myself, without a military escort, nothing, like a crazy man all by myself, telling them they can open their stores. I think it was on a Sunday or Monday. It was actually a really nice scene.

---

*The area in Hebron under full Israeli control.

Aside from the Shalala roads, did the other places that didn't have injunctions, and weren't given new injunctions during the reorganization, did they remain closed?

We didn't finish the reorganization during my time there, and I don't know what the situation is like today, but yes, they remained closed, without injunctions. That I know.

What about closing houses, or preventing residents from returning to their houses if they're next to Avraham Avinu, for example . . .

Are you talking about welding? Oh . . . welding was done without an injunction, and afterward welding was done with an injunction. After we saw that places were being welded over without an injunction, they started issuing injunctions, which, if I'm not mistaken, came from the brigade commander. But when they came to weld the places, they'd already been welded, so they just went over it again. By that point no one was living in those houses anymore.

134. Each time they went to evacuate the place, an order came from the minister of defense

Unit: Civil Administration
Location: Hebron
Year: 2002–2003

What do you remember from Hazon David?*

Apart from the nights in Hazon David, they finished me . . .

The evacuations started during your time there . . .

I remember I evacuated them a few times. Each time, we tried to trick them a different way, do you remember all that nonsense? To show them they were being evacuated? We tried all kinds of tricky things, they never worked.

---

*An illegal outpost in Hebron, which was ordered evacuated and destroyed—more than thirty times.

Tell a story.

There isn't much of a story, Hazon David is still there.

How did the evacuations start? When? Why wasn't it ever really evacuated—how did that play out?

First of all, I don't even remember how many times they told me to evacuate the Hazon David outpost, but I think at least a few. There's a court ruling on it.

When was Hazon David first established?

I don't remember exactly. During my time there, end of 2002, beginning of 2003, something like that. It was clear why they put it up. They always had a dream to connect the western gate of Kiryat Arba to the Jewish settlement. They'd say it to you directly. It was clear why they were doing it. Hazon David is a bullshit story—every time the army went to evacuate it, an order was given by the minister of defense not to evacuate. Whenever they evacuated it, the outpost would reappear, and that was the story. I don't know what the dirt there was. If I were serving the settlement's interests I'd be able to tell you a story about it, but I wasn't interested in that. I don't know what happened there.

Were there times when you went to evacuate Hazon David and the minister of defense ordered you not to do it?

The night we were supposed to evacuate it, they canceled the evacuation once, they canceled it a second time, and the third time we did evacuate it, but the outpost was put back up the next day. I don't remember what happened there. I wasted so many nights on Hazon David.

Did you guys know from the beginning that the outpost was on private Palestinian land? Private property?

That's not relevant, I don't remember, I don't know what to tell you. I don't know whose land it was, I don't remember. But it doesn't matter.

Why is Hazon David still not evacuated, do you have any idea?

Because . . . listen, here's what happened. In the middle of 2003 some Knesset members visited the Jewish settlement in Hebron, after Hazon David was established, you can check the papers. I escorted their tour. Tzachi Hanegbi was there, Ruby Rivlin,* and all kinds of people like that. And there was Hazon David, a fact on the ground. Listen, when you get verbal legitimization from a Knesset member . . .

Knesset members visited the settlers?

They visited the whole Jewish settlement, they went on the tour, the western gate, they really did the whole tour.

They came to Hazon David and said . . .

I remember Tzachi Hanegbi said that one of the goals was to connect the western gate and the Jewish settlement. He said it to the settlement leaders. Look in a newspaper, *Ha'aretz*, from that period, and you'll see. Sometime in 2003.

135. They spat on me and cursed me

UNIT: FIELD INTELLIGENCE
LOCATION: ELON MOREH
YEAR: 2006

After a few months doing various missions, you continued with the squad commander course and went to Nablus. What kind of operations did you do there?

We were also in Elon Moreh, and operations there were about protecting the settlement itself, defense against terrorist activity.

How do you do that?

You look out on the slopes that lead up to Elon Moreh, and everyone who comes close to the settlements from below is suspect.

*Members of the government, from the right-wing Likud Party.

And what do you do then?

I can tell you stories from the sector, but during the time I was there, no one came up to Elon Moreh.

But what were the orders if someone did?

If you identify a suspect, you shoot to kill. If he's armed—you shoot to kill. If it's just someone—you deploy the forces, the settlement security coordinator, whoever you need.

You deploy a civilian force?

The settlement security coordinator is like an employee of the IDF. In any case, he's connected to the military, and any report that goes over the radio he gets as well.

If in theory you see a person coming up the slope without anything on him, do you inform the settlement security coordinator?

No, first you inform the brigade operations room. But the coordinator is the first responder, that's his assignment in the settlement. I can tell you that we once identified armed men going up the slope, and they turned out to be guys from the settlement who decided to train their kids there, a kind of training camp where they taught them how to sneak into places. They didn't coordinate this with the army, of course, and it created a big mess.

Who was armed?

The teenagers and their camp counselor.

How old were the teenagers?

Fifteen to seventeen, something like that.

And what happened?

We reported it to the operations room, and then they sent out a team, and in the end it turned out okay, I don't remember exactly what happened, but the guys were identified as Israelis, and so nothing happened. It was pretty stupid of them to do something like that, because another force would have shot them.

What other missions did you do aside from that?

From the Elon Moreh post itself you also look out over the eastern neighborhoods of Nablus, and there you mostly accompany arrests. The distance is relatively big, so basically, you provide security on the roofs, the windows, and accompany arrests. And, of course, roving security.

What does that mean?

It's a fixed mission, it's not the result of anything special, rather it's just a military force protecting the settlements, the security of the surrounding settlements, whether it's Gidonim, Yitzhar, Har Bracha, or Elon Moreh itself. Mostly roving security. That's more or less the kind of operations we had there.

And did you encounter any settler action around the settlements there?

One time, for example, we were supposed to provide security for them on a Shabbat morning hike in the valley between two villages. A whole company was attached to their hike just to provide security. Really, I'm talking about families on a picnic. A military force escorted them because their hike went through a Palestinian area. We were part of their security.

They really set up a lookout force and an escort company just for the hike?

Yes.

Were you stationed specifically in Elon Moreh?

Part of the force was in Elon Moreh and part in the central brigade itself.

Were there missions where you were stationed in Yitzhar, for example?

Yes. The force that's stationed in Elon Moreh stays in Elon Moreh. It doesn't move from there. The force in the central brigade goes to Yitzhar, Har Bracha, Gidonim, to all kinds of points in the sector.

Did you encounter real terrorist activity while you were in these settlements? From incursion attempts to burning their land?

No. I was there for a short time. I imagine there were stories like that, but not in my time.

And what about the opposite? Settlers against Palestinians.

No. Not in my time. But there were stories there—it was a relatively sensitive period with respect to the relationship between the IDF and the settlers, because it was after the disengagement. I remember one story. I wasn't there when this happened, but I heard that the deputy regional brigade commander of Shomron came to a Passover seder with a black eye, which he got from a settler. There were all kinds of confrontations like that. Things like that happen, though I personally didn't see any of it. There were stories about settlers even damaging military property, slashing tires, and there was a terrible story from Yitzhar, which caused the army to remove its security detail from the settlement. Masked men from the settlement came to the gate, there was a private there who was on settlement security detail, and the masked settlers came and beat him up and took his radio. This happened a few months before I got there, I think. From my own experience, once I was in Elon Moreh and about to go on a run in the settlement when I was hit with spit and cursed at, the settlers said things like "A Jew doesn't expel a Jew" and like that. It's really two-faced, because on the one hand they'll bring you cake, and on the other hand, you feel the tension and you put up with what you put up with. If I wanted to hitch a ride from the Tapuach intersection, which is forbidden but everyone does it, a resident of one of the settlements would stop for you, and the first question he'd ask was where you were during the disengagement. It's like a ticket to get into the car. Either you justify yourself, or you hide information, or you do what I did—I closed the door and told him to keep driving.

Did you talk about it with your commanders? That the settlers were spitting on you.

You tell them what happened, but the deputy brigade commander got punched by settlers in Yitzhar. Everyone knows that the situation is fraught. Nablus, Elon Moreh, Gidonim and Itamar and Yitzhar are known for being the toughest sectors, really a tough place. Ariel isn't one of those places. You know the character of the population, so you try to cause as little friction as possible. The settlers used to visit the posts, and so the army put out an order that it's forbidden for any civilian from Elon Moreh to be near the posts anymore. There are a few posts around there, and I believe the orders were for all of the posts.

136. They stomp on the *mitzvot* and morals

UNIT: IDF SPOKESPERSON'S UNIT
LOCATION: YITZHAR
YEAR: 2005

Were there any unusual incidents that occurred during your service which really left an impression on you?

Yes. The first was the evacuation of the Shalhevet Yitzhar outpost on January 3, 2005. It was the first time there was serious photography of the event. I'd never photographed anything really journalistic before, where the events were so intense and so detailed. Do you want me to describe what happened?

Yes. Why did you choose that event specifically?

Because the incident affected me personally, and because I was involved in it, I wasn't just a spectator. And also because it was really the first time I was in such an intense situation, and it made me interested in the whole political situation in this country. Why are we like this, how did we come to this, who are these settlers, how did they get so powerful, who are these people, what's going on here?

And you didn't know any of this beforehand?

It interested me, but it wasn't at the front of my mind, I didn't go and read books about it. Now I'm at the point where every—I mean, it doesn't really convey the point—but now every settler I see in the street I turn around . . . So what happened there? I got there in the morning with the photography crew—a videographer, a soundman, and a stills photographer. I was the stills photographer, and we went up with a convoy of soldiers from the settlement, from the settlement gate to the outpost, which was a bit farther down. Now, at a certain point we became separated from the convoy. In short, there's a slope leading down to the outpost, where they were evacuating it and where there was this huge mess. When we got there, it was really chaotic, lots of hitting, it was a rampage.

Between the IDF and the settlers?
Between the IDF and the settlers.

Were the police there?

The police were there, and they'd brought all kinds of heavy machinery to evacuate the outpost, which was just a caravan. And then, at a certain point on the slope, we got separated. Somehow the soldiers got away from us as we were going down. The photography crew wasn't moving, the videographer and the soundman were standing right at the start of the incline, and they were filming something that didn't interest me, so I started going down. I was alone and I had a camera and a uniform on, and they saw I was a female soldier. And then while I was walking down, five or six settlers came and surrounded me and started yelling at me and all kinds of stuff. The photography crew didn't see me, and the settlers were surrounding me and yelling at me, and I couldn't say a word, I just stood there and I didn't move and I didn't say anything. I had two cameras, one around my neck and one on my shoulder, and at one point, one of the settlers grabbed the camera on my shoulder and pulled. I pulled, he pulled. It went on like that for ten seconds or so, only he was stronger. He grabbed it, ran away, and that was it. And then I started screaming, I think. I was more in shock.

Settler children destroying the wall of a closed Palestinian store, Hebron. The photographer, Noam Biberman, took this image while serving in Hebron.

Did they touch you?

No, but it was a very scary situation. They surrounded me and I wasn't able to speak, I couldn't move. But I remember I was more in shock from what a soldier did. There was a soldier near me, and I started saying to him, "Help me, they stole my camera," and he kind of—I imagine he was afraid, because he didn't do anything—he kind of turned away.

Turned away?

Yes, turned away. And then I started yelling to my friends from the unit, "Come, see," and they started to run.

How did you carry on working after that?

I had another camera.

I imagine you didn't record the crowd.

Actually, that made me want to. I wanted to take photos much more afterward, because it infuriated me. After I . . . I was still in shock, but it infuriated me, they annoyed me. What is this? All these morals they claim to have, just like that they discard them. All the *mitzvot* and morals that they do all this in the name of, here, they just stamp on them. You get it?

137. The settlers in the administration do whatever they want

Unit: Civil Administration
Location: General
Year: 2000–2002

Did you have anything to do with issues regarding outposts and land?

No. I personally didn't, that was all the administration's domain. Let's say, 90 percent of the work is done at the level of headquarters, in the infrastructure branch. The head of infrastructure, a lieutenant colonel, was arrested. He was a settler himself. He was arrested because he did some land sales of absentee property to Jews. Everything there is corrupt to its core, because they're settlers who do whatever they want.

The people who work there?

Yes. It's shocking. Really. And I think everyone knows it. I don't know how he was only arrested just now.

138. Evacuating an outpost? It takes years

Unit: Civil Administration
Location: General
Year: 2007

You get calls from the settlement council heads, "Why'd you do this, why'd you do that . . ."

What do you mean?

They want to know why we don't approve this or that construction plan, or why construction is delayed.

The DCL approves construction plans?

The administration is the planning authority, and it's responsible for planning and construction in the Territories, as its name says, Civil administration. And we'd also get complaints from the other side, why don't you evacuate this outpost, why don't you evacuate that outpost.

Complaints from—

From left-wing organizations, yes. Why doesn't the administration evacuate this or that house? In the Civil Administration you really see all of the complexities of an issue, because you deal with all of the things that happen there, and you get reports on all of the things that happen. And you see the bureaucracy, and how the administration is so firmly entrenched. We've been there for forty years, for heaven's sake—either annex it or leave. Israel can't continue like this, and there's so much . . . you know that the law in the Territories isn't Israeli law. It's Jordanian.

Jordanian? I thought that it was a hybrid of Israeli law . . .

No, it's like this, the law is Jordanian.

For which cases?

For all cases. It doesn't matter which.

Criminal cases, too?

Criminal, too. But security ordinances signed by the major general, injunctions of the major general can override Jordanian law. The major general basically rules the area. Now, with issues of planning and construction, the law is Jordanian for every case and issue. Meaning, the whole process of building permits—not all of them, there are also ordinances which came afterward—but Jordanian law is still the foundation.

You really learn the Jordanian law?

I don't. But there are authorities in the administration who do. The planning department knows it fully. And you understand that basically . . . it's like a purgatory that's been going on for forty years. You need never-ending legal opinions for every single subject, and nothing ever gets done. There's such turmoil that in the end you get annoyed, even though you're part of the system. "Come on, for heaven's sake, decide already." The administration doesn't decide anything.

What do you mean by that?

They don't decide anything, and they have discussion upon discussion upon discussion and you never reach a decision.

Discussions about which issues?

Every issue: construction and planning, electricity, water.

But with regard to illegal outposts, from what I see in the field, it's pretty fast.

It's complicated. It's very complicated.

What? For roads, electricity . . .

Just evacuating an outpost is complicated . . . it's very complicated. You have to submit injunctions, and then they can submit an appeal against the injunction, and then it goes to the military appeal committee, and it gets stuck there for months sometimes. And until you get approval to evacuate, then they go to the Supreme Court. And then you have to wait for the Supreme Court to finish. It's so complicated that you say to yourself, "I'll take a bulldozer and destroy it, just to end this whole thing." There are outposts that generate legal correspondence of seven, eight, nine, ten binders. The Beruchin outpost has . . . in my office there were ten binders and the legal adviser had even more.

The evacuation process is really so complicated?

Yes. They're complicated legal proceedings, and you have to prove many things for them to let you evacuate at all.

But you have maps that show that these outposts are not on your land . . . isn't it simple?

Not at all. There's a lot that I can't even explain to you.

Did you deal with outposts in the South Hebron Hills, for example?

Not so much. I dealt more with Beruchin . . . in principle, there are a few types of lands. There's state land, which for the most part is abandoned and managed by the Israel Lands Authority. And there are private lands—Palestinian and Jewish.

The first type of land is equal in all legal ways to land, say, in the Hadera and Modi'in areas, Netanya and Rishon Letzion?*

State land? In terms of planning and construction?

Yes.

No. There are a few other things. You can't build a house in the Territories like you can in Hadera.

What's the difference?

You need approval from the minister of defense, and all kinds of things like that. But the more problematic outposts are those on private Palestinian land. There it should be simpler, as it were, but it's much more complicated. Let's say I build a house on state land—so the state comes and sues me because I built the house illegally, but it doesn't really care. It's less problematic. The more urgent issue is evacuating outposts that are on private Palestinian land. And going through all of those proceedings quickly is impossible.

Why?

It's impossible. Because it's protected by the law. I present you with an injunction to evacuate the house, and you come and say, "I have proof that the house and the land are mine." Come and prove it. You submit the proof and I have to postpone.

*Towns within Israel.

But the proof . . . what proof?

The proofs are not definitive, because don't forget that the maps from 1948 are not exact. Meaning, the maps showing land demarcation are not exact.

But you have maps . . .

They aren't precise.

And the DCL doesn't have . . .

There's no precise map.

So how can you do your work?

There are old maps, there's what's called "the blue line team." The blue line team is a unit that redefines the borders, with corrections, of all of the land in the Territories. In the end it's supposed to redefine the borders, not for areas where there's no argument, but in the majority of the problem areas. There are, for example, settlements which were built on the basis of a military injunction. That's something different entirely.

Settlements on the basis of a military injunction?

Ma'ale Efraim—a military seizure injunction.

What does that mean?

A seizure injunction. The military takes possession of the land.

But there's a base there.

No, they built a settlement there.

With the support of the army?

On the basis of an injunction signed by the major general. The major general signed the seizure injunction on a certain piece of land, and they built a settlement there.

Is that a process that moves more quickly?

Yes. Much faster. The moment the injunction is signed, you just have to submit building plans, and on the basis of the injunction it's approved. Because it's a seizure injunction. If we're talking about a civil proceeding, it's much more complicated.

But the injunction has authority over what land?

Only over state land.

Is there more state land than private land?

Yes, much more.

Say I come to you with a group of people and we want to establish a settlement. What happens if I come without an injunction?

Without an injunction?

Right. Isn't that a long process? Would you suggest I do it with an injunction?

But they don't give injunctions. They don't exist anymore, they're only for bases. It's a legal problem to approve an injunction for building a settlement. Now there's just a legal process.

Which is the same for everyone?

Yes. But the chances that you'd be approved for a construction plan in the Territories are so low, because there are always private lands in the middle. Let's say this is land for my settlement. I developed a plan on all the land, but here there's some private land—they won't approve that plan. And try finding land that doesn't have private land on it. Good luck with that.

But settlements are still built.

They don't build legal settlements anymore.

What about the neighborhoods in Efrat, for example?

I don't remember exactly what Efrat's status is.

It's settlement by settlement?

Yes, but the construction plan exists, so there's no problem with adding to it. If you have an approved construction plan, then there's no problem with building another neighborhood, if the neighborhood's approved. You also need a building permit, but they'll give it to you—because the plan has already been approved. There's no building of new settlements, just expansion of old settlements. There aren't really any new settlements.

What about Giva'at Sal'it in the north?

I think Giva'at Sal'it is an outpost.

It's considered an outlying neighborhood.

But it's an outpost. Giva'at Sal'it is an outpost.

It's been there for years—does it really take years to evacuate it? Is there an evacuation order for Giva'at Sal'it?

I'm not sure about Giva'at Sal'it. But Migron, near Ramallah, is an outpost which has had an evacuation order on it for three or four years, and the case is still in the Supreme Court.

Were there Supreme Court rulings during your time? Did they evacuate any settlements?

A few caravans and things like that. I closed a few.

Which ones, do you remember? For example, I was there for the evacuation of Gilad Farm.

No. But what was Gilad Farm? A trailer, not a permanent structure.

But every outpost is pretty much just trailers.

What are you talking about?

How else do they get up on a hilltop?

Ofra is one big outpost.*

*An iconic settlement of 3,200 residents, one of the first, established in 1975.

Ofra is an outpost?

The majority of Ofra is an outpost. You think you can evacuate Ofra?

No.

Not on your life.

But from an administrative perspective, I don't understand what an outpost is. If you were to tell me that Ariel* is an outpost, I'd believe you.

Ariel is 90 percent legal. There are a few isolated houses in the industrial area there, it's not that it's illegal, but there's some kind of problem there. But Ariel is legal.

But you told me that Ofra is an outpost—it's huge.

The whole settlement was built on an outpost.

When?

Twenty years ago.

Twenty years ago? There are Supreme Court cases going back twenty years?

There's no case. No one's going to evacuate it. Where are you living? Everyone knows it's illegal, but no one's going to evacuate it. You can't. You can't evacuate places like that.

139. It wasn't clear where the settlement begins

UNIT: CARACAL BATTALION
LOCATION: SOUTH HEBRON HILLS
YEAR: 2008

What was your experience of the Territories like?

I was there while doing post officers' training.

---

*The fourth-largest settlement in the West Bank, established in 1978, with a population of 17,600.

When was that?

Last Shavuot. I remember because it was holiday time.

You were there as a cadet in the officers' course?

Yes.

Officers' course, specialization training.

Yes.

And you were deployed there for what purpose?

We were brought there to guard the Susiya settlement. There were also noncombat women cadets in our group, who had been squad commanders during basic training and had gone through the officers' course. It was kind of weird to do guard duty with them.

Why?

Because they don't usually do guard duty. They don't really know the routine, getting briefed and getting instructions on the ground and stuff like that. It's not part of their life.

But guard duty at Susiya was kind of routine security procedure, wasn't it?

Yes. We were inside the settlement. We didn't leave the settlement. And that's the point—it's kind of a strange settlement, especially considering where it's located. It raises many questions—like if there weren't all these situations there, it could even be a really pretty kind of place. It gets you thinking. Every few hours you go on guard duty and you think. And then, in our first round of getting familiar with the guard posts, the local settlement security coordinator came and tried to define for us a red line, a green line, and so on.

What do you mean?

Where it's okay for the shepherds to graze their flock in the village on the opposite hill, and where we had to stop them. Where the settlement begins and where it ends.

The boundaries of the settlement?

Yes. Susiya has no fence, it's a settlement without a fence. Both because it costs money, and also it's a statement of sorts.

Did the settlement security coordinator explain to you why they don't have a fence?

Yes. First of all, because a fence doesn't actually keep anyone out, it only delays entry—whoever really wants to get in can always find a way in. Second, because they want to feel like they don't need a fence. It's a kind of denial of danger. And the way he defined things, which lines can and can't be crossed, it wasn't really clear what was part of the settlement and what wasn't. Even if he'd said, "The settlement ends here in the wadi, but if you see a person on the hill across the wadi, you still have to keep him away." Like, on the one hand it's obvious why they do that, why it's like that. They're being extra cautious so that no one will dare come into their settlement, and they don't want to have to wait until the person is actually at the border. On the other hand, what gives me or him the right to tell a person, "Get off that hill"?

The hill is where you see the rock cairn?

Yes, where that water hole is.

So you're stationed there, or was the rock cairn the boundary?

The other way around . . . there was one post where the boundary was really unclear. The terrain there is lower, and actually the post only guards one family, one of whose members had been murdered.

Jews?

Yes. They're from the settlement. The post is right next to their house. Because of what happened to them, the guard post was placed right there, to give them a sense of security. It's on the lower end of the ridge. So the definition of where [Palestinians] aren't allowed is, everywhere you see.

That's what the settlement security coordinator said?

Yes. All the way to there . . .

Within the boundaries of the settlement, is there anything that belongs to someone else? A water hole, a tree, a grove?

I don't think so.

Houses?

I don't think so. There was nothing there.

There wasn't a single water hole in the area you guarded that was out of bounds?

I don't think so.

Are you familiar with the term "special security zone"?

What does that mean?

The settlement security coordinator didn't discuss it with you? How long did you do guard duty there?

A week. Everything was very vague. It was terribly vague whose it was, if it was part of the settlement or not, because without a fence . . . Myself, I didn't trust him. He was kind of slick, you didn't know when he was telling you the truth and when he was giving his own interpretations. I don't know.

Was there a map you could look at?

No.

A briefing room?

No.

Who was the commander at that settlement?

Our commander from the officers' course.

And she showed you a map? What did she tell you at the briefing?

We didn't have briefings. She was from the Border Police, they don't do post briefings. They don't have those at all.

140. It was his settlement, and, the fact was, we were under him

UNIT: GIVATI BRIGADE
LOCATION: GUSH ETZION
YEAR: 2007

They built big houses for the settlers, but the settlers didn't move into them so they wouldn't have to pay income tax, and they continued living for free next to the buildings that were built for them. A gray place, no color, religious people walking with their heads down. A strange and depressing place, with a settlement security coordinator who was scarred from the Vietnam War. There were four of us and a platoon commander who left after one day and came back on the weekend. Another person and I were in command. The settlement security coordinator made it clear that it was his settlement, and, the fact was, we were under him.

He briefed you in the beginning?

Yes.

What did he say?

It was like something from the movies. I don't remember his name, but he said "I was a soldier in Vietnam, I was in the Marines and I see that you're infantrymen, that's good, because I have two boys in Golani." He told us that if anyone wants to come into the settlement, we have to check his ID, and if he's Arab, he can't come in. He starts saying, "I see people in the distance, if they want to come in, I shoot them." He said, "If people drive up in a taxi, you have to check to make sure the driver is Jewish, because one time someone from the settlement caught a taxi in Jerusalem, didn't know who the driver was, the driver came in, and

Settler trailers within the IDF barracks in Hebron.

I catch him in the kindergarten looking for a bathroom. I went up to him, he's looking for knives, I sent him to hell, I don't let anyone with an Arab name into the . . ." The guy's crazy.

What did you do there?

Guard duty. We waited for people to try to enter, and no one did.

It was quiet there.

Yes. One time we had our binoculars and saw that three kilometers from the settlement a boy was bringing his flock from the Hebron area to the valley. The settlement security coordinator came, put in a magazine, emptied it in his direction, as if anything would even reach there.

He shot in the shepherd's direction?

Yes. He said, "That Arab's gathering information, he wants to infiltrate the settlement." You could barely see him. It had just gotten foggy, so we had to use binoculars to see him.

He just fired an entire magazine at someone three kilometers away?

Yes, the guy was crazy.

Did you see the boy afterward?

He wasn't even aware that anyone was shooting at him. He was near Hebron, they empty magazines there all day. He stayed where he was with his sheep. The funniest part is that the Haruv Battalion relieved us, and they all have Arab names, and this settlement security coordinator hates Arab names and anyone who speaks Arabic.

141. The settlement security coordinator got angry, kicked him

Unit: Nahal Brigade
Location: Alei Zahav
Year: 2008–2009

At around twelve o'clock we received a call on the radio to come to Alei Zahav. We got into the Hummer and drove there. I see that a soldier doing settlement security and the settlement security coordinator both have their weapons out. He tells me that a woman heard voices, that he went in with a bullet in the chamber, there were two of them, and now both were tied up, hands on the ground, with restraints.

Who was there?

Two young Arabs, around our age. The coordinator asked them questions, the woman said they stole eight hundred dollars from her, some astronomical number. He asked where the money was. One said "Here, there . . ." The other said to each of us: "You, drink water, drink water, drink water." It seemed like he wanted to annoy us, like to tell us, "Relax." And then the coordinator got angry, kicked him, and stomped on his face. I don't know if the platoon commander saw it, but he turned away, because he didn't want to see it. I said to myself, "Either I stop the coordinator, or I get to work, look for more Arabs." While the coordinator was beating him up, he put the barrel of his gun in his mouth or at his head, and then he said to me, "Take him out and shoot him." He only meant it to scare him. In the end, the Arab really did have a gold chain in his pocket. We checked the documents in their wallets and found an ID. The Arab said, "My friend needs water." After he was beaten, he'd stopped talking, and we were afraid that maybe something happened, but he asked the coordinator again, and he beat him up again. He beat him up two or three times. One of the times, my platoon commander saw the beating, at least once.

This took place in the woman's living room?

Yes.

Who was in the room at that time?

The two Arab intruders, the woman was walking around the house, the coordinator, myself, another soldier, and the platoon commander. Afterward, police came, and neighbors also came. We brought the Arab water and he was dazed, but the coordinator said he was pretending. The Arab's friend said he'd been bitten by a dog and needed to go to the hospital. We checked their papers, and then we saw that they were Abu Mazen's soldiers,* they were soldiers in uniform. When they asked them why they did it, they said they had no money.

Did they speak Hebrew?

One of them did . . . Other forces came, slapped them around, at one point one of the Arab's phones rang, so one of the scouts put a gun to his stomach, so that he'd talk and they could gather information. I gave him water, and there was this really terrible smell coming from him. He stank the whole time while I cleaned foam from around his mouth. I think that he couldn't control his gas, his eyes were open and there was foam coming out of his mouth. Maybe he had something, maybe he didn't. I called an ambulance and two of them came, they gave him a few slaps, I think it was the medic, and he answered some more ques-

---

*The soldier is referring to Mahmoud Abbas, president of the Palestinian National Authority.

tions. He could have been pretending, but maybe he wasn't. He was in shock. They hit him—not fatally, but he kicked him, and stepped on his head—it was mostly humiliating. The settlement security coordinator said he didn't beat him up too hard.

Only the settlement security coordinator beat him up?

Yes. What happened was that until the company medic came, the only medic who was there was this young guy, a bit in shock. We didn't have medics in our company, they always brought us new ones. Before the medic started treating him, I told him what had happened to the Arab. The platoon commander said, "He wasn't hit." I said, "He was." We argued. The platoon commander got angry with me and told me to go to the Hummer. I refused. I wanted to be there because the woman's son had showed up all annoyed, and I was afraid he'd try and beat the Arab up. The police didn't care, the police just wanted their handcuffs back.

Why did you put handcuffs on him?

I put on a nylon restraint, not handcuffs. When the police arrived, we changed it to handcuffs. I didn't want to leave the Arab after I saw he was beat up and maybe sick. I stayed in the house, but I didn't want to talk about it in front of everyone. I said to [the platoon commander], "Let's talk." We went out to the Hummer. I told him, "I'm not going to sit in the Hummer." He threatened me with three days' confinement to the base taken from my leave. I went back home and we never spoke again.

142. The settlement security coordinators think of themselves as our commanders

UNIT: KFIR BATTALION
LOCATION: SUSIYA
YEAR: 2004–2005

Do you remember other stories from Susiya? What was your relationship with the settlers there? What about with the residents of Susiya, the residents of the settlements, and other outposts in the area?

There were ups and downs. For the most part, during that time the settlers did respect us, sometimes they also spoiled us, meaning they invited us to all kinds of places. There were also people who thought that the work we were doing wasn't tough enough, all kinds of slogans like, "We want security, not protection." Sometimes the settlement security coordinators would, how to say this, they thought they were our commanders, not our company commander. They'd try and give us orders, what to do, when and where.

And they didn't have a say?

They had influence, but not a say. Meaning, they'd say: "Your guys didn't turn back the shepherds when they got too close," or they might say, "Next time you're in the same situation, do it right and be more aggressive." It wasn't like they'd tell the company commander what to do, but they definitely had influence. I didn't participate in the meetings, but the settlers had influence both in the battalion commander meetings and certainly in meetings with the company commander. The settlement security coordinators would meet with the company commander at least once a week, both for a situation assessment and as part of a routine, but they'd also say what they thought about what we were doing, and what they thought we needed to do. I don't know how much they cared in the higher ranks. In the lower ranks, there were times where the company commander didn't listen to them at all. And then there were cases where he did exactly what they said. I don't know what was considered as appeasing the security officer, and what was a genuine security consideration, but there were certainly things that were influenced by the settlement security coordinator.

143. The checkpoint's not for Israel's security

UNIT: NAHAL BRIGADE
LOCATION: GITIT CHECKPOINT, JORDAN VALLEY
YEAR: 2006

We had a tough time with this, morally. This whole checkpoint was just there for Palestinians coming to work for Israelis in the Jordan Valley. It was all about Israeli exploitation of Palestinians.

Did you see that at the checkpoint?

You know the date harvest? During the harvest Palestinians are paid something like fifty shekels.

Do you know this from the checkpoint?

Of course. I know how much they're paid. They come every day at four or five in the morning and go back at seven in the evening, exhausted. You see a guy exhausted from having worked hard all day, manual labor, and he gets fifty shekels a day. Great, I mean that's what they get for date picking. That's what the workers get. Not only do I know they only get fifty shekels for a day's work, but on top of that I also, you know, I stand there, they have to wait at my checkpoint and go through the humiliating inspection. I mean, the whole checkpoint is really an economic facility. You feel you're on checkpoint duty not for Israel's security but for Israel's bank account.

How is that connected to the checkpoint?

Who goes through the checkpoint? Only Palestinians working in the Jordan Valley. They've got no reason to go there, just their livelihood. Nothing else. I mean, because they earn their living there, they have families in the area, but the people from Akraba and those villages have no reason to go to the Jordan Valley. They're two separate populations. Now it's very connected, because when you work somewhere you make connections, and you start a family and so on. But I'm at that checkpoint so that Palestinians without work permits don't get through. Why should I care if they don't have work permits? From a security point of view, because it means they weren't cleared. But what does that mean, they weren't cleared? Do you know what stops someone from getting a work permit? Listen carefully—if a relative of the fourth degree, meaning your uncle's grandfather, threw a stone back in 1948—I'm not kidding you, now—then you can't get a work permit.

How do you know that?

Because we once asked a Shin Bet agent about the criteria. We were told there's a very clear definition. If any family member—fourth degree down—has ever been charged with an act of violence against Israel, no work permit. That's one of the criteria. Now show me someone, I mean what's the percentage of the population? Nothing. It's zero. We've been at war with them for over fifty years, so clearly someone, somewhere in the family tree, has thrown a rock at some point, you see? Everything's documented. So you get a sixteen-year-old boy, comes to the checkpoint all smiles, and the grandfather of the father of his brother threw a Molotov cocktail in 1962. So he can't get a work permit. So what does he do? He bypasses the checkpoint. Now, why would this guy bypass the checkpoint—to carry out a terrorist attack? No. To work. So I'm the checkpoint, working for economic interests. Cool. Great. It's shit. Apart from the fact of capitalism, socialism, whatever. Why do I, as a soldier, have to keep watch over the bank accounts of the Jordan Valley settlers? Why? There's not a single reason in the world. That's the corrupt occupation in its clearest form. Pure economic interest.

144. A settlement forbidden to soldiers

Unit: Armored Corps
Location: Ramallah district
Year: 2003

One platoon would get into some eight army patrol jeeps, armored jeeps, and go out on patrol, mainly doing lookouts and checkposts. The checkposts would be more interesting. There were some very hostile villages there, and several illegal settlements that were also very hostile, and we were not supposed to enter them unescorted.

What do you mean?

There was this one hill there, and orders were not to enter because the settlers didn't like soldiers. They're crazy out there.

If soldiers went in, what would happen?

I don't know, we never tried. I guess they'd riot. I don't know. We never go in.

You're talking about a settlement?

Yes.

145. The political ranks are very close to the settlements

Unit: Civil Administration
Location: General
Year: 2001–2004

When you shift roles to work on settlement issues, you basically flip a switch: instead of dealing with the Palestinian population, you deal with the settlers.

Yes.

What does that entail?

First of all, decisions about building settlements aren't made at the Civil Administration's level. For the most part they're directives from the minister of defense's aide on settlement issues. Although later it turned out there was corruption there—it was after I was released from the army, you can look it up on the Internet just like I did. —— left a big mess, it seems that he passed things along, built things, transferred land, all kinds of things like that. —— was the head of the infrastructure division. I'm not sure whether he was even tried. In short, you deal with pretty technical things, moving mobile homes from place to place, trailers. Expanding a specific settlement's territory, dealing with the fence around Efrat or the security for Kiryat Arba and its fence.

What does that mean, "dealing with"? Budgeting?

If only the Civil Administration had money for things like that. It's money from the Ministry of Defense.

Organizing requests?

Organizing requests, sitting with the [settlers], seeing what's reasonable, what's not, all kinds of defensive measures, and so on. You deal with all kinds of Israeli incursions, Israeli breaches, all kinds of disturbances. Overseeing an injunction issued by the oversight branch, that it's really being enforced. It's a supervisor's job, it wasn't . . .

After organizing the requests, were decisions made?

The branch commander can make recommendations, but we were inconsequential. Really inconsequential . . .

Does the recommendation play a role?

The recommendation plays a role . . . The head of the administration says what he thinks, yes or no, but the security recommendation of the branch plays a role. What can you do? He approves the location of the fence.

And such action needs approval from the minister of defense.

You need approval from the minister of defense for settlement issues. You just need approval from the aide, and he's supposed to inform the minister. Supposed to, but I don't know if it happens.

Do you also deal with defining the legal borders of settlements?

Yes. That's totally the Civil Administration. You think we do that just for the Jewish settlements, but we don't. The Palestinians also make trouble: destroying homes, infiltrating territory that then has to be evacuated, uprooting groves. Of course we deal with all that.

Meaning the supervision of lands and infrastructure and settlement—

Settlements in Area C, and some B, although we don't really deal with Area B, but sometimes we do.

Okay, so let's start with the settler trailers. How do you move a trailer? What does it entail? Do you need a permit? Who issues it?

Again, that's the role of the minister of defense's aide for settlement issues, only he can approve each trailer. Each trailer has the potential to expand a settlement. Think about it, there's nothing you can do. So any change, the aide to the minister of defense announces an injunction, which is brought to the Civil Administration, who verifies that the change was implemented the way it's supposed to . . . that the trailer was moved to the right place, and that it didn't somehow get moved to a different settlement—that actually happens. Sometimes trailers appear without you knowing why.

How does that happen?

Because the soldier at the checkpoint doesn't necessarily know that a trailer needs a permit, and the settlers sometimes move a trailer without a permit, either one of their own trailers, or a trailer they move from one settlement to another. There are a lot of settlements in the Territories with junkyards, mostly in the Nablus area, where they take stuff from there and use it to build another settlement. It happens.

And what happens when you find out?

The oversight unit takes out an injunction. First you take out an injunction to investigate, and then they come to the committee and verify that there really isn't a permit for that trailer, and why not. If there's no permit, then there are two options—either they get a permit, which is a completely plausible option . . .

Does this happen a lot?

Yes.

Who sits on the committee?

A representative of the Civil Administration, from the infrastructure division. There's a representative from the Ministry of Defense, a representative of the oversight unit, and the committee is subject to the head of the Civil Administration. Each decision is subject to the head of the Civil Administration, he knows the decisions before . . .

But the players, the representatives are normally—

Very senior people, clerks.

Are there people from the settlements on the committee?

I don't know who's there today, but in the oversight unit there are a lot of people who live in Judea and Samaria, there are people from the army.

But there are more than a few people on the staff who are from the—

Yes, from the settlements, knitted *kippot*, yes, you find them there. If you look, you'll find them. But that's how it is in any group.

But the question is whether the settlers on the committee influence the decision-making process, because you say, for example, that many trailers located in places that don't have permits receive permits retroactively.

Who do they get permits from retroactively? Not from the committee.

Okay. Then who?

The committee hears the case and passes it on. What the committee does is it says, This trailer doesn't have the whatever, we need to clarify its status, so the committee calls for a clarification, and informs the aide to the minister of defense.

Who's called for the clarification?

Whoever . . . there's no such thing as signing off on a trailer, it's not the army's role.

So who does it?

Normally, if it's in a settlement, then the head of the settlement council does, but . . .

The same settlement where they put the trailer.

Right, the settlement where they moved the trailer to . . . in most cases a trailer doesn't stay by itself, it's usually joined by other trailers. They don't decide, with this kind of thing they just say that there's a trailer in . . . we'll take out a demolition or evacuation injunction, it doesn't matter, it's normally a demolition order, but it doesn't matter. A trailer is a depressing thing, it just reappears somewhere else and then they send the case on to the minister of defense's aide, and he can say that it's okay for the caravan to stay there. That's within his power, and that happens.

In your experience, does this happen more or less than demolition or evacuation orders for a trailer?

Listen, this whole question of settling Judea and Samaria isn't discussed in writing. Many things are decided verbally, and not at our level. Because things are agreed on verbally, maybe we'll find seven illegal trailers, and the case will go to the minister of defense's aide, and he'll say, "Okay, the oversight unit found these trailers, but actually I approved the caravans verbally," and so he lets them be there. That's just how things work, that's the process.

Meaning, you often get cases where things were agreed on verbally, without . . . ?

Yes, there's lots of verbal agreements. By virtue of the fact that the political ranks are very close to the settlements, there's nothing you can do about it.

You never saw a document that was signed by anyone? Say, a document approving a trailer?

No. And I think that if you found such a document . . . during my time it was Fuad,* the agreements were normally reached in a compromise with the settlement, they weren't put in writing, and you won't find them in writing, if you tried to find them, you wouldn't.

So there's no official document, not even . . .

I imagine that there are internal documents in the Ministry of Defense. But they don't come to us. "There's a Ministry of Defense order in light of the agreement, evacuate X, Y, Z." But the document? Maybe the Ministry of Defense has its own procedures.

But you don't have it.

It's a political body, it tries to be apolitical, but . . .

What are the parameters of a settlement's jurisdiction? How is the settlement's jurisdiction established? Who determines it? Why?

What do you mean? A settlement's jurisdiction, it's surrounded, by virtue of the fact that it's surrounded it has a defined jurisdiction, we're talking about existing settlements here. During my time, there was maybe Migron, which I think doesn't have a jurisdiction even today. But I remember that we never established any new jurisdiction, rather it happened because of settlement expansion. When a settlement expands because families want to join it, the settlement's jurisdiction is defined accordingly.

*Labor Party minister of defense Binyamin ben Eliezer.

Do you also work in coordination with the settlement security officers?

No. The brigade commander works opposite the security officer. The brigade commander is the security officer's best friend. The Civil Administration doesn't deal with security officers.

I want to go back to the topic of fences. What's the story behind the fence in Efrat? What period are we talking about?

We're talking about sometime in 2002. The deal with the fence in Efrat is that it's a well-established settlement, and the shepherds in the area were coming into the settlement, and this constituted a threat to the settlement, so they requested special resources there, and I think that even now it's still the most advanced system in the Territories— enclosure, observation, cameras, sensors, the system is very advanced. In Gaza at least this advanced system was used to approve security measures. And they approved it for Efrat.

What about agricultural areas harmed by the fence? Efrat is a good example: were agricultural areas belonging to Palestinian farmers enclosed by the fence?

You need to have ownership, so the question is who owns the land.

Say you carried out an investigation, and now the settlement . . .

It's not that hard, there are all those custodian maps, it's not that difficult, you don't have to do an investigation. There's the Ottoman period, the British, whatever you want, crumbling maps in the, whatever, you see whose land it is. It's not such a big deal. If the land is very important for security routes, it happens . . . a few *dunams* . . . it'll be limited. If they decide they need the land, then you can expropriate it. Yes, for security reasons.

Who can seize the land? Could you?

Yes, it's for the public need, so to speak, it's a bit different.

Whatever the need, do you issue an injunction?

The legal adviser issues the injunction, and it's signed by the Civil Administration. But the source that approves it legally is the . . . legal adviser, he has to be sure that they'll receive compensation for the land, and he'll know how to answer to the court when it gets to court. He's subject to the government legal adviser, through the Military Advocate General, but yes.

And what happens when land like that is enclosed by the fence? How do you deal with it? Is there access? No access?

No, there's no access. You'll bring that land into a settlement. But again, I didn't see active farmland, and I don't believe that there was fertile land annexed to the settlement. It's usually farmland that hasn't been used for a certain amount of time, and they can see for how long according to the weeds there. It's not such a big deal. There are people from the oversight unit who know how to determine whether the land hasn't been worked for two, eight, or ten . . .

How do you handle, what's the policy toward Israelis who've infiltrated land in the Territories, breached roads, and so on?

Israelis? What's the policy? First, the oversight coordinator has to see it. The oversight unit, coordinators, all kinds of people who are familiar with the area. The policy is to issue an injunction that states that the breach is not . . . I'm talking about people who know the area incredibly well. The youngest of them has been at the same job for twelve years, sometimes in the same place. You issue an injunction for the breach, you see if there is someone you can summon for the breach, if it's an incursion into a settlement, then there's definitely someone you can summon. If it's just any old breach—and there are breaches which signal an opening to something else, you see the breach widen and a road slowly emerge . . . then if there's someone to call, you call. If there's no one to call, then you set up surveillance and look for the tractor that made the breach. You pay close attention to when there's a tractor there and when there isn't, and then you catch the tractor and you investigate what's going on, who sent him, who did it, and you bring your findings to an investigation.

And what happens if along the way you identify the beginning of a new outpost?

It depends on the period. During ——'s time, even if they were to establish an outpost, no one had the balls to come out and say so to the political ranks. There was no "fresh incursion." Even if there was a fresh incursion, no one had the balls to say, "Here's a fresh incursion, I'm going to destroy it." The period after that, during ——'s time, I don't know if there was a policy change or if it was his own initiative, but there was a different policy in place, and fresh incursions were destroyed. That really did happen.

Can you give some examples?

A good example of a fresh incursion is a trailer. A house is not considered a fresh incursion, because if you built a house, and spent time building the house, then it's a "veteran incursion," which means it has approval from the political ranks. Yes, I remember a few examples, but for the most part it was with tents. I can't remember something specific, but it happened.

Do you remember in which areas it happened?

In the Ramallah area. This was later on, and I was in Hebron by then, but I remember that it happened in the Ramallah area. It was actually with this issue that the [settlers] were . . . by this point it was in 2003, and they'd gotten smart.

Why at the moment when they defined something as an incursion was it not defined as a fresh incursion? Did they look the other way?

No, they weren't looking the other way. No one would take it upon himself to do that. Looking the other way is something you have to choose to do. Even the oversight coordinator wouldn't do that. Maybe he didn't see it, that kind of thing happens, he's not walking around in the field all day. There's one coordinator for each sector, and it's not a small area. He sees each area once in a . . . he sees each piece of land once every month, month and a half—it's a problem. If anyone's looking the other way, it's the higher ranks. Don't look for it with the clerks, it's not there.

Meaning the clerks record and report everything. A stone moves—another report.

If he sees it. There's a report, and it's passed on to the commanders. The division commander knows that a stone moved, right? Or the head of the Civil Administration finds out that a stone moved, and even if he has the authority to move it, he'll speak first with the settlers and tell them he's moving it, and he'll get the opinion of the aide to the minister of defense. And if it's a stone that was moved a long time ago, he won't deal with it. He won't take it upon himself to carry out an evacuation. You need balls to do that kind of thing.

How does it work if we're talking about Palestinians, not Israeli settlers?

Same thing. It works the same way, only the upper ranks approve the evacuation . . . "Fresh," it's nonsense, it goes from the head of the Civil Administration, the division commander, the general of the Command, the decision to evacuate passes, no problem . . . if they tell the aide, that's it, it's done. But a Palestinian incursion, there's a ton of illegal Palestinian construction, a whole sea of it, you can't begin to grasp the scope of it. How does it work? Oversight, injunctions, an investigative committee in Bet El, they come, they set up a committee, they decide what to do, or until it's settled, it goes to the head of the Civil Administration and the general of the Command. There was a time when illegal construction went to the minister of defense. That was a tense time.

As opposed to cases involving settlers, where the aide to the minister of defense for settlement issues . . .

Yes, it's a lower rank for approval.

Here it's the head of the Civil Administration?

No, it's the general of the Command.

The implementation? How much illegal Jewish construction . . .

There is no point in comparing the quantities. If you ask how much illegal Palestinian construction has been destroyed compared to Jewish construction, it's a certain amount. I don't know, I haven't checked. Also, in terms of violations, if I were to take you on a trip around the Hebron area, I could show you fifty points of illegal construction along the way. That's just how it is.

What about permits and the like in Area C?

You can get them, but it's a long process.

Do you know of proceedings where they got them?

They get them, not for a new settlement, they get them for settlement expansions, but it's a very long process. It can take five or six years.

Do you have an example?

I remember times when construction was approved. I remember reading documents where things were approved. It would go past me in the paperwork chain . . . it was approved by the infrastructure oversight unit, so it didn't get to the head of the Civil Administration. It's not a decision, if it's in a strategic area, it's a decision that goes up to the higher ranks. But it really takes a long time, during the Intifada it took even more time, and there were cases that lasted five years, but they'd eventually approve it. They'd get it. If it's an existing settlement, you can't say no. But the settlers don't normally ask our permission: the process was long, and they decided we wouldn't evacuate illegal construction, or they hoped.

The settlers usually do ask?

For expansion of an organized settlement? Yes.

And what about a new outpost? They don't ask you?

Certainly not the Civil Administration. Certainly not during ——'s time, no way, the settlers hated him, they despised him. They spat on him. All the connections the settlers had with the Civil Administration during ——'s time, all of that nonsense was gone once —— got there. It didn't exist any longer.

Do you remember waves of violence? Settler violence toward the Civil Administration?

Yes, in Hebron I was hit with rocks, eggs, certainly, of course, sure. Racist comments, everything.

Glossary

8/8 (or any other numbers): The ratio between hours of duty and rest (which includes various chores).

APC: Armored personnel carrier. There are several varieties: the standard APC is known as Bardelas and is fairly vulnerable, although used widely in the infantry. Heavy APCs—the Puma or *Achzarit* (evil lady) model—are less common and more heavily armored.

battalion: Three hundred to four hundred soldiers commanded by a colonel.

brigade: One thousand to fifteen hundred soldiers, commanded by a lieutenant general.

company: Fifty to one hundred soldiers, commanded by a captain.

D9: A military bulldozer used by the Engineering Corps to demolish houses, among other things.

DCL: District Coordination and Liaison, also called the DCO, or District Coordination Office. These are branch offices of the Civil Administration of Judea and Samaria, a military body charged with oversight of the day-to-day affairs of Palestinians in the West Bank and Gaza Strip.

deployment: The period when a unit is sent out into the field to engage in routine security. Combat units are generally in deployment or in training.

front command squad: A small band of soldiers accompanying a senior officer, usually a driver, a medic, and a radioman.

gate guard: A guard at the entrance of an army base or post.

H1/H2: Administrative areas in Hebron defined in the Hebron Accords of 1997. H1 comprises most of the city and is administered by the Palestinian Authority; H2 is the city center, which is under Israeli military rule and is also inhabited by Israeli settlers.

MAG: Acronym for machine gun, deployed at the platoon level; also ubiquitous on armored vehicles and guard posts. It provides medium firepower and is not accurate.

orders group: An officers' meeting. Before any military operation, a meeting of officers is convened to discuss orders, objectives, procedures, and possible incidents.

platoon: Twenty to forty soldiers, commanded by a lieutenant.

regional brigade: A brigade comprised of rotating battalions that maintains logistical and tactical control of operations in a specific region.

rubber bullets: Bullets cased in a layer of rubber. They are considered to be less lethal than standard bullets and are supposed to be fired in groups of three held together by plastic wrap. They are more lethal when separated and fired individually.

Ruger: A sharpshooting weapon used for riot control. In 2001 the Military Advocate General decreed that the Ruger is lethal and should not be used as a means of riot control.

security officer: A civilian charged with the security of a certain area or institution.

settlement security coordinator: Also known by the Hebrew acronym "Ravshatz," a civilian employee of the IDF charged with a settlement's security.

special security zone: A buffer area around a settlement or other Israeli installation in the Territories.

squad: Five to ten soldiers, commanded by a sergeant.

straw widow: A Palestinian home occupied by force and used as a concealed post.

wet: Slang for live shooting, as opposed to "dry," i.e., with no fire.

Acknowledgments

Grateful thanks are due to the many volunteers and supporters who made the work on this book possible. Without their assistance, these important testimonies would not be able to reach those who need to know them. We would also like to thank Shai Efrati, who created the maps; the people at B'Tselem and Peace Now, who supplied the information on which they are based; Tal Haram, J.R., Amit Gvaryahu, Alexandra Polsky, Jerry Haber, and especially Clare Needham for help with the English translation. Finally, our thanks as well to Riva Hocherman at Metropolitan Books, whose devotion to the project has allowed our book to live in translation.

About the Author

BREAKING THE SILENCE, one of Israel's most internationally lauded NGOs, was established in Jerusalem in 2004 by Israel Defense Forces veterans to document the testimonies of Israeli soldiers who have served in the Occupied West Bank and Gaza Strip.